THE UNDERGROUND SHOPPER®

A Guide to Discount
Mail-Order Shopping

Sue Goldstein

Andrews and McMeel, Inc.
A Universal Press Syndicate Company
KANSAS CITY • NEW YORK

Text illustrations by Marty Leigh.

The companies appearing in this catalog were selected because they sell merchandise at a lower price than full retail stores. A few select companies, although they may not be considered discount, were also included because they offer items which are not available in most stores or because they give the user a chance to save money by doing a portion of the construction himself. (Find these companies in sections titled "Kits and Kaboodle" and "Hard-to-Find.") The merchants paid no advertising fees to be listed and *The Underground Shopper*® makes no endorsements of these businesses. As of publication date, these companies were selling by mail at the time we contacted them (June 1982 to February 1983).

Goldstein, Sue, 1941-
    The underground shopper.

    Includes index.
    1. Mail-order business—United States—Directories.   2. Mail-order business—Directories.   3. Discount houses (Retail trade)—United States—Directories.   4. Discount houses (Retail trade)—Directories.   I. Title.
HF5466.G6   1983   381'.1   83-3828
ISBN 0-8362-7915-8

First printing, April 1983
Second printing, June 1983

To Josh, the best male-order ever delivered

ACKNOWLEDGMENTS

Several years ago, at the American Bookseller's Convention in Atlanta, I stood mesmerized by Ziggy as he was autographing at the booth of Andrews and McMeel/Universal Press. Simultaneously, I noticed John McMeel and his president's nametag and I thought, why not!

How lucky I am to have dreams. Dreams that materialize into blends of euphoria and everyday reality. Impossible dreams, still to be dreamt, with visions of more plums dancing in my head. Having a real live publisher and syndicated column and more plans on the drawing board is almost too good to be true.

If I didn't have the team and their talent to help produce the books and columns as well as the in-between daily projects which demand attention, and the faith and love which permeates it all, there would be no glory.

To the Andrews and McMeel/Universal Press family: John McMeel, Kathy Andrews, Donna Martin, Tom Thornton, Lee Salem, Alan McDermott, and the entire able-bodied creative cast and crew who made visible my vision, my sincerest gratitude for the opportunities presented.

To Aaron Priest, my friend first and now my literary agent, who finally said he'd represent me alongside Erma Bombeck.

To the commitment made by my staff to make it happen, to their enthusiasm, their energy, and most of all, their skill in maneuvering the many assignments, deadlines, deadbeats, and deadbolts, my thanks. Especially to the top bananas: Debra Goldie, managing editor, and our writers and researchers-in-residence, Tom Schneider, Beth Kisor, Pam Murphy, Pamela Rainville, Kelly McCoy, Richard Dosher, and Alexa Carole.

And lastly to my family—and my family of friends, Josh and my dad, who always dream with me; KaMylle, Bob, Joan, Ginger, Toy and Tom, Mel, Don, Jeff, Ben, and Ellen who have always listened to my dreams.

And to Bob and Margie who knew it would take the edge off!

CONTENTS

INTRODUCTION

Welcome to the age of mail-order shopping. It's one of the most exciting times to be a consumer because of the tremendous opportunities to have it all for less time and money.

Talk about variety. As you will see on the pages that follow, there's no end to the merchandise available by mail. We have sources for message recorders and massage wands, flannel sheets and futons, monogrammed towels and monorail passes, Chevy vans and vin ordinaire, soda syphons and sphygmomanometers, gardenia bushes and the greenhouses (complete with ladybugs) to grow them in.

Convenience is the name of the mail-order game. Toll-free 800 numbers (be sure you dial "1" first) and credit cards make ordering virtually effortless. There's no crowd, no gas bill, no pushy salespeople, and you can shop any time of day or night with a catalog in front of you. In spite of their discounted prices, certain catalog houses did not spare any expense. You'll experience some of the most beautiful catalogs with detailed product descriptions included and most are free for the asking.

Most of all, you'll be saving up to 90% off retail. Often it doesn't cost as much to sell direct to you as it does to have a physical retail outlet; some manufacturers prefer to avoid the middleman just like the consumer.

How do you get started? We had the same fears you might have setting out to research this book a year ago. "How can I order if they don't have a catalog?" "Where do I get the manufacturer's style number?" "What if my custom suit doesn't fit, how can I rectify this?" "What if my order never arrives when I've already paid for it?" Happily, after many orders and few ordeals, these apprehensions have been alleviated.

Our staff sent for catalogs, requested price quotes, ordered merchandise, returned merchandise, and digested over a thousand questionnaires completed both by phone or by the company's personnel. Most impressive were the number of multimillion-dollar companies whose answers to our inquiries were in the president's own hand. In the end, our conclusion was positive. For the most part, mail-order merchants (at least those listed in this book) were just as concerned about our satisfaction as we were.

We hope you will enjoy this book and use it whenever you have to buy something. Who says you need a brother in the business to shop at wholesale prices? Just sit back and let your fingers do the working. You'll be ringing in the savings with your first call.

Sue Goldstein

TEN QUESTIONS ABOUT MAIL-ORDER

1. When ordering apparel, how can I be sure I get the right size?
You may be a perfect "10" but if the manufacturer cuts his garments small to save fabric, they won't fit. It is always wise to send your measurements so that if there is any variation due to fabric, style, etc., whoever is filling the order will know how to compensate and get the correct size. Lands' End offered the following tips on taking your own measurements in their catalog:

- Neck—Take a shirt with a collar that fits you well. Lay the collar flat and measure from the center of the button to the far end of the button hole. Number of inches = your size.
- Sleeve—Bend elbow, measure from center of neck (backside) to elbow and down to wrist. Number of inches = your size.
- Chest or bust—Measure around fullest part, keeping tape up under arms and around shoulder blades. Number of inches = your size.
- Waist—Measure around waist, over shirt, at the height you normally wear your slacks or skirt. Keep one finger between tape and body. Number of inches = your size.
- Seat and hips—Stand with heels together and measure around fullest part.
- Inseam—Take a pair of pants that fits you well. Measure from the crotch seam to the bottom of the pants. Number of inches (to the nearest ½ inch) = inseam length.

2. I've never shopped by mail, how do I get started?
We've coded the listings in this book so you will know if a company has a catalog **(C)**, offers a brochure **(B)**, or operates on a price quote or price list **(PQ)** basis. When writing or calling a company for the first time, mention *The Underground Shopper* as the

source of the inquiry. Once you receive the catalog, read the order blank carefully. Make sure everything is clear to you. Note product information such as size, weight, color, contents. Specify all of these details on the order blank. Give substitutions and second choices. (You must authorize companies to do so.) Observe minimum orders. Many companies can only offer a discount on quantity purchases. Include shipping or other charges indicated on the order blank. Always request insurance if it is not included. Include sales tax. (Note: in general, sales tax applies only if you live in the state where companies are headquartered or have retail outlets. This should be explained on the order form.) Don't mail your order until you understand the return policy. Give your credit card number or enclose a check. Personal checks often delay shipment until they clear. *Never send cash.* You'll have no proof of payment in case problems arise. When you've done all this, mail the order. When ordering by phone or by mail, always keep complete records (date order was placed, name of order taker, receipts). When requesting a price quote, sending an SASE (self-addressed, stamped long envelope) will speed up the process considerably.

3. What is a price quote and how do I get one?

Many of the companies listed in this book have access to thousands of products from an electric toothbrush to a talking bathroom scale. If cataloged, these products would fill a book the size of the Manhattan Yellow Pages. The price quote system is an extremely cost-efficient way to let you know a) that the item is available, and b) what the current discount price is. Don't be afraid of price quotes. Suppose you want to buy Christian Dior panties, which normally cost about $7 a pair in the department store. Find the stores in this book that sell lingerie and write each one like this: Today's date, "Dear Sir, Do you have Christian Dior (manufacturer) Intimates (model) #82500 (style) size 6 panties in beige? If so, what is the cost per pair, per six, per dozen?" (Limit your requests to three items since most clerks are pressed for time in this business.) Also ask, "What is the extra shipping cost and when will they be shipped? Thank you and I look forward to your prompt reply." Remember, include a self-addressed, stamped envelope even if it is not specified.

4. My porcelain heart is broken. Can I return it?

The first thing to remember is *never* send anything back without first writing the company and requesting permission. Wait for their answer. If you telephone, record the name of the person who gave authorization and the instructions you receive. Some companies will pay postage, most won't. A surprise to us was the existence of "restocking" charges—as much as 25% of your order—that some companies use to protect themselves. It's always best to ask for the return policies if they are not spelled out in the catalog. Save the original packaging if you think there's a chance you'll return something.

5. Where do I find the manufacturer, model, and style number?
Catalogs will generally have this information included in the write-ups. Or, go to the retail store and look at the price tags, which will usually have the model number (although it might be coded). Asking the retail salesman for this information is kind of sneaky but . . . better yet, send an ad or photograph clipped from a magazine of the item you want.

6. My order never arrived, the company's phone is disconnected, my check's cleared. Help!
A normal delivery time is six to eight weeks. Companies are required by law to either ship the goods or advise you of the delay within 30 days of receiving the order unless otherwise stated in their catalog. They must also offer to refund your money and give you a cost-free method (either an 800 number or collect call) of canceling if they cannot ship within the 30-day period. One trade organization that will intervene or put you in touch with the proper agencies is the Direct Marketing Association, 6 E. 43rd St., New York, NY 10017, (212) 689-4977. While *The Underground Shopper* cannot solve problems with companies listed in this book directly, we will keep your written complaint on file and eliminate a listing if it proves necessary. (See the Reader Response page in the back of the book.)

7. After I pay the shipping charges, am I really saving?
If the item you want is available at a local discount store or is due to go on sale soon, perhaps you would do better to buy it locally. Some companies have charts in their catalogs for figuring postage, others charge by weight or by price. Always determine what the extra shipping charges are before comparing prices. There are three ways an order can be shipped: 1) Parcel Post (PP). The United States Postal Service charges from 45 cents to $4.70 to insure parcels valued up to $400. You must register packages valued over $400 and send them First Class. These can also be insured. *Parcel Post is the only way goods can be shipped to a post office box.* Mark both your order and check, "Deliver by Parcel Post Only" if you want delivery to your post office box. C.O.D. orders are more expensive since the carrier collects the amount of the order, postage, a C.O.D. fee ($1.20 to $4.50), and a money-order fee (75 cents to $1.55). 2) United Parcel Service (UPS) automatically insures each package for $100 in value and charges 25 cents for each additional $100 in value on the same

package. UPS charges should not include insurance unless the cost is greater than $100. This carrier is considered to be the most efficient and reliable. The cost is determined by weight and measurement, location of firm, and location of customer. 3) Truckers are used for nonmailable orders (goods over 50 pounds) and combined orders (nonmailable goods with those under 50 pounds in weight). Weight and distance determine the charges. The shipper specifies on the bill of lading the amount due, if any, and form of payment to be collected by the trucker upon delivery. On C.O.D. orders, for example, the shipper must specify that a personal check is acceptable. This may not include the freight company's charges, in which case, an additional check may be required. You will often see the abbreviation F.O.B. or "freight on board." "F.O.B. factory" means you pay the shipping charges from the point of origin or from the time the goods leave the factory.

8. Will the trucker's charges eat up the savings on large purchases such as furniture?

Deregulation has caused the freight companies to lower rates on long-distance and local hauls. For example, three years ago it cost approximately $2,800 to ship a truckload of furniture from Texas to California. That same shipment would cost about $1,400 today. Remember, too, you'll save about 50% of freight charges on items such as book cases if they are shipped "knocked down" or disassembled because they take up less room in the truck. Residents of the East and Southeast should look for companies in the North Carolina furniture district that have their own trucks and crews since their rates are generally lower than those of common carriers.

9. The idea of ordering from a foreign country scares me. What if I send my money for a kaftan and get back an afghan?

Getting catalogs with exotic stamps, quaint idiomatic letters, and unusual products is like taking a small trip to a foreign country. Read the catalogs closely and look for such things as insurance, duty (each item is different), returns, and delivery information. You'll pay a premium for air mail delivery but the alternative is "slow boat" surface mail. The method of payment should be explained in the catalog. If not, write to the company before sending any money and be sure you understand their payment policies. Because of the fluctuating market, Deak-Perera, a currency broker with offices in most major cities, suggests the company bill you in their foreign currency and you then pay in that foreign currency. Currency brokers and most banks will issue a check based on the current rate of exchange.

You can obtain a currency conversion table for approximate values from Deak-Perera, 29 Broadway, New York, NY 10006. If you must return your purchase for damage, write for instructions first to avoid double payment of duty.

10. Please explain customs duties. How much extra will I have to pay?

Any purchase made outside of this country is subject to customs examination. The U.S. Postal Service sends all incoming foreign packages to customs for examination and duty assessment. Individual commodities are charged a percentage of the appraised value assigned by the exhaustive *Tariff Schedules of the United States.* The duty on a silk blouse might be 18% while that on a cotton blouse may be 25%; it's a complicated business. After the duty bill is written, the parcel is returned for delivery and collection of duty and a $1.75 postal handling fee. In Canada, you will be notified by customs that your package is ready for pickup. Canadians pay slightly higher duties than U.S. citizens along with a 9% federal sales tax. "Duty-free" items included in the Generalized System of Preferences (GSP) come from over 140 underdeveloped nations and include approximately 2,800 items ranging from cameras to wood carvings. In order to take advantage of GSP, you must acquire the eligible article in the same beneficiary country where it was grown, manufactured, or produced. Even bona fide "unsolicited" gifts are dutiable and not exempted under the laws for returning travelers. If you're interested in learning about duty charges on specific commodities, pick up "Pocket Hints" available at your local customs office or by mail from the U.S. Customs Service, Box 7118, Washington, DC 20044. Canadians can request a copy of "I Declare" from Customs Office, 360 Coventry Road, Ottawa, Ontario K1K2C6.

1.

APPAREL AND ACCESSORIES

Children's Wear

Dress your little ones in natural fibers from Europe. Buy diapers at wholesale prices, suits for your little prince, pinafores for the princess, and hand-knit clothing for everyone at way below retail prices. If you're planning on more than one child, better quality clothing will last longer. Also, consider buying quantities of items like sleepers and diapers. You'll have them when you need them next time, and you'll save money, too.

COTTON DREAMS
P.O. Box 1261
Sebastian, FL 32958
(305) 589-0172

End the polyester nightmares with sweet dreams for the whole family, in 100% natural fiber clothing. They carry hard-to-find items like 100% cotton knee socks, panties, slips, baby clothing, and children's sleep wear. Oshkosh overalls were available in a variety of colors for $12.75. The Nichols family owns, operates, and models for the seasonally-issued catalog. Watch them grow with each issue. Shipping costs $1.25 for the first item, 25 cents for each additional item. **C**

NATAN BORMAN CO., INC.
157 Havemeyer
Brooklyn, NY 11211
(212) 387-2983
(212) 782-0108

Natan Borman carries boys' clothing from infants to size 20; girls' clothing, infants to juniors, preteen sizes 4 to 14; and women's clothing sporting tags and fabrics from the finest domestic and European manufacturers made expressly for Borman. Open Sunday through Thursday, 10 a.m. to 6 p.m.; Friday, 10 a.m. to 2 p.m. with week-long savings of 25% to 50%. Borman's offers a 14-day refund policy and tacks on $2 for shipping. **PQ**

RUBENS BABY FACTORY
P.O. Box 14900
Chicago, IL 60614
(312) 348-6200

"Baby place, you've got the cutest little baby place . . ." If you want your chubby cherub to be truly Rubenesque, you'll find you don't need crib notes to do well here. We saw savings on short-sleeved snap or tie baby shirts (two for $1.99), kimonos (two for $4.99), training panties (two for $1.99), and bibs ($1.99 each) to clothe your sleeping sweetie (or screaming demon). Knit stretch diapers were $8.50 per dozen, or three dozen for $24. Some items were half off retail, although these were seconds. Send a stamped, self-addressed envelope for a flier. When you order send a minimum of $3 or 10% toward your order (whichever is more), for UPS. Rubens' products have been used on newborns "since 1890 in hospitals all over the country," their flier cried. There's a free bumper sticker (for your baby buggy bumper?) with each order. Exchanges—no refunds. **B**

THE YOUNG IDEA LTD.
Aylesbury
HP 202JA England
Phone: Despatch 88068 (dial "01" for operator assistance with this call)

We don't know if this is where Lady Di buys the royal Di-apers, but busy mums can select reasonably priced children's wear from Young Idea's own or Ladybird label. Everything from pinafores, school wear, cord jeans, pj's, and nightgowns to baby rompers and crawler sets. Free catalog is delightful reading, but prices are listed in pounds and pence. Remember to get the right size to keep these London britches from falling down. **C**

Family Wear

One catalog for the entire family? Many companies believe they can make clothes for the little ones using the same fabrics and in the same styles as clothes made for adults. Sousa & Lefkovits, one of the biggest direct merchants of prep wear in the mail-order business today, recently added a children's division to their operation. The Finals catalog was a real find for us. It's devoted entirely to swimming and jogging apparel for men and women. In this section, you'll find a variety of bargains from authentic military surplus to the trendy, functional clothing by Lands' End.

BEMIDJI WOOLEN MILLS
P.O. Box 277
Bemidji, MN 56601
(218) 751-5166

Play ragtime with a ragg knit cap, the perfect winterizer. (And you better believe they know how to winterize here—it's *cold* in Bemidji!) This mill has carried men's, women's, and children's clothing as well as yarn and batting, for over half a century. Popular brands carried include Woolrich and Pendleton, and prices are about 20% lower than comparable retail. Their Paul Bunyan Jac shirt is available in all sizes and it's very popular. There's a 100% satisfaction guarantee: They'll exchange or refund purchases (with no restocking charge) upon request. Write for their free catalog and check out their clothing and gift ideas. **C**

D & A MERCHANDISE CO.
22 Orchard St.
New York, NY 10002
(212) 226-9401 or 925-4766

D & A owner Elliot Kivell's the king of underwear and he's having more than a brief reign. For many years, D & A has been treating their customers royally—25% or more off on a wide range of merchandise: Men's and women's robes by Christian Dior were fit to be tied. Other name lingerie queens were seen, such as Bali, Olga, Warner, and Lily of France. Bra sizes to 48 and panties to size 12. For men, BVD and Munsingwear underwear to size 60. T-shirts to XXXXL and X-tall are discounted for all the king's men. Be sure to be specific when requesting a price quote. Ask for the brand, style number, size, and color to facilitate delivery. All shipping charges are $1.75. **PQ, SASE**

THE FINALS
21 Minisink Ave.
Port Jervis, NY 12771
(800) 431-9111
(914) 856-4456: NY residents call collect

When you're serious about swimming, don't forget to take The Finals. Make a splash for less cash in these factory direct swimsuits priced from $10 to $20 for women, $6 to $10 for men. The scantily clad models in the catalog would get on swimmingly at our pool anytime.

We tracked down running gear made from brightly colored nylon: shorts (lined), $8 and matching tank top, $6. Warm-ups in 12 attractive colors were $45. The 50% polyester/50% cotton polo shirts helped beat "la cost" of living at $11, or three for $30. Goggles, bags, swim caps, and other accessories, too. Team discounts are 10%. Credit card minimum, $25. **C**

HARVARD TROUSER CO.
2191 S. Main St.
P.O. Box 217
Pittsford, MI 49271
(517) 523-2167

Park your car in the Harvard yard because they carry that classic from the fifties, the car coat. We found a limited selection of men's, women's, and children's insulated nylon jackets, coats, vests, and for those who like to go dashing through the snow, snowmobile suits. Women's sizes ranged from 8 to 34; children's sizes were 2 to 18; and men's sizes ranged from small to XXXXX-large. Since H.T.C. manufactures and sells their own line, prices are about 25% off retail. Unused merchandise can be exchanged or refunded. This company's been around since 1926. **B**

HOWRON SPORTSWEAR
295 Grand St.
New York, NY 10002
(212) 226-4307

How, Ron! We spendum heap pile of wampum at the reservation. Next time we lay A-pache and ride to the Big Apple for 25% to 50% off. Chief labels you promise in latest smoke signal really Sioux-ted our tribe. Squaw likum when she can Chippe-way for my clothes by Oscar de la Renta, Stanley Blacker, Damon, Members Only, Sansabelt, Givenchy, and many more. Me Hopi she gets herself ladies' dresses and sportswear (sizes 4 to 18 or 38 to 48) by Act III, Villager, Breckenridge, Prestige, Stuart Lang, and Lee. If you must be an Indian giver, they give store credit only on returns. **PQ**

I. BUSS & CO.
738 Broadway
New York, NY 10003
(212) 242-3338

We caught the Buss and rode for half price. Located in Greenwich Village, this family-run business began as a uniform company in 1892. Today, the military surplus clothing from Europe and the United States enjoys a "rapid transit" from the shelves. Pleated English army drill shorts in khaki (used), 100% cotton, wrap waist were $16, long trousers, $24.95 (new). Also available in copies. Darling French sailing shirts, white with red stripe or ecru with blue stripe, 100% cotton, were $24.95. Prices do not include shipping. Wool coats, flight jackets, Swedish army coats with fleece lining . . . we're on the Buss for good. Major credit cards accepted; no checks. **C**

I. TUSCHMAN & SONS, INC.
61 Orchard St.
New York, NY 10002
(212) 226-4318

Tuschman has clothing for the tush, as well as the rest of the body. Men's, women's, and children's name-brand underwear, sleep wear, shirts, jeans, socks, sweaters, and more at a 25% to 35% discount—a veritable Lower East Side experience next time you're in the City. We don't know how they find time to send out notices with some of their current brands and prices with all the local business. Billy the Kid, Geoffrey Beene, Cambridge, Carter's, BVD, Botany 500, Hanes, Hang Ten, and many others. One of the few places to get original Grand Slam golf shirts by Munsingwear (penguin logo) at a discount. Hang Ten colored briefs, BVD white briefs, T-shirts, and boxers, and Hanes regular size, plus a full range of big size underwear up to size 60 on some items, XL-XXXXL on others. **B**

JANTZEN INC.
P.O. Box 3001
Portland, OR 97208
(503) 238-5000

It's that one Jantzen a life time to get many of the swim and sportswear lines at up to 50% off. This store is the only Jantzen outlet with ready-to-wear. Men and women can choose from a wide variety of bathing suit styles, cover-ups, and casual clothing by finding the model number in a local store. They also carry stretch velour, T-shirt, terry cloth, blouse, and trouser fabrics. Send a sample of the fabric you are trying to match and they will send a price quote for the asking. **PQ, SASE**

LANDS' END
Lands' End Lane
Dodgeville, WI 53595
(800) 356-4444
(608) 935-2788: WI, HI, AK residents

Look shipshape in sharp clothing from Lands' End. We saw beautiful cotton sweaters for men and women, colorful polo and rugby shirts, twill pants, Madras shirts, women's tops and shorts and shoes along with belts, shoulder bags, and nautical gifts fit for the most pre-possessing preppy. Even boomerangs are offered (certainly an item no fashionable American family should be without). While not really a discounter, Lands' End does offer high-quality clothing at reasonable prices. Satisfaction is guaranteed or they'll refund complete purchase price. Their spectacularly photographed 92-page full-color catalog makes great reading in the captain's quarters. Yacht'a order one today. **C**

LOUIS CHOCK, INC.
74 Orchard St.
New York, NY 10002-4594
(212) 473-1929

Chock-ed full of nuts who love this heavenly coffer, we found savings of 25% off hosiery and underwear for the whole family—from new-borns to grandparents. Carter's pj's, undies, blankets, Danskin tights, Hanes briefs and boxer shorts, Burlington socks, Mayer panty hose, and much more. The tall men will find a "T" shirt in their size (up to XXL) for $4.50 each (retail, $6). Shipping is $2 per order anywhere in the United States. **C $1**

MELNIKOFF'S DEPARTMENT STORE
1594 York Ave.
New York, NY 10028
(212) 288-2419

Melnikoff's calls itself a department store, even though it's really more a neighborhood emporium, simply because they've got so much stuff jammed between their four walls. A mecca for money-saving, savvy New Yorkers have long made financial pilgrimages here. Quality clothing for men, women, and children is offered at well below retail prices. Sweat clothing in Adidas or Nike labels (for men and boys) occasionally is discounted as much as 40%, while ladies can find Maidenform and children can find Carter's. Ralph Lauren Polos also gallop their way to Melnikoff's periodically (Melnikoff's merchandise fluctuates). Fine labels such as Izod, Lee, and others are available at 10% to 25% Melnik-off. Write or call with a description. **PQ**

MORRIS TRENK
90 Orchard St.
New York, NY 10002
(212) 674-3498

Cheaper by the dozen is the policy, so T-shirt and sweat shirt aficionados unite! Never before have you been able to stock up on your every T-shirt need. Scoop necks, V-necks, short sleeves, French cut, etc., to match every t-aste. Witty sayings or clever observations of your choice can also be printed on a shirt and the final product delivered to unsuspecting friends (or enemies). Use your imagination! The little league, bowling team, school groups will love them at such low prices. **C**

PAGANO GLOVES
3-5 Church St.
Johnstown, NY 12095
(518) 762-8425

When it's spring, a young man's fancy turns to thoughts of gloves . . . Pagano Gloves, Inc. sells men's, women's, and children's deerskin gloves, coats, jackets, and accessories at 50% and more off retail store prices. They offered a Texas-size selection of ladies' handbags priced from $22.50 to $75. And for the rough and rednecks, they offered "rough-out" cowhide jackets and vests beginning at $52. Slip into a pair of feather-light slippers or moccasins for as little as $6.50, for around the house. No refunds, exchanges only. **C $1.50**

RAMMAGERDIN OF REYKJAVIK
Hafnarstraeti 19
P.O. Box 751-121
Reykjavik, Iceland

Question: What's the favorite comic strip of an Icelandic sheep shearer? Answer: Mutton Jeff! This company offers clothing for the whole family made from wool and fur, as well as ceramics, souvenir gifts, and knitting products. Prices on their woolen sweaters, ponchos, coats, caps, mittens, shawls, and vests are about 50% less than U.S. retail for comparable quality (around $35 to $40 usually, versus $70 to $80). If you've been hankering to weave your own bargain, they also sell Lopi undyed yarn in single and triple ply, spun and unspun, already washed and mothproofed. There's a minimum yarn order of eight skeins. **B with samples $1**

ROMENES-PATERSON LTD.
Edinburgh Woolen Mill
Langholm, Dumfriesshire
Scotland DG130BR
Phone: 054180092 (dial "01" for operator assistance with this call)

Are you on a kilt trip about spending too much money? Don't skirt the issue, address it (and send it off to Scotland). You'll be coming back for moor. Tweed and tartan skirts and suits for men and women are priced well below those found in comparable stores in the U.S. Classic Shetland sweaters by Pringle, Lyle & Scott, and their own brand cost from $20 to $60 ($35 to $100 retail). Satisfaction is guaranteed 100% and they will gladly accept exchanges on items purchased by mail or at one of their 65 retail shops in Britain. Since all prices are in pounds, it is best to get a pounds sterling certificate for the proper amount. The company will honor its catalog prices for one year following the catalog's publication date. A £5 (surface mail) or £10 (air mail) postage fee is required on any size order. **C**

SOUSA & LEFKOVITS
621 S. "B" St.
Tustin, CA 92681-4389
(800) 854-6177
(714) 731-7183: CA, HI, AK residents

Whether you love or hate preppies, everyone knows you can't look tacky when you're wearing khaki. This popular retailer entered the mail-order business in 1981 by offering 20% to 40% savings on traditional men's and women's clothing such as wool blazers, cotton Oxford shirts, tailored linen dresses, and colorful Madras shirts made from fine-quality fabrics by the best manufacturers. The spring 1983 catalog featured a high-tech Norman Rockwell-like approach depicting activities in everyday life and using S & L employees to model hundreds of outfits. (There are retail stores in Tustin and West Los Angeles.) Satisfaction is guaranteed or you can return the items at the company's expense for refund or replacement. Shipping cost on all orders is $3.50. **C $1**

SPECIALTY LEATHERS AND BAGS
1139 N. "D" St.
San Bernardino, CA 92410
(714) 884-2216

Here's a manufacturer with something to hide: 50% off leather coats, jackets, and vests in semi-western to dressy styles. Made from distinctive materials (cabretta, glazed lamb, or polished calfskin), these garments are lined with satin acetate. Ladies' coats ran from $99.45 to $165.45 for full-length wraps. Men's coats and jackets ran from $91.45 to $139.45 for regulars, up to $189 for sizes 48 to 52 and longs. Vests, also lined, were priced from $39.45. Assorted leather bags for travel, tennis, and workouts were priced from $12 for an Adidas tennis bag to $70 for a five-piece set of luggage. The company will respond within 21 days of receipt of the order. Minimum order (four) in bags only. They guarantee articles to be free of damage or errors in workmanship or they will replace them up to 90 days provided the article is unworn. **B $1**

STRAND SURPLUS SENTER
2202 Strand
Galveston, TX 77550
(800) 231-6005: charge orders only
(713) 762-7397: TX residents

If your mother wears combat boots, get 'em here for $44.95 ($61 government cost). The Strand calls itself 'the only genuine surplus store in the country." No doubt this bold self-appraisal originated from the company's "belovedly wise and cool leader" Colonel Bubbie who looks like a cross between Sad Sack and Abe Lincoln on the price lists (sent monthly). Strand salesman Oscar, a major sales force by himself, told us of British WWII camouflage pants of cotton, "unused and perfect," for $49.95, Italian army pullover sweaters of 100% wool for $85, and many more items, including tools and mess kits. Their $1 price list (updated every 30 days or so) mentions bargains at up to 70% off. **B $1** (refundable)

WINONA KNITTING MILLS FACTORY OUTLET
910 E. Second St.
Winona, MN 55987
(800) 328-7298
(800) 642-6038: MN residents
(507) 454-3240

Bundle up the family without spending a bundle. You'll find better sweaters in such styles as crew neck, V-neck, cardigan, pullover, and turtleneck made from such wearable fibers as ragg, merino, cashmere, Shetland, lamb's wool, and berber at savings of 40% to 50%. Wool blends are also available, along with chamois and buffalo plaid shirts by Woolrich, and Cellar stoneware. We saw a beautiful ladies' V-neck cashmere sweater (beige, heather, white, or scarlet) for $64 listed in their 24-page full-color catalog. All merchandise comes with a 100% unconditional guarantee, so if you're knit-picky about your order and change your mind, you can get off the hook with their liberal exchange or refund policy. **C**

Menswear

Interested in investment dressing without cashing in all your blue chips? Check out the stock marketed here and get everything from Adolfos to Zeros at bargain margins. Classic clothing is always in style. Natural fabrics wear better and last longer. If you're looking for Arrow shirts, Bass shoes, Brooks Brothers suits, Dior robes, Sansabelt slacks, or Hanes underwear we've got you covered at less than over-the-counter prices.

A. RUBENSTEIN & SONS
63 E. Broadway
New York, NY 10002
(212) 226-9696

Unlike the late great musician, this A. Rubenstein's no pianist, although his prices on men's clothing definitely struck a responsive chord with us. This family's been playing our song for 60 years with a wide composition of suit sizes (from 34 short to 52 long) and key manufacturers (Adolfo, Cardin, Givenchy, Stanley Blacker, Yves St. Laurent, Oleg Cassini, and Zero King—not to mention San Remo, Marzotta, Damon, and London Fog). Shirts, ties, sportswear, rainwear, and outer wear also were available at 20% to 30% discounts. There's a $25 minimum order, and no restocking charge. The refund policy is to make a full cash refund in two weeks after delivery. No wonder note-able New Yorkers have kept in tune with the times by making this store their fashion forte. **B, PQ**

CUSTOM COAT COMPANY, INC.
227 N. Washington St.
Berlin, WI 54923
(414) 361-0900

Pass the buck to Custom Coat after your successful deer hunting trip, and they'll tan your hide! Custom Coat transforms raw hides into deerskin jackets, coats, vests, gloves, purses, hats, moccasins, and many other leather accessories. They've got many styles to browse through in their free catalog, and their prices averaged 25% lower than other retail sources, so you'll save some doe. If you need extra leather to complete your order, they'll supply it at $2.75 per square foot. And if you don't hunt, Custom Coat can furnish ready-made leather goods from their stock of skins so you can be dressed out, even if a deer wasn't. **C**

THE DEERSKIN PLACE
283 Akron Road
Ephrata, PA 17522
(717) 733-7624

Those who don't run with the herd can let their fingers do the stalking through this brochure. You can fawn over jackets, coats, handbags, shoes, moccasins, sheepskins, gloves, and wallets for men and women at 30% to 50% off retail. (Bargains like that belong on our trophy rack—our interest is mounting!) A women's belted leather jacket was $189; a pair of men's fringed or unfringed moccasins was $28.95 ($39 elsewhere). We set our sights on a pair of women's unlined gloves for $19.98, and bagged a coonskin cap ($5.95) for the Bambi-no. There's no minimum order; no restocking charge on returns; but there is an exchange-only policy (no refunds). If stiff leather prices dis-suede you from buying, you won't lock horns with these prices, and you just might save some bucks. **B, PQ**

DEVA COTTAGE INDUSTRY
303 E. Main St.
Box US
Burkittsville, MD 21718
(301) 473-4900

"Deva is an attempt to humanize work and integrate it with home life," according to the catalog, and manufacturing natural fiber clothing for men and women is the means they've selected. Deva drawstring pants, $16, close kin to the surgical team look, are extremely comfortable. They come in many colors and are perfect for running, lounging, or meditating. They also make shorts, $10; T-shirts with insignia, $7; wrap skirts, $18; a wonderful "Spring Moon" kimono, $35; and many other products. Clothing comes in small, medium, large, extra-large, or special ($5 extra) sizes. Unconditional guarantees (exchange or refund). They also sell wild herbs and books and records for devotees of Eastern philosophy and culture. *Natural Fibers Directory,* $3, is an excellent source for household goods and clothing made of natural fibers. **C**

DORSETT DISTRIBUTING CO.
11866 Dorsett Road
Maryland Heights, MO 63043
(800) 325-4155
(314) 291-8565: MO residents

Another sports Cinderella story . . . Tony's toes were twinkling at the Foot Ball in celebration of Dorsett's contemporary designer men's and women's clothing (which was free from offensive price hikes). "Exquizitely (football players can't spell) tailored" stars such as Oleg Cassini, Givenchy, Corneliani, Halston, and Bill Blass were suited up, with prices huddling at 30% to 40% lower than retail. A line-up of fabrics included pinstripes, herringbones, tweeds, solids, plaids, Ultrasuede, and sharkskin (but no pigskin). Ed was trying to sell a van, but instead announced he'd got a "really big shoe," (since Allen Edmonds' AAAA to EEE widths were carried in sizes 5 to 16 at 25% off). With 100% money back if dissatisfied, no restocking charge, a free catalog, and a 100% warranty both from Dorsett and the manufacturer, we had to cheer this mail-order team. In fact, the only person not smiling at this gala event was Tom Landry—perhaps he'd been told that at the stroke of midnight the coach would turn into a pumpkin. **C**

FACTORY WHOLESALERS
United Ramex Division
P.O. Box 938
Litchfield, MN 55355
(612) 693-3413

"Workers of the world unite" should be the slogan for this outfit. We gave high Marx to their used men's work clothes including pants, shirts, coveralls, jackets, socks, and white shirts, and ladies' smocks made from washable Lenin. A bundle of five pants and five shirts was $16.50 plus $3.50 handling. Men's premium-grade cotton tube socks were 10 for $14.50 plus $3 shipping. Shop coats were three for $8 plus $4 shipping. This company says they will save the working man a minimum of 90% over a year, and there's 100% satisfaction or your money is refunded. It's Stalin a day's work for this industrial clothier of over 10 years. Pricewise, these czar the good old days. **B, PQ**

GELBER'S MEN'S STORE
630 Convention Plaza at Seventh Ave.
St. Louis, MO 63101
(314) 421-6698

The St. Louis Cardinals may make us see red, but Gelber's is far from our Arch enemy. The inventory of discounted men's clothing changes weekly at this 91-year-old company. All merchandise is first quality and is discounted 30% to 70% off regular prices. Current styles are available in such names as Cricketeer, Curlee, Raffinatti, and Misty Harbor. They sell factory overruns and salesmen's samples at low prices: suits, $79.50 to $114, sport coats, $59 to $79. They even do alterations at little or no charge. Send them a style description for prices. **PQ**

G & G PROJECTIONS
53 Orchard St.
New York, NY 10002
(212) 431-4531

Gosh, Golly, and G whiz. They'll take the shirt off their racks and mail it to you. Tell GiGi she can order name-brand and designer shirts and sweaters sporting such names as Hathaway and Christian Dior through their affiliated stores across the street at 58 Orchard St. called Penn Garden and Liberty Menswear (212) 966-5600. All shirts, sizes 14½ to 18 and suits and jackets by such notables as Geoffrey Beene, Stanley Blacker, Yves St. Laurent, Adolfo, Pierre Cardin, and Calvin Klein. You'll save 35% and they pay the shipping with no G-strings attached. Orders by phone only with credit cards, Sunday through Friday. If you call on Saturday, guess you're plumb out of Gluck. **PQ**

HARRY ROTHMAN, INC.
111 Fifth Ave.
New York, NY 10003
(212) 777-7400

I'm just wild about Harry and Harry's wild about men. Rothman is the granddaddy of the discount men's business; the male counterpart to Loehmann's. Save 25% to 50% on suits, jackets, shirts, ties, rainwear, and haberdashery in a wide variety of styles and sizes (36 to 56) plus extra-longs and extra-shorts from many top men's manufacturers. Low prices will blow you away. Though they won't reveal labels to us over the phone, we know that many a Hick-ey has become a Free Man after leaving his shop. Write to their mail-order department describing your size, weight, height, and waist measurements, and preference of patterns and fabric. They will provide you with the top of the line in menswear. Over 40,000 square feet and 35 employees. Accepts major credit cards and checks. Returns also accepted (if not worn or altered). **PQ**

JOS. A. BANK CLOTHIERS
109 Market Place
Baltimore, MD 21202
(301) 837-8838

For investment dressing, this is a manufacturer you can Bank on. Savings of 25% to 30% on fine-quality traditional men's, ladies', and prep clothing and accessories were more than suit-able, and were definitely tailored to fit our budget. Scrutinize this 75-year-old Bank's holdings: $12.50 silk ties; $18 men's Oxford shirts; men's 100% wool worsted suits, $210; $26.50 for women's khaki slacks; and $20.50 for ragg wool sweaters. Other assets included shoes, belts, rain gear, handbags, hats, and caps. There's no restocking charge on returns (within 30 days for exchange or refund, if not worn or altered or specifically cut), satisfaction's guaranteed, and their catalog's free. If you need to put a finger on the supple fabrics they use, ask for samples. **C**

LEE-McCLAIN CO.
U.S. Highway 60 West
Shelbyville, KY 40065
(502) 633-3823

Tired of jockeying for clothing at retail? (You bet!) Well, you can't get a Kentucky derby here, just suits, sport coats, and slacks at 40% to 60% off. This 50-year-old company manufactures its own line of "Strathmore" suits, as well as sewing on private labels for retail buyers. Summer-blend suits were 55% dacron and 45% wool, while winter suits were 100% wool. One suit style available: a two-button front with center vent in the back. Prices on Strathmore suits ranged from $145 to $185 (comparable quality suits run $285 and up). Suits are stocked in sizes 36 to 50 in extra-long, long, regular, and short, with custom suits $100 more. Send them your suit size and they will send fabric samples (since not all fabrics are available in certain sizes). Make your decision, and you'll be off to the races (looking like a thoroughbred) with their finished lines. **PQ**

MASTER FASHIONS
5318 Normandy Blvd.
P.O. Box 37559
Jacksonville, FL 32205
(904) 786-8121 or 786-8770

Strictly a-men of the cloth store, this company is geared to serve preachers, pastors, or Christian groups. Bless their hearts, they offered basic black, brown, and navy suits at $69.95 and $99.95 (the brochure shows only two styles to choose from) that they say would retail for $129.95 to $194.95. Savings graced out at 40% to 60%. Their offering also included a simple two-button blazer in electric blue, orange, red, green, gold—as well as dark blue (we're not passing judgment but we must confess, that's not our style). They also tithe one free suit for every 10 religiously ordered. **B**

MILTON'S CLOTHING CUPBOARD
163 E. Franklin, Dept. 1
Chapel Hill, NC 27514
(919) 968-4408

Thanks to Milton, Paradise can be regained and men don't have to go around wearing fig leaves anymore. In fact, we found top designer suits, sport coats, shirts, pants, and outer wear from heavenly creators such as Pierre Cardin, Hart Schaffner Marx, Christian Dior, College Hall, Eagle, Browning King, and Sussex. Milton Julian is a personable man who circulates a mailer about twice a year to 25,000 customers. His other retail store locations (which also accept mail orders) are at 3934 W. Market St., Dept. 2, Greensboro, NC 27407 and 6631 Morrison Blvd., Dept. 3, Charlotte, NC 28211. **C**

PALISADES OUTLET
7601 River Road
North Bergen, NJ 07047
(201) 861-1115

For out-of-pocket savings that are completely out of hand, try this outlet. No more will you be Roman the stores looking for clothing by Damon, or paying prices only a king can afford. You can leave your chariot at home and get first-quality sportswear at close to wholesale. This store is owned by Damon and (predictably) carries their own brands: Damon, Bill Blass, Mirelle. Prices are a whopping 40% to 60% off retail. They offer a five-day refund, 30-day exchange policy. Isn't it a Pythias so many are in-slaved by their ignorance of this outlet? **PQ**

QUINN'S SHIRT SHOP
Route 12, P.O. Box 131
North Grosvenordale, CT 06255
(203) 923-2589

What a Quinn's-cidence! Prices 40% to 50% lower in the same shop with high fashion. Me and my Arrow, shirts that is, and my Enro just slightly irregular from the straight and narrow. Owner Robert Fian is a pleasant man who's been in this business for over 30 years. He requests you specify short or long sleeves, color preference, and line (Dover, Brigade, Cottonese, Kent Collection, etc.) when requesting prices. Exchanges only. Order sent C.O.D. **PQ**

SAINT LAURIE LTD.
Mail Order Dept.
84 Fifth Ave.
New York, NY 10011
(800) 221-8660
(212) 242-2530: NY residents

Halo from the Saint who can save you pennies from heaven on classic business suits. After Christmas, Saint Laurie's took out two full-page ads in the *New York Times* so you know they must be doing something right. Discounts of 33% and more are religiously given on men's suits, $139 to $245, and women's suits, $192 to $267, shown in their 32-page, full-color catalog. Fabric swatches of tweed, herringbone, serge, worsted wool, and camel's hair give you a feel for what you're buying. The customer service department thoughtfully ships UPS orders to the busy exec's office from 9 a.m. to 5 p.m. We don't want to make a suit-case out of this, but here is where the worst-ed can be the best. **C** (twice a year)

STANLEY M. MIRSKY
2770 Irving Blvd.
Dallas, TX 75207
(214) 634-7249

Stan's the man to see since "I can get it for you wholesale" is his standard operating procedure. Behind the sleek black blinds of this jobber's elegant shop are beautiful designer suits and sport coats selling for 50% less than retail boutiques. Another room had coats including distressed leather jackets, down parkas, sheepskin coats, raincoats, even leather pants. We had to give in to a Givenchy tuxedo, on sale for $135 in any size. Silk ties $10, cotton shirts $17, designers like Nino Cerruti . . . just tear a page or two from the latest issue of *GQ* and send it to Stanley. Chances are good he'll "get it for you wholesale." **PQ**

SUSSEX CLOTHES LTD.
895 Broadway
New York, NY 10003
(212) 260-1910

Dress for Sussex means power dressing for Wall Street or Washington. The model pictured in this company's ads is Ivy League all the way—to the bank. But you can have the same suit Brooks Brothers or any other preppy proprietor sells for almost half-price. This prestigious manufacturer sells "retail to the public at wholesale prices." For $2, we received samples of herringbone, camel's hair, flannel, pinstripe, plaid, tweed, and solid wool in shades that made us think of English lords. Also carries 100% silk sport jackets; trousers, sizes 30 to 40, $42.50; two-piece suits, $199; three-piece suits, $224; tuxedos, $234—all bearing the Sussex label. Shipping costs $5 for the first suit and $1 for each additional garment. Send for their Yale-order brochure and swatches. **B** $2 (refundable)

Women's Wear

Shop around the world in these pages and save on airfare. Go international with wooden clogs from Holland, Irish hand-knit sweaters, or fine woolen clothing from the famous looms of Iceland. Stay home and get Anne and Calvin Klein, Diane von Furstenberg, and original Levi jeans at dress-for-less prices. Be an informed shopper. If you're on the smallish side, you can save $$$ on your Izods by buying them in the boys' department. Here are the size conversions: boys' 20 = women's large (38 to 40), boys' 18 = women's medium (34 to 36), boys' 14 to 16 = women's small (30 to 32). No matter what you're looking for, use your ingenuity. You can usually get your upstairs wardrobe at bargain basement prices.

A. ROSENTHAL INC.
92 Orchard St.
New York, NY 10002
(212) 473-5428

One of the seven wonders of the off-price world is New York's Lower East Side. Blossoming forth from innocuous-looking store fronts along Orchard Street are some of the finest bargains in the land. A. Rosenthal is definitely one of our favorites for underwear, bras, lingerie, robes, nightgowns, and panty hose discounted 20% to 50%. A firm supporter of over 50 brands of lingerie such as Maidenform, Lily of France, Vassarette, Lady Marlene, Formfit, Kayser, and many more. Sizes 32A to 40DD. All first quality. No returns on special order merchandise or worn, torn, or soiled items. Tickets must remain on. Minimum order $20 on MasterCard or Visa. Write for brochure or send manufacturer and style number for a price quote. **PQ, B**

BREAKAWAY FASHIONS INC.
88 Rivington St.
New York, NY 10022
(212) 298-4455

Looking for your big (price) break? You can Breakaway from high retail prices on designer lines like Anne Klein, Silk Farm, Jack Mulqueen, and harvé bernard at this place. Items carried include women's designer dresses, suits, coats, accessories, and evening wear. They also take custom fur orders and will soon feature a "fur catalog." (We can hardly wait—while we've seen a lot of catalogs, including catalogs of furs, a "fur catalog" will surely be unique to the industry.) Their 20% to 40% discounts were liberating, to say the least, and caused us to break out in song. The minimum is one garment per order, and merchandise can be exchanged if all tags are still attached to the garment and the garment has not been worn. Furs are warrantied for one year against natural defects. **C $1** (refundable)

CAREER GUILD
6412 Vapor Lane
Niles, IL 60648
(800) 228-5000: member orders and new memberships
(800) 228-5454: retail orders
(312) 492-1405: IL residents

We promise not to guild the lily regarding the Career Guild, 'cause we don't want to feel guild-ty later on. This is their firm offer: You may purchase their catalog items at retail prices or, for $7.50, become a member and be eligible for an average 25% discount on coordinated fashions for working women. (Members are under no obligation to buy.) Examples of savings to members include a silk blouse, $27 for members and $36 retail for nonmembers; silk trousers, $31.50 versus $42 retail; a jacket dress $41.25 versus $55 retail; and a wool-blend suit $57 versus $115 retail for nonmembers. (As any apprentice will tell you, it pays to pay your dues.) Members also receive a 7% Hertz rental discount, bimonthly newsletters, and credit plan eligibility after four months. There's a 15-day exchange or refund policy, and the membership fee is refundable if ever you should become dissatisfied with the service. There are four free catalogs yearly. **C**

CHARLES WEISS & SONS, INC.
38 Orchard St.
New York, NY 10002
(212) 226-1717

Charles' sons may be Weiss guys, but after 30 years ladies still love their lines. We found 20% to 50% discounts on ladies' lingerie and bras having such top-of-the-line labels as Bali, Maidenform, Formfit, Kayser, Vassarette, Olga, Lily of France, and Christian Dior. (The teddies may bare a lot but the savings are far from skimpy.) This company wants it known they take checks and credit cards. With such a supportive price policy, you can shoulder your sagging fortunes and keep from going busted. **C**

DOWN GENERATION/SYLVIA & SONS
725 Columbus Ave.
New York, NY 10025
(212) 666-0631

Get down, get down! More than 35,000 down-filled garments, including jackets, vests, and full-length coats are discounted 20% off retail. We found enough skiwear to outfit Jean-Claude Killy for ten seasons and that's no snow job. Exchanges or refunds made within two weeks. **C**

GOHN BROS.
P.O. Box 111
Middlebury, IN 46540
(219) 825-2400

Going, going, Gohn to the brothers from Middlebury! This 85-year-old company sells Amish men's and women's clothing, plain clothing, underwear, hosiery, yard goods for quilting and supplies, and notions. (Their *Amish Country Cookbook,* $7.95 featuring 600 old-fashioned Amish farm cooking recipes, was one notion that really whetted our appetites.) Clothing brands carried included such names as Hanes, Health Knit, Gerber, Red Wing (shoes), Cannon (towels), and Chatham, and prices were about 30% off retail. They carried a good line of sewing supplies in their eight-page, very functional newspaper brochure listing their merchandise. Amish suits were made to order. This company will exchange merchandise, but won't charge or make refunds, so once you spend your money here, what's gone is Gohn's. **B, PQ**

GOLDMAN & COHEN
54 Orchard St.
New York, NY 10002
(212) 966-0737

Call for the finest names in lingerie and lounge wear. Orders for in-season top liners filled by a personable sales force with savings of 20% to 70% (average discount 40% to 50%). Mostly first-quality, an occasional select irregular (like select irregular Lollipop panties that Macy's sells for $1.49; G & C price is 99 cents). Bras and lingerie by Yves St. Laurent, Eve Stillman, Vassarette, Kayser, Bali, Lily of France. We even asked for John Kloss but were informed he has not been designing for years. (See how up-to-date we are.) Sizes in bras from 32A to 44D; lingerie P, S, M, L, and XL. Exchanges only on bras and girdles with receipt, tickets on, and clean; no exchanges on lingerie. Minimum of $10 on credit cards. Shipping costs $2.50 for orders under $50; $3 shipping charges on orders up to $100. **PQ**

THE ICEMART
P.O. Box 23
Keflavik Airport
235 Iceland

Dyed-in-the-wool sweater freaks yearning for undyed yarn will find their fancy looming on the horizon. Coats, caps, jackets, mittens, socks, scarves, and sweaters are made of wool shorn from descendents of sheep brought to Iceland during the ninth century. (Perhaps they were on the lam-b from Beo-wolf.) The hair has evolved to produce softer, glossier, lightweight wool. No dyes, artificial colors, or bleaches are used—just natural wool in muted earth tones of creamy white, pale brown, and charcoal gray. You won't get fleeced either—prices are not Baa-d! One hundred percent wool blankets were $37 to $43; ladies' knitted fully lined jackets and coats, $84 to $92; ladies' hand-knit pullovers with hand-twisted yarn in one-of-a-kind designs, $54. They also have sheepskin rugs, Lava-Ceramic ware, silver jewelry, and fish and dairy products. Warning: If ewe miss this, you might feel sheepish! **C $1** airmail, free by surface mail

IRISH COTTAGE INDUSTRIES
44 Dawson St.
Dublin 2, Ireland

You can't churn a living making cottage cheese, so the Irish churned to making fine quality sweaters. It o'curd to them that the cottage industry could churn out homemade wool-you-be-mine's faster than granny could say, "Bring me another glass of warm milk, dear." And their prices on hand-knit Aran sweaters, scarves, and mittens won't get your Ire up. Save about 25%. With luck and a buck, you can get a charming catalog. **C $1** airmail, free by surface mail

KENNEDY'S OF ARDARA
Ardara County
Donegal, Ireland

Shawl be comin' round the island when she comes. Savin' up to 50% on world famous hand-knit Aran Isle sweaters. Kennedy's also carries shawls, scarves, mitts, and other items at 30% to 40% off. **C $2**

LADY ANNABELLE
P.O. Box 1490
Boston, MA 02205
(617) 242-3825

Ladies in weight-ing will find their designer teddies, camisoles, slips, bras, and other shining nightgowns in hard-to-find sizes 38 to 48. While not a discount store, they do offer savings over custom clothing with lines like Formfit, Vassarette, and others. They have a full money-back guarantee—all exchange and refund requests are honored. The catalog price is refundable with the first order. **C $2**

L'EGGS SHOWCASE OF SAVINGS
P.O. Box 748
Rural Hall, NC 27098
(919) 744-3434

A L'egg-acy from the Consolidated Foods Company, try this on for thighs: slightly imperfect L'eggs panty hose, Hanes underwear and socks for men and boys, Underalls and Slenderalls panty hose, and others at up to 55% off. We also found many first-quality panties, bras, and slips discounted with names like Bali busting out. The colorful catalog featured style and size charts for easy ordering and tagged pages indicating first quality and imperfect merchandise. Plus there was a large selection to choose from. L'eggs regular queen-size panty hose were $1.17—$1.79 retail. Most items have minimum of three pairs. Postage varies with amount of purchase: under $10, pay $1.05, under $20, pay $1.55, etc. **C**

LINDA'S HOSIERY OUTLET INC.
311 Trindale Road
High Point, NC 27263
(919) 431-2568: Call collect when ordering

Got everything under control? If your tummy isn't too sure, Linda's Hosiery can help you "suck it in" with their control top panty hose without sucking it out of your pocketbook. No need to drop names, the highest-quality brands can be found at discount prices in a variety of colors. The low prices on socks won't sock it to you, and the ladies' panties will leave you panting for more. Discounts of 30% to 40% are the rule, and there's a $10 minimum. If you're ready for seconds, "repaired" socks are also available. **PQ**

THE LINGERIE SHOP
8230 Forsyth
Clayton, MO 63105
(314) 721-7982

Does this place have your size and manufacturer? Of corset does. Firm believers in uplifting experiences will find Formfit Rogers, Lily of France, Barbizon, Lisanne, Lorrdine, Niki Lu, Olga, Round the Clock Hosiery, Vassarette, Warner's, Dreamaway, Henson Kickernick, Iris, Christian Dior, Lucie Ann, Maidenform, Periphery, Robes of California, Slumbertogs, Travel Lite, and Val Mode in lingerie and hosiery. Without stretching the truth, prices are typically 15% to 20% off retail. They warmed our heart with their exchange or refund policy, and there's no restocking charge to pad the company's . . . coffers. **PQ**

THE LOFT DESIGNER SPORTSWEAR
491 Seventh Ave.
New York, NY 10018
(212) 736-3358

When we saw the Loft's less-than-lofty prices on designer sportswear, we didn't hit the roof. With 33% to 60% discounts, we found prices much less steep-le than we expected; and even though we had a ceiling on our budget, we could put a designer on our back. Nothing comes between us and our Calvin's (Klein's, that is), except high price tags. We found Perry Ellis, Ralph Lauren, and even Anne Klein-ing the walls here, with their latest designs available in this to-be-watched tower. **PQ**

MAYFIELD CO. INC.
303 Grand St.
New York, NY 10002
(212) 226-6627

Mayfield knows hose, and theirs go for 20% to 25% off retail. Berkshire, Bonnie Doon, and Christian Dior are among the selection. Men's underwear as well as ladies' lingerie (in such brand names as Barbizon, Vassarette, Olga, Warner's, and Bali) are also carried. All are guaranteed first quality; there's no restocking charge on returns; refund within 10 days; and there's a $25 minimum order. You may have to do some stocking up to meet the minimum. **PQ**

MENDEL WEISS
91 Orchard St.
New York, NY 10002
(212) 925-6815

Weiss up and become bosom buddies with Mendel Weiss. His 25%

discounts will keep you abreast of inflation. A treasure chest of lingerie lines: Lily of France, Dior, Olga, Maidenform, Bali, Playtex, Warner's, Formfit Rogers, and more in bras, girdles, panties, garter belts, slips, camisoles, caftans, robes, body suits, swimsuits, cruise wear, car coats and raincoats, hostess gowns, and peignoirs. They also carry mastectomy forms and bras. Refund or exchange within 30 days. Handling and insurance, $1.75. **PQ**

MID-SOUTH FACTORY OUTLET
6215 Highway 305
Olive Branch, MS 38654
(601) 895-4050

OK, so maybe their name doesn't set us quivering with curiosity. Maybe that's our mis-shake, 'cause their prices certainly set us to trembling (with anticipation!). This high class discounter carries no seconds or imperfects and has prices at least 20% off retail, and generally much more (30% to 70%). Lines carried include Damon, Inron, Hallen-St. George, and Flying Scotchman. Send a written request for price quotes on familiar and designer clothing lines, and start shimmying with panache. **PQ**

MRS. RUBY'S BOUTIQUE
7904 West Drive #2
North Bay Village, FL 33141
(305) 756-6433

Located across from the Harbor Island Spa, Mrs. Ruby's exclusive designer outfits and accessories have shaped the images of actresses and celebrities alike. Aiding and abetting many recently reduced women who steal in for a quick change of clothing (down or up a size, whichever the case may be) gives Mrs. Ruby the opportunity to seek out undiscovered young designers of haute couture clothes in sizes 12 to 24 for the "richly endowed" woman at lower prices. Save at least 15% on sportswear and dresses, cover-ups, sweaters, belts, blouses, handbags, hosiery, and semiprecious jewelry. Imitation is the sincerest form of flattery, so she seeks out designs similar to those in the fashion magazines that have "a look with movement." A stunning woman herself, Mrs. Ruby will coordinate a luscious wardrobe for you at no extra charge. The outfit we bought looked like we paid thousands for it. Send photo, size, occasion, and price range and leave the shopping to Mrs. Ruby. Enclose SASE for order blanks. **PQ**

NATIONAL WHOLESALE CO. INC.
Hosiery Division
Lexington, NC 27292
(704) 246-5904

Do you get crotch-ety paying thigh prices for lingerie? All your dollars don't have to go to waist. Brief-ly, they carry lingerie, hosiery, and socks, from tummy tamers, body slimmers, surgical hose, ankle-, thigh-, and knee-high hose. Don't let the camisoles and slips slip by. We found sheer savings from heel to toe (and on up!) with queen-size control top panty hose. Regular panty hose are available at good prices ordered half a dozen or a dozen at a time. Men won't fight their prices on boxers, T-shirts, or socks, either. Everything has a money-back guarantee. **C**

O'CONNOR'S YANKEE PEDDLER WAREHOUSE SALE
1731 N. U.S. 23
East Tawas, MI 48730
(517) 362-4631

If you want to be the tog of the town, the answer is just around the O'Connor. They carry last season's stock along with first run close-outs from manufacturers such as Pendleton, White Stag, Jantzen, College Town, Calvin Klein, Levi, Misty Harbor, and more at 30% to 70% discounts. They also carry men's clothing, gifts, and furniture. They do have an exchange policy on returns and will honor justifiable returns. Write for a price quote. **PQ**

OPULENCE
19 E. Main St.
P.O. Box 1186
Uniontown, PA 15401
(800) 245-1195
(412) 439-8900: PA residents call collect

What's Op, doc? Opulence is a catalog of exquisite designer fashions with a twist. After making selections from the catalog (four per year), customers may call the toll-free number. Ask for weekly sales on select clothing in sizes 4 to 24. About 30 days before a new catalog is issued, you can garner closeout discounts from the previous issue of 25% to 33% on their entire catalog inventory with the exception of jewelry, accessories, or lounge wear. Iron out the bugs, Bunny, and put an Albert Nipon, Geoffrey Beene, Bill Blass, Jack Mulqueen, and more in your wardrobe. Elmer won't be a Fudd-y duddy when he sees the bill, either. A silk taffeta blouse with gold trim was $88, on sale for $59. **C** $2 (refundable with first order)

THE PRISCILLA CO.
69 Alden St.
Fall River, MA 02723
(617) 678-7553

If your yarns are getting a little worn from the adventures you've been having (not to mention the stories you've been weaving), and your sweaters have seen better days, latch onto this Fall River Knitting Mill outlet for discount sweaters. Prices here generally run 30% to 50% lower than retail. Machine washable and dryable Shetland crew neck sweaters were $10.95 for women and boys, $11.95 for men. They also stitch monograms or full names in 19 colors in different styles. Identical Shetland crew necks for ladies, monogrammed, were $14 at Priscilla's, and $40 elsewhere. Get hooked on 27 colors for cardigans, V-necks, and crew neck sweaters. **B**

RAYMOND SULTAN & SONS, LTD.
47 Orchard St.
New York, NY 10002
(212) 966-3488

We did an under-study and found this to be a class act for Broad-way sizes (32A to 50DD) in current and discontinued bra styles. If you know your lines, you'll score 20% savings on lingerie by Bali, Poireet, Maidenform, and many more. Supporting cast includes a large selection of black bras and girdles. Send a postcard with manufacturer, style number, and size and get your tickets to comfort. **PQ**

REBORN MATERNITY
1449 Third Ave.
New York, NY 10028
(212) 737-8817

For a pregnant pause that refreshes, try on these born-again bargains in sizes 4 to 20. Revive your maternity wardrobe with moderate to better sportswear and evening wear. You'll sing its praises and, after you've seen the 10% to 50% discounts on first-quality clothing, you'll know you've been saved. Liberal exchange and return policy. Shipped UPS. **C**

ROYAL SILK
Royal Silk Plaza
45 E. Madison Ave.
Clifton, NJ 07011
(201) 772-1800

Although Royal Silk isn't a bona fide discount company, excellent values can be found on silk fashions in blouses, dresses, and menswear, with prices around 40% off comparable retail lines. (Royal Silk carries only their own line!) The *Royal Man* catalog exhibited a Shantung silk tuxedo shirt for $45, silk shorts for $18, a black silk sweat shirt for $25, and several styles of cotton shirts. The women's Royal Silk catalog featured a colorful array of tastefully elegant silk blouses, most from $30 to $60. The Madras kimono of cotton was eye-catching and $22. The Royal Silk *Dress Collection* catalog displayed a dozen brightly colored dresses. The ad for the "Tempest" dress read: "A swirling ballet of color and frill. The redder the better. The message: vibrant. The mood: pulsing with fire. The impact: maximum." (Sounds like a Tempest in a teapot, boiling.) There's a 100% guarantee: If not satisfied for any reason, they'll refund, exchange, or credit. **C $1**

SACHA LTD., INC.
Loehmann's Plaza
18777 Biscayne
Miami, FL 33180
(305) 931-0737

Sacha deal! Save on name-brand shoes like Andrew Geller, Natural Comfort, and Casadei. Anybody would want an Enny or Judith Leiber handbag at the prices here. Tell them the size and style you want and they'll take care of it. We bought a black patent leather and mola shoulder bag that has been the talk of Texas—retail $145; their price, $116. Most unusual collection of collage bags, appliqued sweat suits, and though their phone reception to our inquiries was cool, their in-store service was not as limited. **PQ**

SHIREY'S
1911 Stanford
P.O. Box 1649
Greenville, TX 75401
(214) 455-8895

Send your SASE and stretch your money while stretching out your body in Danskin tights and leotards at a 20% discount. Plenty of famous-name panties and other lingerie for ladies. But don't kid yourself, children's lingerie (Shirey) and Danskins are also available at the same discount. Family sportswear (infants' to ladies' and boys' to size 14) will keep you looking in tip-top shape without paying top dollar prices. Other brands carried include Koret, Levi, Billy the Kid, and Health-Tex; prices averaged 20% to 50% off. There's a $10 minimum order. Send manufacturer, style number, and size for prices on Danskin and Shirey lines. **PQ, SASE**

SWEETWATER HOSIERY MILLS
P.O. Box 390
Sweetwater, TN 37874
(615) 337-6161

Are hose afraid of the big, bad wool? Nope, not as long as they can run faster. At this 86-year-old sock shop, you'll be out of the woods with 40% off men's over-the-calf zephyr wool and nylon blend socks for $2.25 a pair. Ladies' support panty hose irregulars were $1.10 a pair, with girls' and boys' cotton and nylon blend crew socks three pairs for $1.25. Men's athletic shirts (well, they are in good shape) were three for $4.99 and were regularly three for $7.47. My, what big T-shirts they have! Tis better (heh, heh) to save you money, my dear. **C**

TAFFY WRAPS
600 N. Central
Cameron, TX 76520
(817) 697-2226

Take the wrap and go directly to the "Best Dressed" list with lovely evening skirts drag printed on taffeta by a Texas artist. Cameron may be the "Wrap-City in Blue" but there are three basic colors to choose from: dark peach background with print in earth tones, Chinese red background with print in blues, yellow background with print in pastel colors. These one-of-a-kind skirts of art (sizes 6-8, 8-10,

12-14, 16-18) are $95 unhemmed, or send waist-to-ankle measurements, and they will hem it for $5. Add $5 for shipping plus tax and you've got it made. Send for sketch and fabric swatches. (Note: We have one and it's particularly appealing immediately after that big, we mean big, meal.) **PQ, SASE**

V. JUUL CHRISTENSEN & SON
Strandboulevarden 96
DK-2100 Copenhagen Ø
Denmark
Phone: 26 60 00 (dial "01" for operator assistance in making this call)

How Swede it is! Jackie Fleecen would have loved working for this knitwork. These Eider Knit sweaters are top-quality Icelandic wool clothing. The sheep used are from a 1,100-year-old breed. We're not trying to pull the wool over your eyes when we tell you how gorgeous their jackets, coats, and accessories will look on you. **C**

WACO THRIFT STORE INC.
P.O. Box 143
Waco, GA 30182
(404) 537-2702

I dream of jeanies with the light brown wrappers. Men's and women's first-quality jeans for $16.95. Goose-down jackets, from $49.95, children's clothes for school or play. Many gently worn by gentle people. Write with labels and styles in mind for a prompt reply and then make three wishes. **PQ**

WEST ORANGE HOSIERY MILL, INC.
225 Stiger St.
Hackettstown, NJ 07840
(201) 852-1700

This Orange hosiery has no orange hose, but rather beige, taupe, French coffee, white, and cha-cha. (What color is that?) Try this on for size: A box (six pairs) of first-quality regular panty hose was $7. Other styles including queen, support, control top, seamed and no seam, knee-high, and thigh-high varied in price. Buy several boxes and besides never "running" out, you'll save postage: $1.25 first box, 25 cents each additional box. Request their price list when inquiring.
B

W.S. ROBERTSON LTD.
1315 High St.
Harwick Rorburghshore
Scotland, TD9 9DB

This Scottish company has the goods for what ales you. Drink a hearty toast to their fine luxury woolens by such makers as Pringle and Lyle & Scott. Aye, you'll pay lass for it here with 30% to 50% discounts. Moor for your money and well worth the price. **C $5**

Jewelry

Jewelry can be many things to many people. It may be one woman's mystique and another man's fancy. If you know what you're looking for, you ought to be able to find it here. We offer everything from low-cost gems and cultured pearls from the Orient, to high-grade diamonds from New York's famed jewelers on Forty-Seventh Street. The more specific you can be, the more pleased you will be with your selections. Remember the higher the carat and the purer the gold, the higher the price.

AH, ZAHAVA
8041 Walnut Hill Lane
Dallas, TX 75231
(214) 696-1700

Zahava! Sound like an exclamation at the end of a joyful folk dance? Or a toast at some gala occasion? An obscure Gabor sister? Well, Zsa Zsa and company would feel right at home with all de-luxury designs, dahling. One-of-a-kind jewelry creations and fair prices took our breath, but not our money, away. She breathed new life into some of the old jewelry we dredged up from the bottom of our jewelry boxes. Flat-fee appraisals are another plus for this Israeli designer. Devoted customers love her works of art and the way she artfully dodges the heavy-handed mark-up of many of her competitors. Call or write for further information. "You vouldn't vant to miss dis experience, dahlings." **PQ**

BATIKAT
P.O. Box 226022
Dallas, TX 75266
(214) 386-4869

Batikat, Batikat, Seth Hersh is the Batikat man. He trades exclusively in Southeast Asian gold work. Each piece of jewelry is completely handmade and is guaranteed to be 22K (92% pure) gold or higher. The soft rich color of this jewelry expresses the mystique and lure of gold for people all over the world. Mr. Hersh has traveled extensively throughout the Orient and by combining direct purchase with minimal overhead in the U.S., he is able to offer 22K gold jewelry at 14K gold prices! **C $1**

BMI
1617 Promenade Bank Building
Richardson, TX 75080
(214) 234-4394

If you're thinking about getting into gem-nastics, this company will make you sit up and take notice. Time out—they stock Pulsar and Seiko watches, and will order and drop ship (at a minimum of 20% to 35% off) such watch-ables as Rolex, Concord, Corum, and Piaget at customer's request. Nothing but 14K and 18K jewelry from diamonds to semiprecious stones. Gold chains in serpentine, cobra, herringbone, and beveled herringbone varieties are about 50% off. This former veteran Zales employee and jewelry rep also offers add-a-beads, fashion earrings, ear jackets, pearls, studs, and a promise that if you can describe it, he can get it for you. Prices fluctuate with the gold market. All jewelry is a guaranteed sale—guaranteed to be represented accurately. No returns. **PQ**

CROWN CULTURED PEARL CORP.
580 Eighth Ave.
New York, NY 10018
(212) 947-0540

How do you tell if a pearl is cultured? Easy. Cultured pearls rest in Queen Anne oyster beds. We found pelicans, hippopotamuses, rhinoceroses, and exotic birds inhabiting the pages of this typed mailer. Pearls from Japan and China, along with jade, ivory, coral, carnelian, onyx, malachite, and other gemstones were formed into rings, necklaces, pendants, earrings, and bracelets. We shook our buddhas until they were thoroughly jaded, hoping they would give us some fresh pearls of wisdom. The prices we saw in their stapled price sheets ranged from $14 to $1,250, with everything discounted. **B**

EMPIRE DIAMOND CORP.
Empire State Building, 66th Floor
350 Fifth Avenue
New York, NY 10001
(212) 564-4777

This company is building an empire. In business for over 52 years, this well-known and trusted diamond cutter and wholesaler offers jewelry to the public at a 25% to 40% discount. Included in their inventory were fine quality diamonds, cultured pearls, colored gems, and 14K to 18K gold jewelry ranging from $20 charms to diamonds costing thousands. Gold seal guarantee to insure your complete satisfaction. Refunds within 60 days and there's no minimum order. Their 96-page catalog is a visual feast. **C**

FORT WORTH GOLD AND SILVER EXCHANGE
600 Houston St. Mall, Suite 203-A
Fort Worth, TX 76102
(800) 433-5668
(800) 772-8556: TX residents

We thought Emmylou Harris was the Queen of the Silver Dollar till we discovered this one. Save 40% to 75% and even more on jewelry, diamonds, precious metals, and rare coins. They pay top dollar for coins and other gold and silver pieces. Time honored Rolex watches were sensationally priced: Men's Pavé Diamond Rolex watches listing at $33,950 were $10,500; the Ladies' Presidential Rolex was $3,750 ($5,600 list); and Seiko gold and regular watches were 50% and 25% off list. There's a 30-day refund period (plus $10 if you can find a better deal elsewhere), a credit period to 90 days, and if you should become dissatisfied at any time after 90 days, they'll repurchase for at least 70% of the purchase price. Inventory fluctuates rapidly. Their catalog was stunning, along with their prices. **C, B, PQ**

HOUSE OF ONYX
#1 N. Main St.
The Rowe Building
Greenville, KY 42345
(800) 626-8352
(502) 338-2363: KY, AK, HI residents

This house is built on the premise that onyx-sty is the best policy, so if rocks are your quarry, you'll find craft-quality agates, loose diamonds, opals, sapphires, emeralds, tiger eye, malachite, and blue topaz here at 50% less than retail, minimum. A green jade solid bangle was $6; Mexican onyx 6-inch horsehead bookends, $7.75; onyx English chessmen, $25; and a cloisonné pendant on woven nylon cord, $10. All stones are genuine; satisfaction's guaranteed; the minimum order's $10; and the catalog's free. At half the price of retail, we could afford twin purchases of these Gem-in-eyes, and still be able to bask in the lapis of luxury. Last year, over 2 million orders were processed and not one complaint was registered through the P.O., Action Lines, or other consumer protection agencies. Onyx-sty. **C**

JAY KAY JEWELERS
2512 Program Drive, Suite 109
Dallas, TX 75220
(214) 358-1586

If diamonds are a girl's best friend, does that mean she's got a heart of stone, or are her friends just multifaceted? Rubies, sapphires, emeralds, opals, diamonds, and pearls all receive the royal treatment in this king-size (and brilliantly photographed) catalog. Jay Kay sells fine jewelry at about 50% less than retail; in fact, if you make a purchase and get it appraised for less than you paid (within 10 days), you can get your money back. Obviously, they really carat this place. If you're "setting" around and thinking about your next engagement, you might give these folks a ring. **C $5** (refundable with first order)

L & R WATCH CRYSTAL CORP.
11 Eldridge St.
New York, NY 10002
(212) 925-3690

We don't know about the opinion of Manwatchers, but watch watchers will note that all the faces here are hands-ome. (And we don't need a "seconds" opinion!) This company offers first-quality watches in names like Pulsar and Movado discounted 10% to 30%, which makes their watches more than mere faces in the crowd. Jewelry is affordable at a sparkling 50% off retail and they'll even custom-make to your specifications. Watches are guaranteed for one year but there are no refunds or exchanges on jewelry unless there is something physically wrong. A catalog's in the works, but right now, call for a price quote. Time flies, but at L & R, they help keep high prices at a standstill. **PQ**

M & I HABERMAN INC.
380 Lexington Ave., Suite 521
New York, NY 10168
(212) 697-5270

M & I Haberman has been selling jewelry at discount prices since 1918. They have diamonds, pearls, and precious stones, as well as watches by Seiko, Bulova, Pulsar, Accutron, Citizen, Longines, Movado, Cronns, Omega, Jules-Jurgenson, Heller, and Keepsake. Prices are generally 25% to 50% less than retail. Exchanges and refunds are offered, although shipping charges are deducted. You can send for their attractive full-color catalog (the price of which is refundable with your first order), or you can write them with the model number of the item you desire. **PQ, C $2** (refundable)

THE NECKLACE SHOP
P.O. Box 421
Redwood City, CA 94064

The Necklace Shop sells necklaces, pendants, and earrings of genuine semiprecious natural stones including amethyst, tiger eye, citrine, and mossy agate. The difference, in case you're wondering, between "precious" and "semiprecious" is largely one of rarity and price. A diamond is considered precious; a tiger eye, semiprecious; and a topaz can go either way. The stones offered by this retired geologist are all good quality. Necklaces come in varying lengths and range in price from $4.50 to $40. Discounts from 10% to 50% off. Our order for a $14 necklace arrived promptly. Returns and refunds made within 10 days. **B**

P.M.C.
P.O. Box 1519
Pebble Beach, CA 93953
(408) 373-1848: call collect

This company is one of the finest sources around for investment quality diamonds and colored stones. Prices are low, quality is high, and their advice is the tops. All purchases can be handled safely through the mail. They also publish a free newsletter that gives investors the latest information. **PQ**

RAMA JEWELRY LTD.
987 Silom Road
Bangkok, Thailand
Phone: 011-66-2-234-7521 (dial direct)

Oh Mama, Rama is the Thai that binds you with wholesale gems, jewelry, Thai silks, silverware, bronze ware, leather goods, teakwood carvings, and other local products. Princess rings, diamond rings, and ruby and sapphire rings are their mainstay. They'll create a design from a picture, sketch, or description of what you want. Minimum order is $100 in U.S. dollars. Deliveries usually take one week if sent airmail, and about two months for sea-mail. **C, PQ**

R/E KANE ENTERPRISES
15 W. 47th St. #401
New York, NY 10036
(212) 869-5525

More than a good citizen, Kane is a good entrepreneur as well. While you likely won't find them muttering "rosebud" on their deathbed, you may, if you listen closely, hear the words "Cubic Zirconia" pass from their lips. This company delivers Cubic Zirconia for $10 per diamond carat, compared to $85 elsewhere. A round CZ was $10 per diamond carat and $30 for a marquise cut. Send a self-addressed, stamped envelope for mail-order information. **PQ**

RENNIE ELLEN
15 W. 47th St. #401
New York, NY 10036
(212) 869-5525

If, as Frank Sinatra sings, New York is a city that doesn't sleep, does it follow that this jeweler rocks round the clock, to quote Bill Haley? Perhaps we should just say, "Bill Haley won't you please come home?" and leave our comedic gems behind. We left no stone unturned in a fruitful search for bargain diamonds in the Big Apple. Happily, we found Rennie Ellen in the perfect setting. As one of the few women in the industry, and a consumer advocate, Rennie's wholesale diamond cutting business will polish approximately 75% off the price of all jewelry items. A pair of diamond earrings, 43 points, with 14K white gold setting was $500. The 16-page catalog also offered pendants, necklaces, bracelets, and chains sparkling with sapphires, rubies, and amethyst stones. **C $1**

SAMARTH GEM STONES
P.O. Box 6057
Colaba, Bombay 400 005
India

Holy cow! We found out Bombay is the world's largest market for gemstones due to the cheapest labor charges. Don't moo-ve. They offer 10 8mm gemstones ready for mounting in gold jewelry or presentation for $60: faceted aquamarine, tourmaline, peridot, amethyst, golden citrine, garnet, cobochon ruby, opal, moonstone, and diopside. Your gems will be sent air postpaid. **C $1** (refundable)

VANITY FAIR
55 E. Washington St.
Chicago, IL 60602
(800) 235-3000
(312) 977-0318: IL residents call collect

Since 1921, S.A. Peck has been specializing in jewelry design and diamonds. Because they import and manufacture fine jewelry and eliminate the middleman's profit, they offer savings from 30% to 50% through their Vanity Fair catalog. We found a beautiful 14K gold cowboy boot necklace trimmed in diamonds for $247.50 (retail $370) and ogled over a one-of-a-kind $15,480 brooch with 14 pear-shaped diamonds, four full-cut diamonds, and 60 tapered baguettes cut to $9,750. Their 15-day money-back guarantee is underwritten by Lloyds of London. They also offer, to their customers, the free service of inspecting and ultrasonically cleaning your jewelry for you. Send it to them for service and they pay return postage including insurance and handling. Notarized appraisal on all purchases. **C**

THE WHITEHALL CO.
P.O. Box A3425
Chicago, IL 60690
(800) 621-0771
(312) 782-6800
(312) 787-9500: IL residents

Fake it till you make it with low-priced counterfeit diamonds from Whitehall, or dig into a good selection of real diamonds, 14K gold, and semiprecious stone jewelry at 25% to 50% off retail. Refunds within 60 days if not completely satisfied; they accept mail and phone orders. They also accept trade-ins if you'd like a larger diamond, and offer other unusual guarantees if you would prefer a redo on your setting within one year. There are 35 stores around the U.S. **PQ**

Luggage and Handbags

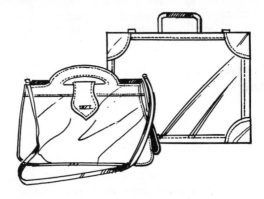

Shop here for your traveling companions. If you want to bag a lasting bargain, consider buying the most durable luggage you can find. Airlines put baggage through a lot of wear and tear—you'll save money in the long run. If you're a woman in business, try buying a handbag that doubles as a briefcase. Some of the listings insist on a description and model number. Be specific. You'll be more likely to receive the olive snakeskin bag by Dior that you requested rather than relying on the whims of the clerk who thinks you'd like a straw satchel.

ACE LEATHER PRODUCTS
2211 Avenue U
Brooklyn, NY 11229
(212) 891-9713

With 25 years in the business, Ira Horn holds a wild card in the bargain game. He's an ace at selling all types of top-grade luggage, briefcases, attachés, small leather goods, handbags, gift items from manufacturers such as American Tourister, Lark, Hartmann, Meyers discounted from 20% to 40%. Mr. Horn believes that discounts should be calculated by comparison to "real retail" prices and even blows his own Horn a bit by adding that he does exactly that. Request the "mail out" of current merchandise. Exchanges made within 10 days of purchase. **B**

AL'S LUGGAGE
2134 Larimer St.
Denver, CO 80205
(303) 295-9009

We shouldn't have to quote scripture to you about the strength of Samsonite—if you've watched the TV commercials you've probably seen a testament to its durability. Al's offers some commanding discounts of 40% to 50% off retail (pretty standard discounts everywhere) on all the most popular styles (except the Silhouette 200 line, which was 35% off). This place is a source for irregular, but perfectly respectable luggage, soft side and hard side casual bags, and attachés. If you're planning a trip to visit the Phil O'Steen's of the Middle East, you can profit with honor from the savings in this country first. **C** $2 color, $1 plain; **B; PQ**

A-Z LUGGAGE
4627 New Utrecht Ave.
Brooklyn, NY 11219
(212) 435-6330

How do you spell relief? S-a-v-i-n-g-s! We found everything from attachés to zippered manicure sets at one of their six stores in New York. Christmas comes but once a year and when it comes it brings A-Z's only catalog. The brimming book contained various styles of luggage and travel accessories from famous makers such as Hartmann, Zero Haliburton, Rolf, Ciao, Tumi, LaCoste, and Samsonite discounted 20% to 40%. An additional 5% will be deducted from the bill if you mention *The Underground Shopper.* By calling the company before placing the order, we found out which catalog items were on sale for further reductions. If you are looking for something special, send a detailed description for a price quote since the catalog represents only a portion of the A-Z inventory. **C, PQ**

THE BAGMAN, INC.
924 Windsor St.
Reading, PA 19604
(215) 372-6237

Reading about bags, man, can be a real drag—unless of course they're a bargain. Here you can buy quality leather handbags and accessories by such brand names as John Romain, Borelli, Christian Dior, Frye, Stone Mountain, Tano, Phillippe, Tumi, and others from this company at 35% to 60% off. They don't have a catalog, however, so you must write or call them for a price quote with a description of the product you want and if possible, the model number. **PQ**

BAGS 'N' THINGS
220 N.E. First Ave.
Hallandale, FL 33009
(305) 454-7674

If the romance has gone out of your life and you're tired of the old bag, trash it and clasp a new one to your heart. This company offers ladies' handbags, accessories, and belts at a 20% discount. Such top designers as Leiber, Moskowitz, Fiori, and Stephan (among others) were carried. Formerly G.L.C. Inc., Bags 'n' Things requires the manufacturer's name, style, and model number along with full postage before they'll ship your order. No refunds, but they do give credit where credit is due. **PQ**

BER SEL HANDBAGS
79 Orchard St.
New York, NY 10002
(212) 966-5517

Remem-Ber, Sel-dom do you get anything in this world for nothing. But you can get up to 35% off on a wide variety of leather, exotic skin, and fabric handbags, wallets, belts, and gloves from top manufacturers such as Anne Klein, Dior, Pierre Cardin, Lisette, Stone Mountain, Isotoner, and Totes. The man who answers the phone is friendly but your inquiries must include the manufacturer's style number. **PQ**

CAROLE BLOCK LTD.
1413 Avenue M
Brooklyn, NY 11230
(212) 339-1869

Carole has a mental Block about charging full price, so she psyches up her customers with 15% to 20% off list in the final analysis. What's more, during her twice-a-year sales, we saved 30% to 50%. The reputation of her merchandise is secure, even if her prices are a bit depressed. Ladies' handbags and small leather goods were available from Italy, the U.S., and South America in such brands as Halston, Susan Gail, Aldana, and Visona. Carole's bag has been shrinking prices for 27 years, but she's still feeling pretty Jung. Write or call for price quote. **PQ**

CARRY ON LUGGAGE
97 Orchard St.
New York, NY 10002
(212) 226-4980

A Lark in the hand is worth two at the baggage claim when you can save 30% to 35% on first-quality luggage, garment bags, portfolios, and wallets. Besides Lark, we found Ventura, Wing, Lane, Samsonite (up to 50% off), and Christian Dior carrying on with attachés by Rona, Yale, Atlas, Scully, and many Italian lines. The owner, Mr. Rubin, told us he can special order anything with manufacturer and style number and have it in about two weeks. Shipping is by UPS, usually $5 to $8 for a 14-pound order. **PQ**

CREATIVE HOUSE
100 Business Parkway
Richardson, TX 75081
(800) 527-5940
(214) 231-3461: TX residents

Before you become unhinged and pack it in on finding luggage and attachés, check out these discounts from 30% to 60% on the moderately crafted World Traveler and Mastercraft lines. Their free catalog features briefcases and attaché cases in many styles and colors at about a third off retail and also a line of leather luggage and garment bags. They had a $200 leather attaché case for $80. Handbags, wallets, and other leather products are also carried. Familiar names we saw included Samsonite, American Tourister, Amelia Earhart, and Verde. Add $3.75 to your bill for shipping. **C, PQ**

EUROPEAN LEATHER SHOWCASE CO.
P.O. Box 204
90 Bates Road
Great Neck, NY 11022
(212) 224-2623

It isn't right to take Fernando's hide away. If you have to hide legal-size documents, Paul Orlow has the portmanteau for you. Prices from $19.95 to $54.95 won't turn you into a poor man, too. All items are crafted in Holland, West Germany, and France. Payment by money order or bank check and orders are shipped immediately. Personal checks take 14 business days to clear and will be shipped three weeks after receipt of order. **C**

FINE & KLEIN
119 Orchard St.
New York, NY 10002
(212) 674-6720

Julius Fine and Murray Klein opened their New York shop some 38 years ago and today feature a "tremendous selection" of exclusive, first-quality ladies' handbags, attachés, and accessories. Their Fine Klein-tele includes many international celebrities. Currently the talk of the town is the new, better ladies' shoe department above their store aptly called Sole Above 119. All merchandise was 33% off the retail price. Mr. Klein welcomes everyone to write him for price quotes on particular styles and brands of merchandise. If you see something in *Vogue,* it's in the bag that Fine & Klein can get it for you at a substantially lower price. Orders are shipped same day. Enclose an SASE for immediate responses. **PQ**

ROBINS BAGS, INC.
141 Orchard St.
New York, NY 10002
(212) 475-9280

We thought pigeons were the only birds on the streets of New York these days, but we gave this bird a call and found out she carries famous-name handbags and small leather goods by Lisette, Susan Gail, Ronora, Stephan, and many Italian imports at a 33% discount. Clip magazine ads or send manufacturer's name and style number for a quote. Prices still are not chicken feed so don't fowl up by ordering the wrong bag since Robins gives no refunds. Exchanges must be made within "a reasonable amount of time." Robins' likes to "service their bags" even years after they've been purchased, a nice touch. **PQ**

TRAVEL AUTO BAG CO.
264 W. 40th St.
New York, NY 10018
(212) 840-0025

Traveling salesmen purchase their soft-side luggage from this company and you can, too. That way, lugging around your samples won't be the death of you, Willie, low man. These prices are low! These functional Herculon tweed bags are extra-heavy stitched and are available with large casters for greater mobility. A 26-by-20-by-7½ piece was just $32 (approximately 25 pounds to ship). Greater discounts when buying in quantity. Prepaid orders receive first priority. **B**

Shoes

We think you'll take a shine to the fancy footwork listed in this section. Maybe you've never been to Gilley's but that doesn't mean you shouldn't get a pair of Texas boots just for kicks. If Chief Big Foot has been on a rampage lately, tell him about the size AAAAA to EEEE shoes available by mail. (Maybe he'll quit his squaw-king.) From the Netherlands come wooden clogs that are comfortable and well-constructed. For loafers, tassles, topsiders, saddles, espadrilles, or sneakers, look here first for special buys. It's a "shoe in."

A.W.G. OTTEN
Albert Cuypstraat 102-104-106
1072 CZ Amsterdam-z
The Netherlands
Phone: 011-31-20-729724 (dial direct)

Let's go Dutch this time. They have a tree of Dutch and Danish wooden shoes and clogs (klompen) for the whole family, at half the price. (They're twice as expensive if purchased domestically.) Besides the matter of sheer unavailability (a pair rents for $10 in the States at a costume shop), wooden shoes usually last forever. Once you have mastered the dubious task of converting your shoe size to inches to something called "maat," you have one foot in the door. Using the conversion chart supplied by A.W.G. Otten, an 85-year-old company, we guessed a pair of ladies' clogs would cost around $10.55. Feel the difference of having shoes from a Nether-land. Allow four to five weeks and add $6.50 (U.S.) for postage. Ask for their free brochure, "The Story of Dutch Wooden Shoes." **B**

BOOT TOWN
5909 Belt Line, Dept. 101
Dallas, Tx 75240
(214) 385-3052 : Call collect

One of Dallas' finest boot merchants mails his boots out of town for the same 25% to 40% discounts. Top-quality brands like Lucchese, Tony Lama, Rios, Justin, Dan Post, Nocona, Acme, Larry Mahan . . . in the most exotic skins of lizard, snake, ostrich, antelope, cowhide, and more. Sizes 6½ to 13 for men, 4 to 10 for women, and children's sizes. Call for customer assistance with the brand and size and Boot Town will ship within a few days. They also carry the popular "name blank" belts, hats by Resistol and other major brands, and a variety of buckles ($8 to $50) including Crumrine initials. Plus Western shirts and jeans by Levi, Wrangler, Lee, and Panhandle Slim, to boot. **PQ**

HILL BROTHERS
99 Ninth St.
Lynchburg, VA 24504
(804) 528-1000

Put your best foot forward with your feet out-footed in shoes by Hill Brothers. Dealing exclusively in women's shoes, they have shoes to fit feet from sizes 3 to 13, widths in AAAAA to EEEE (although the range of sizes varies with the individual shoe style). No more will sufferers of five-digit inflation have a Cinderella complex about the size of their hard-to-fit feet. Shoes carry such ritzy names as Chloe, Cher, and Audra, as well as more mundane names as Verna, Agnes, Bernie, and Rona. Satisfaction guaranteed. If within 14 days you wish to return your shoes, you can receive an exchange or full refund. Their 48-page, full-color catalog is perking with savings. **C**

J.W. BRAY
P.O. Box 189
Dalton, GA 30720
(404) 226-2729

We've got some good news and some bad news. First the good news: You can slip into women's soft slipper scuffs and slip off half the retail price. Attractive women's terry and tricot wedges and scuffs were offered for $4.50 to $5.50 ($9 to $11 suggested list). Men's, women's, and children's leisure and casual footwear in their own lines are available at 20% to 30% less than retail. The bad news is: There's a $100 minimum order, so unless you're a centipede, you're going to really have to stock up. (Buy a closet full, gather orders from your friends, set up a table at the flea market, or it's your scuff luck.) This company's been in business for 40 years, and they guarantee 100% customer satisfaction or you can return merchandise with no restocking charge. Their motto is, "We try softer." **B, C**

NELSON'S
201 South Park
Fairfax, MN 55332
(507) 426-7216

With Wings on your tootsies, your soles can take flight. (On the other hand, who wants soar feet?) This firm is not afraid to put a full-Nelson on high prices, especially on Red Wing boots and casual shoes. Lace up a $13 discount on insulated leather lace-up boots, $10 on Pecos boots, and $9 on work boots. The owner says he "handles the mail-order business at my store during my work day so I do not have additional help for this business." Prices are about 15% below retail and include shipping and handling costs. We're no arch-enemies of Nelson's, in fact, we'll stomp up a storm on one heel of a good buy. **C, B, PQ**

ORCHARD STREET BOOTERY
75 Orchard St.
New York, NY 10002
(212) 966-0688

Boots for fruits? No way—there's nothing seedy about this establishment. Pick from Orchard's crop of shoes for the well-heeled woman. Select Golo, Stanley Philipson, Palizzio, Jacques Cohen, Colormate, and more in leather and vinyl "slush boots," loafers, sandals, slippers, and evening wear at 25% to 30% below retail. Harvest a 20% savings on shoes to cover sizes 5½ to 10 in B and C widths. Write or call for more information or with style and model number. **PQ**

PL PREMIUM LEATHER BY HANOVER
P.O. Box 340
Hanover, PA 17331
(800) 345-8500 ext. 33
(717) 632-7575: PA residents

You'll save money Hanover foot with factory direct prices averaging 25% off retail for first-quality men's and women's shoes. In business since 1899, PL is owned by a well-respected manufacturer, Clarks of England. You'll get a kick out of the selection: Hanover, Nettleton, Candies, Streetcars, Clarks, Revelations, Keds, Grasshoppers, Sperry. The sizes: 8½ A to 12 EEE for men, 5 to 11 for women. Classic styles included wingtips, loafers, tassles, topsiders, saddles, espadrilles, and sneakers all with a free 10-day trial. Shirts, jackets, socks, ties, belts, and attachés were also featured in their color catalog. **C**

SHOE STRING
1120 N. Memorial Drive
Lancaster, OH 43130
(614) 687-1657

When you're living on a shoe string, you know tying times are ahead. But not to worry: Now you can get men's and women's comfort shoes at a comfortable 20% to 40% less than retail. This company carries men's dress and walking shoes (they're discontinuing men's work boots), while 90% of their inventory is all-leather women's dress and comfort shoes, including orthopedic oxfords, pumps, and sandals. They carry factory seconds and closeouts in Footsaver, Lockes, Cantilever, Drew, DeHiss, Dickerson, and Walkover. There's a 30-day return policy (exchanges only, no cash refunds), no warranty on closeouts and seconds, and no restocking charge on returns. Write for style and sizes needed. Occasional catalog. **C**

SPIECE BY MAIL
1150 Manchester Ave.
Wabash, IN 46992
(219) 563-3281

No spiece-ious bargains here, just solid values. Although pronounced to rhyme with "geese," Spiece is noted for less-than-high-flying prices. ("Honk if you love Spiece's!") This 32-year-old family-owned company sells jeans, tennis shoes, and boots at about 25% off on such brands as Levi, Wrangler, and Lee (in jeans); Nike, Adidas, and Converse (in tennis shoes); Frye, Dingo, Dan Post, Puma, Bass, Sporto, Timberland, Herman, and Chippewa (in boots). These folks will refund or exchange if you're unhappy with your purchase (barring extreme wear), and there's no restocking charge. Their catalog's a freebie. There's just one thing left we'd like to know: If this family opened another store, would that be a sub-Spiece's, or an entirely new Spiece's? **C**

2.

LOOK GOOD, FEEL FIT

Cosmetics and Beauty Aids

If you've always wanted to shop for perfume on the rue de la Paix (and not have to pay), here's your chance. Buy fragrances from the perfume capital of the world without leaving home at savings up to 50%. Even with a small handling fee and duty (usually 8%), the price is still much lower. But remember, most (not all) perfumes are "restricted brands" by U.S. Customs. This means there's an import limit of one or two bottles of each scent per person. And, if you've never tried one of the various clubs listed in this section, you should. Discounts of 50% or more on famous cosmetics are in store.

BEAUTIFUL BEGINNINGS
Spencer Building
Atlantic City, NJ 08411
(609) 644-3300

The corn is as high as an elephant's eyelashes in this catalog, but the savings on cosmetics will get you through many beautiful mornings. We saved from 50% to 75% on nationally advertised beauty products in names like Elizabeth Arden, Revlon, Max Factor, Frances Denney, Coty, Jovan, Helena Rubenstein, Halston. Perfumes, lipsticks, eye shadows, even a ceramic bunny that dispenses cotton as you pull its tail. Parfum spray by Yves St. Laurent was $4.95 (retail $20), and Rive Gauche was $4.50 ($13 retail). This company can sell less expensively because they serve to introduce manufacturers' products to the public (so hopefully you'll find the scent that suits your fragrance fancy). **C**

BEAUTIFUL VISIONS
810 S. Hicksville Road
C.S. 4001
Hicksville, NY 11802
(516) 822-3760

The visions here aren't cosmic, but cosmetic, although you do have to "think big" to mentally grasp all the major labels they carry. This division of Unity Buying Service offers prices from 40% to 85% off retail on nationally advertised cosmetics in their 48-page, full-color catalog. Best values were Charlie and Jontue perfumes at $1.50 for ½ ounce ($30 retail). Other products displayed were Almay nail enamel, Max Factor lip gloss, Elizabeth Arden foundation pencils, Revlon lipsticks, Vidal Sassoon shampoos. Our favorite item advertised itself (with exquisite subtlety) as Jovan Sex Appeal Perfume ($1.25— a $5 value!) and promised to be "primitive as a jungle, pulsating as excited love." (These days they bottle everything!) Get some, because as Tarzan said to Jane, "It's a jungle out there." **C**

BEAUTY BUY BOOK
65 E. South Water
Chicago, IL 60601
(312) 977-3740

Whether you're into English Leather for him or just going behind the red door with Elizabeth Arden products for her, you'll find an extensive selection of products from Revlon, Orlane, Coty, Germaine Monteil, Vidal Sassoon, available from this company at discounts up to 80%. Also carry jewelry, bags, and other gifts. Products fluctuate; catalogs issued three times yearly. A free gift with all orders. **C**

BEAUTY BY SPECTOR
Dept. USMA-2
McKeesport, PA 15134-0502
(412) 673-3259

In-Spector Clousseau might say, "Hmmm, vot have ve hair?" Wigs, wiglets, cascades, falls, toupees at 50% below comparable retail are this 25-year-old company's crowning glory. Prices in the sales brochures and descriptive fliers didn't dis-tress us: 2-ounce human hair wiglet, $8.95 (retail $18); "Blow Cut" wig, $24.50 (retail $49); man's toupee, $99.95 (retail $200). At these prices, you can wear someone else's hair (or a synthetic) without fear of being scalped. We won't split hairs over hair care items, fragrances, European skin-treatment products, fashion jewelry, or instructional books on beauty and self-improvement priced less than at retail clip joints. Add $3 shipping on each order. **B**

BEAUTY SHOWCASE
840 S. Broadway
Hicksville, NY 11802
(516) 576-9018

Hicksville's fast becoming the beauty buy capital of the world. Eyebrow pencils at 25 cents each? You can't brow beat that! A bottle of Courréges perfume was $9.50 (retail $26). The Loofah nature sponge was squeezed out at $1.50. Special "bonus box" offers can save you up to 80% if you don't mind taking pot luck and trying some new products. A free gift with all orders. Men's products, too. Allow three weeks for delivery. **C**

CAL-RICH LTD.
P.O. Box 707
78 Tenafly Road
Tenafly, NJ 07670
(201) 568-4735

We hate to be nosey, but in this case it's our business. (Thankfully, nose news is good news.) We sniffed out some o-dorable fragrances here, and at prices that made us nose-talgic for the days of yesteryear. This company offers copies of such famous perfumes as Joy, Charlie, Bal A Versailles, and many others at prices far lower than the originals. For men, they have reproductions of Aramis, Canoe, and Oscar de la Renta also at considerable savings. Ask for sample cards saturated with their fragrances and smell for yourself. There's a $12 minimum order, and a full money-back guarantee if not satisfied (no restocking charge). Perfume reproductions may be scorned by the snooty, but for our money, these are scent from heaven. **PQ**

CATHERINE
6, rue de Castiglione
Paris, France 75001
Phone: 011-33-1-073-81-49 (dial direct)

Parlez vous Fran-savings? Catherine's "tax-free" shop afforded quite an "Eiffel" of perfumes, cosmetics, and gifts at about 50% less than retail in the States. For example, if you wished to buy Patou's Joy 1 ounce perfume in a retail store, the price would be approximately $170. By mail from Catherine, the cost would be $91.05 plus $5 surface mail postage and a possible customs duty not exceeding 8%. This boutique specializes in shipping business gifts from Paris to individual addresses. Besides famous perfumes by Balmain, Chanel, Deprez, Gucci, Lanvin, Nina Ricci, and many others, you can get Orlane, Stendhal, Lancome, Dior, and Chanel skin care products at the same low prices. Viva la differ-France! **B**

COSMETIQUE
6045 W. Howard Ave.
Niles, IL 60648
(800) 621-8822
(312) 583-5410: IL residents

Me and m-eye shadow searched for blemishes in this cosmetic offer but were tickled firefrost pink to find no flaws. Upon request, this company sends you a special introductory coupon. Then, for $1 you'll receive $100 worth of famous-name cosmetics plus a free gift for joining. If you decide to remain a member, you pay $9.93 for each future kit you choose about every six weeks. That makes up a 90% savings off retail and that leaves us at a g-loss for words. Open only Monday through Thursday, 7:30 a.m. to 5:15 p.m. **B**

ESSENTIAL PRODUCTS CO., INC.
90 Water St.
New York, NY 10005
(212) 344-4288

A scent-sational fragrance find! Now you can exude the aromas of affluence without paying the price. Save up to 90% by buying reproductions of 1000 ($245 per ounce retail), Joy ($175 per ounce retail), Bal A Versailles and Opium ($150 per ounce), and Oscar de la Renta ($140 per ounce retail) all for only $16 an ounce for each fragrance, or $9 for ½ ounce, under the Naudet label. Thirty-seven other ladies' perfumes are also available. Men's colognes such as Aramis, Brut, Canoe, Paco Rabanne, Pierre Cardin, and Polo (among others) are copied for $7.50 for 4 ounces. Shipping is by UPS—charges are $2 for the first bottle and 50 cents for each additional bottle. The minimum order is $15, and merchandise returned within 30 days of purchase will receive an exchange or refund depending on the buyer's wishes. Write for five free sample scent cards. For fragrances at prices you won't get incensed over, this place is Essential. **B, PQ**

GRILLOT
10 rue Cambon
Paris 1er, France

Grillot (pronounced Gree-o) sells at prices that are be-low retail. From France, the fragrance capital of the world, come *tres* chic savings on such famous perfumes as Chanel No. 5, Chloe, Gucci, and many others. Men, don't just "promise her anything." Give it to her and save 50% over department store prices. **B** (in English)

HOUSE OF INTERNATIONAL FRAGRANCES
4711 Blanco Road
San Antonio, TX 78212
(512) 341-2283

For scents that make savings (and savings that make sense), order copies of the most popular fragrances under the Touch & Go label. Women can save over 80% on reproductions of Opium, Oscar de la Renta, Chloe, Halston, Chanel No. 5, and Estee Lauder. Men can save over 50% on reproductions of Paco Rabanne, Polo, Lagerfeld, Pour Lui, Van Cleef & Arpels, and Aramis. Many other fragrances are available: They make essence-tially every brand you can think of.

These fragrances last longer than the originals: one drop of 100% essence lasts eight hours; one bottle at $5.99 will last three months used daily. Postage and handling is $1 for the first fragrance, and 50 cents for each thereafter. **PQ**

JEAN-MICHELLE BEAUTY COLLECTION
Lock Box 481
Evanston, IL 60204
(800) 621-1342
(312) 583-4141: IL residents call collect, credit card orders only

This beauty collection sure has polish, as well as mascara, body scrubs, eyeliner, blush, lipstick, perfume, and moisturizers at dazzling discounts of up to 90%. Diane Von Furstenberg cheek color for $1.50 (retail $5), Adrien Arpel eyeliner for $1.95 (retail $6), Zadig perfume by Emilio Pucci for $2.95 (retail $30), and Revlon's Charlie eye color for $1.75 (retail $5) were some of the bargains we noted. They even give bonus gifts with orders over $10. **C**

J.W. CHUNN PERFUMES
43, rue Richer
75009 Paris, France
Phone: 011-33-1-824-42-06 (dial direct)

Atten-Chunn! The pulse point of savings for famous perfumes and toilet waters like Chloe, Arpege, Joy, Opium, Courreges, Bal A Versailles, Chunga (by Weil), and dozens more are discounted 50% or more. Skin care products from Lancome and Orlane were also listed in the brochure. For example, a 6.8 ounce bottle of Orlane cleansing milk was $10.80 (plus $4.80 shipping, plus duty). While this product is worshipped by some of the world's finest beauties, the retail price of $24 in department stores is still prohibitive to the average person. Let's face it, if you do not find the fragrance you are seeking, write with your request. They can usually fill it. **B**

MICHEL SWISS
16 rue de la Paix
75002 Paris, France
Phone: 011-33-1-261-68-84 or 011-33-1-261-69-44 (dial direct)

Ooh la la. Don't throw three coins in the fountain—your Swiss has already come true. Terrific prices on luscious Parisian perfumes.

Franc-ly speaking, you don't knead to pay in French bread since prices are in American dollars. Chanel No. 5, ½ ounce for $34 (retail $65); Givenchy III, ¼ ounce $15.30 (retail $32); Lagerfeld's Chloe, ¼ ounce $20.40 (retail $45); Nina Ricci's L'Air du Temps, ¼ ounce $17.85 (retail $35). Also skin-tillating soaps, crystal limoges, bath oils, body creams, bubble baths, men's colognes, and after-shaves at reasonable prices. However, LaCoste alligator shirts were no jaws celèbre for us, at $23 and $28 (for colors), normally $24 to $25 anywhere. Prices include full insurance and you get a free gift with each order. We almost went in-Seine when we heard it takes two to three months for delivery; airmail, two to three weeks. **C**

TULI-LATUS PERFUMES, LTD.
146-36 13th Ave.
P.O. Box 422
Whitestone, NY 11357
(212) 746-9337: charge orders only

If Tuli was Fuli, would they be F. Latus? (We hope not!) We were fuming at the price of fine fragrances, but once we found Tuli, we were Tuli elated. Tuli-Latus has sniffed out the costliest French perfumes, as well as American designer perfumes, and has created its own reproductions at savings up to 90% of these aromatic blends (using only the keenest ol' factory equipment). They sell reproductions of 26 perfumes, including Bal A Versailles, L'Air du Temps, Oscar de la Renta, Calandre, Opium, and Shalimar from $15 to $40 per ounce. A reproduction of 1000 by Patou (retailing for about $235 an ounce) was their most expensive duplicate at $40. (You can bet we won't turn our noses up at savings like that!) Their perfumes come packaged in beautiful French glass stoppered bottles with French looking labels, as well as in regular bottles at a slightly lower price. Purse spray atomizers also sneeze with a squeeze. **B**

WORLD OF BEAUTY
65 E. South Water St.
Chicago, IL 60601
(312) 977-3700

Try before you buy. It's a fun way to experiment with a wide variety of cosmetics and toiletries. This company sends you a package every six weeks filled with samples of products they select for about $7 to $10. Write for their free brochure and enrollment forms. **B**

Health and Medicine

The next time your doctor writes you a long term prescription, before you rush to the corner drugstore to have it filled, consider sending it to a prescription service. You can save an additional 50% over and above the discounted price, for example, if you substitute generic compounds for the brand-name drugs. Shop around for vitamins and read labels carefully. Here again you can usually find identical formulas with large variations in prices. Visit your local natural foods store or contact a good nutritionist to find out how to combine vitamins for best absorption. Whether you're buying protheses, juice extractors, contact lenses, or hearing aids, compare prices before you buy and be specific about your requirements.

AMERICAN HEALTH SERVICE, INC.
1206 Golf Road
Waukegan, IL 60085
(312) 662-4707

Eh, what's that? WE SAID WE'LL WAX ELOQUENT over the earful of
savings available here, so listen up and we won't have to drum it in.
AHS has got names in hearing aids and health care products we've
all heard before, and at savings of 50% off. You'll get good vibrations
from Audiotone, Bosch, Dahlberg, Danavox, Electone, Fidelity,
Finetone, Maico, Oticon, Phillips, Phonic Ear, Qualitone, Radioear,
Rion, Siemens, Telex, Unitron, and others at unheard-of savings for
hearing aids. Replacement hearing aids are a specialty, so obtain
your first one from a local dealer, and then maintain your financial
equilibrium by getting a replacement through the mail. All hearing
aids come with manufacturer's warranty, and satisfaction's guaranteed. Tune in to a good pick-up—our experience shows AHS to be
prompt and conscientious in shipping. And remember, you heard it
hear first. **C**

BRUCE MEDICAL SUPPLY
411 Waverly Oaks Road
Waltham, MA 02154
(800) 225-8446
(617) 894-6262: MA residents

A professional no-pin-stop sphygmomanometer for $49.95 ($79 regularly) may not be your idea of an im-pulse purchase, but at least you
can get a blood pressure reading without getting the squeeze put on
your wallet, too. This company's 30-page catalog offered a complete
line of medical supplies (in such brand names as Squibb, Hollister,
United, 3M, and Bard) from 20% to 60% savings. Heating pads,
walking aids, bathroom aids, and a wide range of ostomy products
bring medical and monetary relief to those with colostomies,
ileostomies, and urostomies. Bruce gives full refunds within 30 days,
80% refunds between 30 and 60 days, and there's no restocking
charge. They also offer coupons for various items. **C**

CONTINENTAL ASSOCIATION OF FUNERAL AND
MEMORIAL SOCIETIES
1828 "L" St., N.W.
Washington, DC 20036
(202) 293-4821

You don't have to be a dead-icated Underground Shopper to avoid a grave mistake on a funeral. There are over 200 nonprofit memorial societies in the U.S. staffed by volunteers. These folks are committed to "simplicity, dignity, and economy in funeral arrangements." While most members emphasize services with closed caskets and immediate burial (or a memorial service following cremation), you can nail down a traditional American funeral at lower cost with pre-need counseling. Write for the address nearest you, and avoid coffin up your estate in your move from here to the hereafter. **PQ**

FEDERAL PHARMACY SERVICE
Second and Main Streets
Madrid, IA 50156
(800) 247-1236 Mon.-Fri., 8 a.m.-4:30 p.m.
(515) 795-2450: IA residents

One of the largest mail-order pharmacies in the country, Federal expresses the sentiment that "you can save more money buying generic substitutes for vitamins and prescriptions than buying national brands at higher retail prices." Federal's prices on generic substitutes are 25% lower than retail. Compare 100 capsules of Librium 10 milligrams at $17.39 with Federal's price $12.49, and generic formula $3.95. We painlessly substituted generic Darvon Compound 65, $5.69, for the name-brand version, $13.69. They also carry vitamins A through zinc, aspirin, cold capsules, sleep aids, creams and ointments, and even hearing aid batteries and blood pressure kits. Refunds or exchanges within 30 days. There's a 75-cent charge per order as partial payment for handling and postage. **PQ**

FREEDA VITAMINS©
36 E. 41st St.
New York, NY 10017
(212) 685-4980

Feel Freeda gulp these power-packed dietary wonders. Vitamins aren't hard to swallow when they're priced 30% to 50% below usual market prices. Megavitamins, multivitamins, B complex family, C family, children's vitamins, minerals, amino acids, nutrients . . . we felt peppier just scanning their selection. Just about every food supplement on the market today was offered under the Freeda label by this friendly pharmacy. Established in 1928, this family-owned company offers prompt and efficient service. For UPS shipment, add $2. There's no minimum order, and if the item is unopened, you can return it for items of equal value. We got a charge out of discovering a remittance is required with first-time mail-orders to establish credit. **C, B, PQ**

GREAT NORTHERN DISTRIBUTING CO.
P.O. Box 151067
Salt Lake City, UT 84115
(801) 572-1433

Great Northern is no place to get railroaded: If you make tracks here you'll find a collection of sprouters, food dehydrators, grain mills, juicers, bread mixers, and more. Brands carried include such names as Great Northern, Kenwood, Champion, Acme, Vita Mix, Phoenix, and Harvest. Their prices are 30% lower than retail (they sell to anyone by mail at dealer cost), so you won't get all steamed. They have a one-year exchange policy—if you're not satisified you can exchange within that period. Sprouting enthusiasts with a growing interest in "growing their own" will find seed offerings of alfalfa, radish, sunflower, lentil, mung, azuki, and wheatberries in 4-ounce packages from $1.10 to $2.15, as well as sprouting supplies. There's free shipping anywhere in the continental U.S. except on items listed F.O.B. Orders are sent C.O.D. unless noted otherwise. We won't tell Utah do what the folks in Salt Lake City do, but they save Mormon-ey by stocking up on a year's supply of grains and dried goods. **C**

JUST CONTACT LENSES
755 New York Ave.
Huntington, NY 11743
(516) 673-9485

Are you tired of groping around in a futile search for reasonably priced contact lenses? Well, grope no longer. Just Contact Lenses sells (you guessed it!) just contact lenses. Prices are from 50% to 70% off retail, and both hard and soft contact lenses are available. There's a 30-day unconditional money-back guarantee. At prices like these, it's as if we were getting a grope rate. **B, PQ**

L & H VITAMINS
38-01 35th Ave.
Long Island City, NY 11101
(800) 221-1152
(212) 937-7400: NY residents

At L&H, you'll find the ABC's of vitamins in such names as Schiff,

Plus, Thompson, Standard Process Labs, Nutri-Dyn, as well as over 100 other national brands. Discounts are a standard 20%, plus there are several 40% off sales during the year. Their 56-page catalog features every conceivable nutritional supplement, including the kitchen zinc. There's no minimum order, but there is a 20% restocking charge on returns, with no returns after 30 days. The Schiff Acidophilus with Goat's Milk (100 capsules for $3.60; retail $4.50) caught our eye with alluring copy that said: "Natural aid for introducing friendly organisms to the lower intestines—20 million living lactobacilli in every capsule." Yummy! P.S.—Hope none of these little fellows has claustrophobia. **C**

LINGERIE FOR LESS
11075 Erhard
Dallas, TX 75228
(214) 324-9135: open Wed.-Sun., 10 a.m.-6 p.m.

This company sells their own Soft Touch Breast Form for $39.95 (plus $2.50 postage and handling). We couldn't find one comparable for under $75 anywhere (many are as high as $185). A truly unique product developed by a physician who specializes in prostheses from synthetic gels. The molded gel feels soft and conforms to the body like a natural breast. Comes in seven sizes and fits any type bra. Just state your bra size when ordering. Each breast form comes with a one-year unconditional guarantee. Their lingerie items (in many major brands) are 20% to 60% off retail, but are sold in-store only, so local yokels take note. **PQ**

MAJESTIC DRUG CO., INC.
711 E. 134th St.
Bronx, NY 10454
(212) 292-1310

When you're out on a camping trip and your tooth filling plunks into your cup of coffee, Dentemp can fill in for a dentist. This filling mix, developed by a dentist, temporarily replaces lost fillings, loose caps, crowns, or inlays so you can keep on talking while the stuff is caulking. A single application costs $3. They also carry health and skin products comparable to retail, but you get 10% off on a $25 order. **B**

PHARMACEUTICAL SERVICES, INC.
127 W. Markey Road
Belton, MO 64012
(816) 331-0700

Just get a whiff at these prices (priced per 100) and compare: Empirin aspirin 5 grams #250 ($4.67), Benadryl 25 milligrams ($7.60), Dilantin 100 milligrams ($7.10), Fiorinal ($12.30), Inderal 10 milligrams ($7.90), Motrin 400 milligrams ($21), Premarin 1.25 milligrams ($12.90), Tetracycline 250 milligrams ($3.80) to name a few. Be sure your physician writes an Rx that permits the use of generic drugs. They will generally cost about half the price. On the PS price list, generics are highlighted so you can compare. Excluded from mail service are liquid antacids, cough syrups, and mouthwashes. **C**

PRESCRIPTION DELIVERY SYSTEMS, INC.
136 S. York Road
Hatboro, PA 19040
(800) 441-8976
(215) 674-1565: PA residents

How do you spell relief? PDS is a short-cut to savings on vitamins, over-the-counter generics, and regular pharmaceuticals. You can drop your prescription in the mail and they will deliver promptly giving you two weeks to pay. Orders over $100 require prepayment. There's a slight postage charge. We price-checked a local pharmacy and discovered Fiorinaltabs PMP 50, $7.31 (retail $13.55) and Monistat 7, 1.66 ounces, $9.26 (retail $10.85). There are good discounts on epilepsy drugs in large quantities, too. A pharmacist is available on their toll-free number. **B, PQ**

RETIRED PERSONS PHARMACY
510 King St., Suite 410
Alexandria, VA 22314
(703) 684-0244

Just what the doctor mail-ordered. Discounts up to 50% on generic prescriptions, health care products, and on their own label natural vitamins. You must be a member of the National Retired Teachers Association, American Association of Retired Persons, or Action for Independent Maturity to order and receive special additional discounts at leading hotels, motels, and auto rental companies. All orders are shipped postpaid. We'll retire on that thought. **C $1**

RIC CLARK
9530 Langdon Ave.
Sepulveda, CA 91343
(213) 892-6636

You'll grin ear-to-ear to hear of 50% and more savings on nationally advertised hearing aids. Ric can't mention them so he used substitute names in his free catalog. They'll do prescription aids from your audiogram, no custom earmolds, however, so you must buy yours locally. Although we found no savings on batteries, repair costs averaged $35 compared with $60 elsewhere. A $10 deposit is required; one-year guarantee and 30-day trial period. **PQ**

RITE-WAY HEARING AID CO.
P.O. Box 59451
Chicago, IL 60659
(312) 539-6620

Hear ye! Hear ye! Are you oppressed by excessive hearing aid prices? Have manufacturers got you by the eustachian tubes? Rise up, one and all, for the days of lib-ear-ation are at hand. There's economic freedom for those who make a price pilgrimage to a new land of discounts! This company sells hearing aids at 50% less than retail, batteries at 25% off, and makes repairs for about 15% lower than can be found in the retail Homeland. Brand names are eary (Royaltone, Danavox, and others occasionally) all with a 30-day trial and one-year unconditional guarantee (and a six-month warranty on repairs). They'll send you an impression kit for custom earmolds. Select from behind-the-ear, all-in-the-ear, eyeglass, and body aids. You have nothing to lose but your pains (pricewise). **B, PQ**

SALJAC ENTERPRISES
P.O. Box 5337
Beverly Hills, CA 90210
(213) 278-8714

These folks will lend an ear—or a reasonable facsimile. Their pride is a silver zinc rechargeable hearing aid battery and they sell the chargers as well. They promise to save you money—so listen up. **PQ**

STAR PROFESSIONAL PHARMACEUTICALS, INC.
11 Basin St.
Plainview, NY 11803
(516) 822-4621

Twinkle, twinkle, little Star,
Through the mail you're not so far.
If I gulp your vitamin weaponry,
Will my bod, too, become then, heavenly?

No monopoly on the best prices in town even though they sell the game "Medical Monopoly" for $12.95. Prices on their house brand (Star) vitamins do deserve a gold star for being 20% to 50% lower than comparable retail products, but their name-brand goods are comparable to a neighborhood store. They also carry natural health and beauty aids and gifts. Buy original Chanel No. 5, 1 ounce of perfume for $84.75 or their "classique" copy cologne spray of Chanel No. 5, 2 ounce for $5.50. Star guarantees satisfaction: If, after 30 days of use, you are not satisfied, you can return the unused portion for a complete refund. Merchandise shipped directly from warehouse to you, avoiding the possibility of shelf tampering. C

STUR-DEE PRODUCTS, INC.
Austin Blvd.
Island Park, NY 11558
(800) 645-2638
(800) 632-2592: NY residents
(516) 889-6400

Stur-Dee's carries a line of drugstore products like vitamins, minerals, cosmetics, etc., formulated to their own specifications so this company can "keep a tight grip on quality." Prices on house vitamins, minerals, cosmetics, healing agents, aloe vera products averaged a sturdy 15% to 30% lower than most national brands. C

SUNBURST BIORGANICS
P.O. Box 607
Rockville Centre, NY 11571
(516) 623-8478

"Combat dietary deficiencies with all-natural (no preservatives, no artificial flavorings or color) supplements," says Millie Ross. Her family sells the preferred form of vitamin C, calcium ascorbate 550 milligrams, 100 tablets for $3.82 (retail $6.95); and Spirulina 500 milligrams—a new protein food being touted by dieters and joggers,

$6.29 for 100 tablets (special introductory offer). Pep up pets with pet vitamins. Except for a handling charge of 90 cents, customers do not pay postage if shipped within the continental USA. All orders are processed within 24 hours. The catalog offers cash cards so you can obtain a $1-off coupon. Free vitamin and mineral wallchart on first order. We don't want to B complex; C for yourself. C

VITAMIN QUOTA, INC.
21 Henderson Drive
West Caldwell, NJ 07006
(800) 526-2256
(201) 227-5100 ext. 480: NJ residents call collect

Vitamin Quota the Day: "To B or not to B." Here's the healthy tonic you and your wallet need. Wholesome savings up to 40% on their brand of vitamins and natural skin products. Add up your total bill and then deduct a specified percentage (e.g. 25%) off. If you know your ABC's, you can pick out the best alfalfa bets as well as Korean ginseng, papaya ("the miracle digestive aid"), bee pollen, brewer's yeast, or suck on a succulent granule of everyone's favorite flavor: desiccated liver. VQ also offers free gifts according to the dollar amount of your order, or as a reward for soliciting orders from your friends. C

WESTERN NATURAL PRODUCTS
Box 284-U.S.
511 Mission St.
South Pasadena, CA 91030
(213) 441-3447

Whoa down there, podnuh, and don't get roped into paying retail! These Westerners have rounded up a corral full of house-brand natural vitamins and hair and skin products, and have reined in on high prices. We were spurred to savings on multivitamins, mega-vitamins, and children's chewables, along with aloe vera, bee pollen, papaya, enzymes, ginseng, and a whole herd of other items at 30% to 70% off. They've branded their own products (which compare to national labels in quality) so sage shoppers can feel at home on their price range. There's a $2-off coupon on any initial order. All products are unconditionally guaranteed and can be returned with no questions asked. There's no restocking charge, no minimum order, and their catalog's free. You can lick the postal stamp-ede at Christmas if you stock up on vitamins early. C

3.

PERSONAL INTERESTS

Art Supplies

Shop for art supplies without leaving your easel or drafting table. Buy quality products via mail, like Liquitex acrylics, Winsor & Newton designer's gouache, Grumbacher oils, and Rembrandt pastels and enjoy discounts up to 50% off retail prices. If you are a member of an artist's guild or work in a classroom environment, you can buy in larger quantities and save even more.

A.I. FRIEDMAN
25 W. 45th St.
New York, NY 10036
(212) 575-0200

Supplying the fashion industry with markers, paints, and drafting supplies contributes to this man's Fried-dom. Their other clients include publishers, Fortune 500 companies, and even the Muppets. This 54-year-old company featured a complete, state-of-the-art inventory from airbrushes to zipatone in their thick catalog, $3, with many items discounted 20% or more. We were A.I.ded by a special list of discounted items which included Liquitex acrylics and oils, Winsor & Newton watercolors, Rembrandt and Bocour Bellini oils, and a large selection of brushes discounted up to 40%. Canvas panels, watercolor papers, stretchers, canvas, and turpentine were also discounted. Minimum order is $20. Add 10% for shipping, handling, and insurance. **C $3, B**

CROWN ART PRODUCTS
75 E. 13th St.
New York, NY 10003
(212) 673-0150

King Art-hur would have put his royal stamp of approval on Crown supplies, 'cause he used his round table to free-Lance a lot. This company offers king-size discounts ranging from 20% to 65% on silk-screen, artist, and craft supplies. They do have a 15% restocking charge on returns, but no minimum order except on credit cards ($20). We like their metal section frames in silver and gold ranging from 5 inches to 40 inches. (They'll cut them to your specifications, too.) We found a majestic selection of silk-screen inks and supplies, stretch canvas, and craft items in a catalog not soon to be throne out. **C $1**

DICK BLICK EAST
P.O. Box 26
Allentown, PA 18105
(800) 345-3042
(800) 322-9538: PA residents
(215) 965-6051

Use your Bic to write Dick Blick and get the thick red book of creative materials. A leading supplier of high school and university art departments, the best bet is quantity buys of Blick's brand of paints and papers. "Blick City" tempera paints were 20% lower than a comparable brand (a 6-gallon pump kit was $62.90). Crayola crayons were 87 cents (list $1.23) if you bought 72 boxes. Discounted posterboards by Blick in 6-, 8-, and 14-ply were a good sign at 30% below retail. A special *Fine Arts Supplement* offered free shipping with the o-Blick-atory $40 order, of course. Other branches: Dick Blick Co., Box 1267, Galesburg, IL 61401, (800) 447-8192 or (800) 322-8183 for IL residents; and Dick Blick West, Box 521, Henderson, NV 89015, (800) 634-7001 or (702) 451-7662 for NV residents. **C $2**

FRANK MITTERMEIER INC.
3577 E. Tremont Ave.
New York, NY 10465
(212) 828-3843

Whenever Mister Chips goes to the Bronx, he always calls on Frank. He's no chiseler, but his collection of tools will steel your heart away. Over 40,000 tools for woodcarvers, sculptors, engravers, ceramists, and potters plus many how-to books for the knot-so inclined. Discounts of 15% plus a "no charge for shipping" policy on six or more tools whittled away our bill. Dastra woodcarving tools, finely crafted by David Strasmann & Company of Germany, were 15% lower than retail including shipping. A set of four tools (chip carver, skew chisel, parting tool, and gouge) for $34.90. Send for the illustrated catalog because "every whittle bit helps." **C**

JERRY'S ARTRAMA, INC.
248-12 Union Turnpike
Bellerose, NY 11426
(800) 221-2323
(212) 343-0777: NY residents

Trial by Jerry probably means you'll get hung in some art gallery. Winsor & Newton, 3M, Grumbacher, Strathmore are witnesses for the state (of the art, that is) and testimonials to Jerry's "up to 60%" discounts. His sentence: "I'm building a new warehouse so I should have even more inventory space." Minimum order is $25, phone order minimum is $50. Besides the annual catalog, Jerry Goldstein sends out special 32-page issues about six times a year on request. **C $1**

NEW YORK CENTRAL SUPPLY CO.
62 Third Ave.
New York, NY 10003
(212) 473-7705

"We cater to our mail-order customers," says Steven Steinberg, owner of one of New York's oldest fine art supply stores. He offers 20% discounts to support this claim. The paper section encompasses the entire second floor and includes over 1,200 papers from 17 countries. They showed their true colors in 250 lines of paints by such names as Winsor & Newton, Liquitex, Rembrandt, Grumbacher, and Bellini. In addition to a general catalog, $3, there are special catalogs for paints, $2; paper, $2; calligraphy, $1; and a new edition for airbrushes, $2. The price of the catalog is refundable with the first order. **C** $ varies

PEARL
308 Canal St.
New York, NY 10013
(800) 221-6845: orders only
(212) 431-7932: NY residents

Now there's a string of Pearls (Long Island; Paramus, New Jersey; and Fort Lauderdale, Florida, to help you paint the town red, white, or cobalt blue. Considered to be one of the largest suppliers of art and craft materials in the world, their "fine art" catalog represents only 2% of all the products the company distributes. If you send them a product description, they can usually fill it with a 20% to 50% discount. Look what Tex got in the Liquitex line of acrylics: 20% off 2-ounce tubes of color. Robert Simmons red sable hair watercolor brushes let us "sable" little money at 15% below normal retail. Minimum order, $50. **C** on fine art supplies only; all else, **PQ**

POLYART PRODUCTS CO.
1199 E. 12th St.
Oakland, CA 94606
(415) 451-1048

Paint the town and save, but paint your wagon and pay close to retail. We lost our tempera because we had to order $40 of this acrylic artist paint for an extra 10% discount. However, these high-quality paints are already discounted and cost $1.90 for 4 ounces, $4.80 for a pint including shipping. Twelve colors plus gloss clear, gel clear, modeling paste, and gesso. Minimum order of $20 for no additional discount; up to 30% off for orders of $400 or more. **B**

STU-ART SUPPLIES, INC.
2045 Grand Ave.
Baldwin, NY 11510
(800) 645-2855
(516) 546-5151: NY residents

Artichoke you up? Get your framing and presentation supplies cheaper (approximately 50%) and wind up on the Dick Cabbage show. We'll be art-iculate about their discounted museum conservation frames, wood and tenite, shadow-box, and floater frames, mats, d'Arches watercolor paper, and all-media art boards. Minimum orders of $15 on frame sections and $25 on mats (or combine mats and frames for a $25 minimum). Orders over $250 are shipped free in UPS delivery areas only. Refunds if dissatisfied; customer pays shipping and handling to return. **C**

UTRECHT ART AND DRAFTING SUPPLY
33 35th St.
Brooklyn, NY 11232
(212) 768-2528

To etch his own but there's enough of a selection for everyone to draw from 20% to 50% on art and drafting supplies. They carry Utrecht and other major-brand supplies on everything from acrylics, brushes, canvas, and drafting machines to frames, watercolors, and zipper cases. We found a complete line of Pantone products discounted 30% along with Strathmore, Bienfang, d'Arches, Chartpak, K & E, and Design Art Marker products. Minimum order of $40. Quantity discounts on Utrecht products (up to 20% off orders over $450) rounded out their portfolio. Before u trek all over town, u try Utrecht. **C**

Hobbies and Crafts

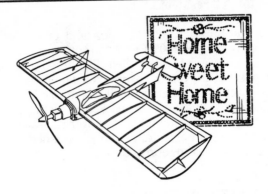

No matter what your special interest is, there is sure to be something here for you. Get yarn, optical accessories, beekeeping supplies, woodcrafting or jewelry making tools, dollhouse furniture, leathercrafting materials, or almost anything to indulge your creative spirit. Be crafty, order by mail or phone and make saving money your new hobby.

A. JAEGERS OPTICS
691 Merrick Road
P.O. Box G
Lynbrook, NY 11563
(516) 599-3167

No optical illusions here. Focus in on their catalog and opt for a bargain on telescopes, beam splitters, mirrors, lenses, eyepieces, prisms, binoculars, and magnifiers. Name-brand telescopes we found in the 50 pages included Muksutov and Azimuth. Best bet: reflector telescope kits starting at $29.75 postpaid ($25 lower than the competition and worth making a spectacle over). **C $1**

AMERICA'S HOBBY CENTER, INC.
146 W. 22nd St., Dept. US
New York, NY 10011
(212) 675-8922

The source for hobby horses who want to assemble 10% to 40% discounts. If you're a model enthusiast—airplanes, railroads, ships, cars—this is your catalog. They advertise "red hot sales" on everything from "little engines that could" to "medium motors that can." If it floats, flies, swims, sinks, roars, or runs, you can bet this center has it. By the way, not only do they accept cash, checks, or money orders, but unused postage stamps as well. It's worth the stamps to give them a try. Ask to receive their bulletins, free to readers of this book. **C $2**

BERMAN LEATHERCRAFT
145 South St.
Boston, MA 02111
(617) 426-0870

Berman has a complete line of leathers and suedes including Gallapava, a fancy name for turkey skin. They also have lizard, snake, and antelope skin as well as the more traditional cowhides (sorry, no buffalo). Hardware, accessories, dyes, and books on leathercraft. Best buys are in quantity, although their everyday prices are still lower than those offered by other firms. Minimum order of $15. They're one of the few companies that sell fashionable metallic leather by the skin, although it's not listed in their catalog. Send for garment, belt, wallet, or bag leather swatches, 50 cents each. **C $1**

CAMBRIDGE WOOLS, LTD.
40 Anzac Ave.
Auckland 1, New Zealand

Knitting yarns by the ounce or pound in earthy, toasty tones as well as cheerful brights. These yarns are hard to find in the U.S. and when available, are often very expensive. They also sell Aran sweaters and sheepskins, along with their knitting, spinning, and weaving supplies. Satisfaction is guaranteed at this 30-year-old company. If you return the merchandise, they'll refund your money. **B $1** (includes samples)

CRAFTSMAN WOOD
1735 W. Courtland Court
Addison, Il 60101
(312) 629-3100

Woody like to pay 15% less for lumber and woodcrafting tools like chisels, shaves, drill presses, coping saws, plus brass finishes for cabinets and doors if he could? Craftsman furniture plans for a gun cabinet cost $8 to $9. Build your own veneer backgammon board from scratch for $23.95. Some ex-sap-tional bargains such as 20 pounds of small pieces of imported wood for $13.98. Brands carried include Bosch, Dremel, Rockwall, and Stanley. Minimum order is $10 for cash; $25 for credit cards. There is a 30-day refund period and no restocking charge except on specially cut merchandise. **C $1** (for postage and handling)

CURRICULUM RESOURCES, INC.
P.O. Box 923
2 Post Road
Fairfield, CT 06430
(800) 243-2874
(203) 255-4538: CT residents

We canvassed this arts and crafts catalog, not missing a stitch, and found hook rug kits to latch onto, calligraphy kits to write for, crewel yarns to weave home for, string art, paints, pastels, acrylics, needlepoint, cross-stitch samplers, wheat weaving kits, instructional class packs, and more. Savings averaged 20% across the board: Familiar brands were Bucilla, Columbia, Minerva, Cathy, and Dimensions. CR, Inc. is especially suited to schools, hospitals, and clubs. Special savings are given to schools and other volume buyers and they even offer discounts upon discounts in periodic bulletins. **C**

DEEPAK'S ROKJEMPERL PRODUCTS
61 10th Khetwadi
Bombay 400 004
India
Phone: 388031 (dial "01" for operator assistance with this call)

Personable Vijaychand Shah also owns Shah's Rock Shop, Vijay World Traders, and Gemcraft India International. His brochure is packed with hundreds of items making it hard for readers to find anything. But if you're persistent, you can string 'em up for yourself or give handmade beaded jewelry to your friends for next to nothing (about 50% to 80% less than retail). Craft-quality lapis lazuli, 40 cents per carat; tiger eye, 9 cents per carat; emeralds, $5 per carat; medium blue Burma sapphires, $11.50 per carat. Also uncovered bone-ivory jewelry, sandalwood and rosewood articles, buffalo horn carvings, mother-of-pearl, brass, and jeweler's tools at inexpensive prices. You save most on quantity purchases. Sea mail parcels take 8 to 10 weeks to arrive. Minimum order is $25 to get free delivery with parcels duly insured by the company. **C**

FORT CRAILO YARNS
2 Green St.
Rensselaer, NY 12144
(518) 465-2371

If you've been weaving lately, straighten up and take advantage of this company's offer. They're no wooly bullies. Yarns for weavers sold by the pound are cheaper bought in large vo-looms. About 30 different colors (bright, pastel, and muted) manufactured by Albany Woolen Mills. All yarns are prepared and spun expressly for hand weavers and craftspeople using a variety of fine wools from Australia, New Zealand, and the United States. Four wool sample cards, $2 a set; 80 cents for cotton cards. Without spinning any tales, we found the savings to be about 30% lower than other imported yarns of the same quality. **SAMPLES, $ varies**

GLORYBEE HONEY AND SUPPLY
1006 Arrowsmith St.
Eugene, OR 97402
(503) 485-1649

When this leading manufacturer of wooden ware discounts 30%, you know they mean bees-ness. Apiarists (a fancy word for beekeepers) will delight in the Glorybee catalog, which sells a complete line of accessories, equipment, and supplies for beekeeping, including, of course, live bees and hives. The catalog is very interesting, even to a bee-ginner, and the prices are bee-low retail. Additional discounts are offered on a per item basis. Another catalog featured bulk and gift packs of honey and bee pollen at wholesale prices and food stuffs like raisins, nut mixes, candy bars. Give them a buzz next time you're in Eugene. **C 25 cents** (both catalogs will be sent for 25 cents)

THE GOODFELLOW CATALOG OF WONDERFUL THINGS
P.O. Box 4520
Berkeley, CA 94704
(415) 428-0142

Here's a source book of handmade items you can mail-order direct from the artisan. This 720-page compendium (priced at $19.95 plus $2.50 for shipping) features 680 selected artisans of jewelry, sculpture, canoes, kayaks, kimonos, teepees, stained glass, roller skates, walking sticks, quilts, rocking horses, photographs, and a myriad of other good and wonderful things. By using this informative book, you can avoid the middleman and deal directly with the craftspeople (and save yourself at least 20% over fancy boutique prices for craft items). Other books from these same goodfellows soon to be available include: *The Goodfellow Catalog of Wonderful Things for Children; The Goodfellow Catalog of Gifts under $50; The Goodfellow Catalog of Wonderful Wearables;* and *The Goodfellow Catalog of Things for the Home and Office.* **C $19.95 plus $2.50 shipping**

GRIEGER'S, INC.
900 South Arroyo Parkway
P.O. Box 93070
Pasadena, CA 91109
(800) 423-4181
(800) 362-7708: CA residents
(213) 795-9775

You may need a Grieger-counter to locate the presence of precious price-saving craft projects: jewelry mounts for earrings, pendants, rings, chains, bead-stringing kits, wax supplies, tumble-polished gemstones, belt buckles, lariat tie slides, clock parts, stained-glass kits, music boxes, wood burning supplies, as well as soldering supplies, adhesives, kilns, tools, and more. No rhinestone cow, boy, but we saw a nice gold-colored unicorn with chain for $2.95, three for $7.79. And a pewter raccoon was just $1.95 ($1.60 if you order six or more). **C**

HOBBY SHACK
18480 Bandilier Circle
Fountain Valley, Ca 92708
(800) 854-8471
(800) 472-8456: CA residents
(714) 963-9881

Hobby Shack's two-part catalog displays hundreds of souped-up, radio-controlled models of boats, planes, and cars bound to stretch the imagination of kids and adults alike. Elaborate designs, bright colors, and assorted scale sizes. Plenty of accessories, tools, and supplies are available at 20% to 40% off. Regular customers acquire special status and receive the *Sport Flyer*, which touts many sales during the year. This company also permits C.O.D. deliveries for $6 extra. There is no minimum order, no restocking charges, and if you place an order, the catalog is free. **C $2** (free with order)

HOBBY SURPLUS SALES
P.O. Box 2170 A
New Britain, CT 06050
(203) 229-9069

You're bound to go loco when you see the great prices and selection of new and used Lionel trains. Chugging along for an equally good deal is a large variety of model ship, car, airplane, and other kits. Create miniature dollhouse furniture for that living doll of yours. The list of war games and fantasy games is out of this world. Try to beat the computer with Avalon Hill strategy games. Who will win the nuclear confrontation? What really happened at the battle of Midway? For answers to these and other questions, send $1 for the Hobby catalog. No shipping charges. **C $1**

THE H.O.M.E. CRAFT CATALOG
Route 1
Orland, ME 04472
(207) 469-7961

Homeowners Organized for More Employment is not only a delightful community group, it's a handicrafter's haven. If you have a fancy for cable-knit sweaters or patchwork quilts like granny used to make, this tabloid offers home work you'll love. A unique approach to marketing the work of Maine's artists with 70% of the selling price retained by the artist. Pottery, leather goods, calico and quilts, toys, woodwork, and Christmas items generally priced lower than machine-made equivalents. Beautiful calico wreath, $12.50; acrylic hand-knit sweaters, $19.50 to $30; all-wood wren feeder, $8.75. Allow four to six weeks delivery on larger items. Contact Virgie Betts. **C 50 cents**

JAY'S YARNS
1-15 N. Central Ave.
Hartsdale, NY 10530
(914) 949-6667

Yarn nobody 'til somebody loves you and Jay's does. Old softies like Bucilla, are discounted at least 20% (up to 50% on closeouts). Pinquoin sport yarn was $1.55 (retail $2). They have a huge inventory of name-brand yarns, discounted 15% to 30%. Jay's carry the largest variety of kits and full lines of materials from Paragon, Bernat, Sunset, Dimensions, Bucilla, and more. Find a kit in one of the craft magazines, write them, and they can probably get it for you for less. We saved 35% on a Sunset Rainbow Balloon kit for $11.99. Mailing charges usually run $1.20 to $3 for UPS. When ordering, buy a little more than you think you'll need—just in case. Jay's will take back extra yarn up to one year and give a full refund. **PQ**

LAMRITE'S
565 Broadway
Bedford, OH 44146
(216) 232-9300

Daisy, Daisy, give me your answer do, I'm half crazy over the love of you. It won't be a stylish marriage, but we'll have flowers all over the carriage. They carry ar-range of silk-like flowers, kits, florists supplies (moss, ribbons, styrofoam, baskets) for those who want to try their hand at flower arranging. You'll save 20% off retail prices for the Pretty Petals line of supplies. There's a 15% restocking charge and the minimum order is $10 **C** **$2** (refundable)

NEW ENGLAND FRAMEWORKS
Route 1, Dept. US 3
Wilton, NH 03086
(800) 258-5480: credit card orders only
(603) 878-1633: NH residents

Seeking frame and fortune? Seek no more but sneak a peek at this manufacturer's catalog; it's free when you send a long SASE with two stamps. These frames and domes are made to display collector's plates. The company also makes display hardware and shelves. Materials range from wood-like polyurethane to solid oak and everything is priced 30% to 50% lower than those marked for full retail. "Ninety-nine percent of the orders are shipped within a week," said Bob Edwards, owner of the 9-year-old company. The catalog has a handy frame finder chart which matches frame to your plate size. **C, SASE**

PINCHPENNY MINIATURES
17 Idaho Lane
Matawan, NJ 07747

The Itty Bitty City Committee buys all their county seats here. Pinchpenny Miniatures can give your miniature dream mansion antique, colonial, or contemporary looks right down to clocks, lamps, newspapers, tea sets, silverware, cooking utensils, food, and anything else you would need, should you shrink to the size of an inchworm. A three-piece 1920s kitchen set is $16; dining table and chairs, $7. Special "surprise" packages, $5 (worth at least $7) and $10 (worth at least $15). **C 75 cents**

THOS. MANETTA
61 Hoffman Ave.
Elmont, NY 11003
(516) 775-2034

Scope out these discounts: 20% to 30% off binoculars, theater glasses, microscopes, and telescopes from Bushnell, Bausch & Lomb, and Swift. A 7x35 Center Focus binocular by B&L, $275 (retail $349.95) was a sight to see. Warranties included on most items. **C** (seasonal, not always available)

VETERAN LEATHER CO.
204 25th St.
Brooklyn, NY 11232
(212) 768-0300

Veteran Leather Co. has a variety of leathers including suede and chamois. They also stock leather working accessories and tools. Most of their everyday prices are lower than retail, with discounts up to 30% on quantity purchases. There's a $15 minimum order, and a 10% restocking charge on returns (unless the material is defective). You can examine their 56-page catalog, or give them a call for a price quote. **PQ, C $1.50**

THE VILLAGE TINKER
377 Boston Post Road
Sudbury, MA 01776
(617) 443-3330

For the little engine that could, you need the imported Peco Track Systems that will be discounted 20%. This tinker is the only U.S. firm we know of to discount these fine imported locomotive tracks by mail. Free price list gives specifications. **PQ**

WALDEN CATALOG SALES INC.
P.O. Box D
Elma, NY 14059

Owner Rosemary Gohn gave us a Thoreau explanation of her company. "Walden sells a variety of needlecraft products including books, yarns, kits, accessories, and more." There is an initial discount of 10% on every item in their catalog. If you become a member of their Preferred Customer Club, you get an additional 10% off all items, bringing your savings to 20%. That's her nature. **C**

Musical Instruments

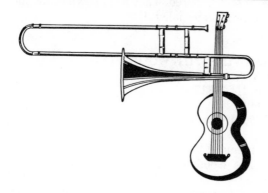

Music-making can be extremely expensive when you pay for music-learning: lessons, instruments, and sheet music. By shopping around, you can usually buy your instrument for less than retail without sacrificing quality. Have a professional advise you on what to buy for your level of skill, then go shopping by mail. Most major manufacturers are represented here. Some stores even offer group discounts, trade-in policies, and free trial periods.

A.L.A.S. ACCORDION-O-RAMA
16 W. 19th St.
New York, NY 10011
(212) 675-9089

Alas! Your key to saving 20% on accordions, concertinas, electronic accordions, and amps. Direct importers of musical instruments for over 30 years, they carry all top brands. Full refunds and all manufacturers' guarantees honored. They are known in the industry as the electronic accordion specialist. **C**

THE BRASSWIND/THE WOODWIND
50741 U.S. 31 N.
South Bend, IN 46637
(800) 348-5003
(219) 272-8266: IN residents

We don't remember the question, but the answers my friend, are blowing in The Woodwind and The Brasswind catalogs. Despite sounding like twin condo developments, the Brasswind and Woodwind are stores specializing in instruments for serious musicians. If you specify your catalog preference, you can rustle through their price sheets and select from a very extensive list of quality instruments. A Yamaha YCL-82 clarinet listing for $1,450 was ony $845, and a LeBlanc L-200 clarinet was $750 ($1,495 list). A Yamaha YCR-231 cornet sold for $199 ($349 list). Other instruments include piccolos, flutes, bassoons, oboes, saxes, as well as accessories in the Woodwind catalog, and fluegelhorns, trombones, trumpets, French horns, euphoniums in Brasswind. They make repairs, too. There's a two-week return privilege, and even an installment plan on some instruments with no interest charged. All instruments are completely tested before shipment. **C**

CARVIN
1155 Industrial Ave.
Escondida, CA 92025
(714) 747-1710

Oh, like wow, man, I'm like freaking out! The original Valley Guy, Frank Zappa, doing product testimonials? How commercial, how grody to the max! (Barf me out, I mean, gag me with a spoon!) Actually such an occurrence is not so totally awesome as you might imagine. This company has been Carvin out a reputation amongst professional musicians for quality products, including mixers, amps, and electric guitars, which are well below prices charged by companies selling comparable name brands. Unlike many other companies, they have a 10-day free trial period, and if not satisfied, you can return the product with "no strings attached" (figuratively speaking). A deal like that, along with a stunningly beautiful catalog (Frank notwithstanding) makes us Moon over a Unit, not to mention a guitar. **C**

FREEPORT MUSIC
144 Wolf Hill Road
Melville, NY 11747
(516) 549-4108

Thar she blows! Moby Dick could have made a euphonious wail playing (and spouting off about) the instruments listed in this catalog. Savings ranged from 30% to 60% on organs, amplifiers, moog synthesizers, and all the musical instruments and accessories you'll need to turn your home into a concert hall or disco (without harpooning your budget). This 52-year-old company harbors such names as Ludwig, Tama, Gibson, Ibanez, Boss, Fender, Ovation, Selmer, Ting, Benge, Armstrong, Signet, and Rickenbacker. There's a $10 minimum order with cash, $25 with charge. Defective items will be exchanged or repaired at no cost except shipping, but there's a 15% restocking charge on returns. The catalog cost is refundable on the first order. Discounted instruments sound pretty fin-tastic to us, and definitely won't set us to blubbering. **C $1** (refundable)

MANDOLIN BROS.
629 Forest Ave.
Staten Island, NY 10310
(212) 981-3226

If strings are your thing, put the finger on these guys and strum up some savings. They've got electric and acoustic guitars, banjos, autoharps, and of course, mandolins at prices that won't make you fret. They specialize in the "vintage" instrument (1850 to 1969) but they also carry the finest brands of new instruments. There are 40% discounts on Guild and C.F. Martin; 41% discounts on Ovation; as well as 30% off Dobro and Washburn. Other brands include Sigma, Yamaha, Gibson, and Kentucky mandolins and Stelling banjos. There's a full approval guarantee on all items shipped, with a 48-hour trial privilege (customers should notify by phone during the trial period if they're dissatisfied, and return via UPS or mail for full refund of purchase price, less shipping charges). A deal like that shouldn't cause any unpleasant reverberations. **C**

NEMC
33 Union Place
P.O. Box 670
Summit, NJ 07901
(800) 526-4593
(201) 277-3324: NJ residents

At NEMC (National Educational Music Company) you can picc-o-lo priced instrument from clarinets to violins at up to 50% off the list price. (Inflation-fighter offers deserve an additional round of applause.) All major manufacturers are represented (Armstrong, Signet, and others) and what they don't have in stock, they'll special order. If your child is taking music lessons, this is a good place to pick up a horn without blowing a lot of cash. **B**

P.M.I.
P.O. Box 827
Union City, NJ 07087
(201) 863-2200

"When you're looking for that big break, P.M.I. can be instrumental" was their line, not ours. We'll toot their horn, too, for other lines of first-quality professional musical instruments and accessories in all major brands at 10% to 25% discounts. Send $3 (which will be refunded with your first order) for their 90-plus-page catalog. Items we noted were VTX amplifier, $328.50 (retail $469.50); and Gibson Les Paul custom guitar, $681 (retail $1,049). Shipped directly from the manufacturer upon P.M.I.'s receipt of order and full payment. Additional freight charges run about 3%. There's a $20 minimum order, 30-day exchange or refund policy, and 15% restocking charge on returns. **C** $3 (refundable); **PQ, B**

RHYTHM BAND, INC.
P.O. Box 126
1212 E. Lancaster
Fort Worth, TX 76101
(817) 335-2561

What's a band without Rhythm? This company principally sells to elementary schools, although they do sell to individuals at the same reduced rates. (There's no minimum order.) Prices ran about 20% lower than retail music stores. Their 60-page, full-color catalog displays a range of rhythm instruments in bells, bongos, castanets, cymbals, drums, glockenspiels, kazoos, maracas, rhythm sticks, ukuleles, and xylophones in their own RBI line. Every catalog item must meet with complete customer satisfaction and approval, and may be returned at Rhythm Band's expense for a refund or exchange within 90 days if unsatisfactory. This company set our hearts to pounding (rhythmically). **C**

SAM ASH MUSIC CORP.
124 Fulton Ave.
Hempstead, NY 11550
(800) 645-3518
(212) 347-7757: NY residents

So-nata bagpipe, marimba, or accordion Sam can't get since he has "one of the world's largest inventories of musical instruments, amplification, sound reinforcement, professional audio equipment, sheet music, and accessories." Founded in 1924 by a prominent New York violinist and bandleader, Sam Ash, the business now offers every important name brand in instruments, synthesizers, and sheet music at low prices. Triple guarantees are offered on all instruments including original factory guarantee, Sam Ash's guarantee, and a guaranteed trade-in policy. They have no catalog or brochure because, in their words, they have "too much stuff." **PQ**

SHAR PRODUCTS COMPANY
2465 S. Industrial Highway
P.O. Box 1411
Ann Arbor, MI 48106
(800) 521-0791
(800) 482-1086: MI residents
(313) 665-7711

The family that plays together, stays together (or at least that's our impression from the photo in their catalog). For over 20 years, the Avsharians have stood for low prices (25% lower on instruments and accessories), service, and selection for those people strung out on stringed instruments. They've got strings, accessories, cases, instruments, and repair supplies at note-iceable discounts, while Suzuki materials, books, and reams of sheet music are available at full price. (Not ones to restrict themselves unduly, their policy on instruments is to "straddle various" manufacturers.) We saw plush

Continental and London Suspensionair and Non-Suspension cases by American Case Company discounted $100 to $200, with less spectacular savings on lower-priced cases by Jaeger, Freistat and Lifton, and M.A. Gordge. Shar's regular discount catalog and catalog of 600 most requested sheet music pieces for strings are free, but the complete sheet music catalog's $2.50. **C** $ varies

SILVER AND HORLAND
170 W. 48th St.
New York, NY 10036
(212) 869-3870

Accord-ion to this dynamic duet, for over 50 years they've been supplying up-and-strumming musicians with the instruments of their trade. (And they're no lyres!) They sell new, used, and vintage musical instruments and accessories at 30% to 50% discounts. (Of course, there is a variance in price depending on age, use, and instrument quality.) There's a $15 minimum order, with a 24-hour full refund period, and a 15% restocking charge after that. Not to leave you on a sour note, when you write and ask for information, there are no strings attached. A catalog is currently in the works. **PQ**

Pets

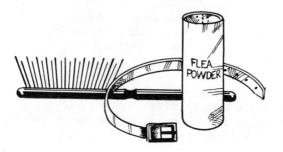

If you recently took up raising St. Bernards, check out these listings. Order dog and cat collars, toys, grooming supplies, vitamins, medical supplies, hair clippers, and even hoof trimmers for your racehorse. Call Wholesale Veterinary Supply and you can even get a veterinarian free of charge.

ECHO PRODUCTS, INC.
335 Mill St.
Ortonville, MI 48462
(313) 627-2877

Echo's a place for resounding bargains in small animal food and hardware, especially for tropical fish. You'll be tankful for the watered-down prices (25% off) on aquariums, fish filters, and live fish. They even have tapes such as, "Successful Fish Photos," or "How to Select a Community Tank Fish" for $2.95 each. (And you won't want to miss the amusing "Tropical Fish Problem Solver Chart" included with your catalog.) They also have "the world's best animal locator service." For $2 you tell them what you want and they send you a computer printout of about two dozen animal breeders, kennels, and individual suppliers catering to the critter you care about. And we're not just talking about ordinary animals (although they can locate all types of dogs, cats, etc.). If you want a hedgehog, wallaby, centipede, seahorse, buffalo, or beetle, these are the folks to find it for you. Give 'em a holler, and wait to hear back. **C 50 cents** (refundable)

LIBERTY LEATHER
P.O. Box 215
Liberty, TN 37095
(615) 597-7999

Buying a good leather collar for your dog can be (yup, you guessed it) a real pain in the neck. This company is at liberty to offer up to 75% savings on a variety of plain and studded styles for any size dog. These collars are all handmade from harness leather. Orders under $20 are retail only. Shipping is $3 on most orders. We'll bow wow-t at this point. **B (SASE and 25 cents)**

NORTHERN WHOLESALE VETERINARY SUPPLY
5570 Frontage Road N.
Onalaska, WI 54650
(800) 356-5852
(800) 362-8025: WI residents
(608) 783-0300

Ro-meow, Ro-meow, wherefore art thou with my chow? Maybe the Montagues and Cat-ulets were fighting it out in Shakespeare's day, but here's a company that offers a happy ending to such problems as worms and fleas. A complete line of animal health products offered at savings from 15%. Orders over $40 are shipped free so gather all ye friends to the court for your first order. They also have a veterinarian on call to answer questions. Major credit cards accepted. **C**

PETCO ANIMAL SUPPLIES
8500 Alvardo Road
Dept. U
P.O. Box 1076
La Mesa, CA 92041
(619) 469-2111

This cat-alog is a purr-fect Santa Claws wish book for felines, canines, and their human pets. Petco carries a full line of supplies for cats, dogs, horses, birds, and fish at prices (10% to 50%) averaging 30% off retail. This company's catalog of grooming supplies, collars, leads, toys, vaccines, remedies, and veterinary supplies also devotes 10 pages to vitamins. Satisfaction's guaranteed; there's a $5 minimum order; and there's no restocking charge on returns. We'll bet your pet can convince you to get something—ours certainly gave us paws. **C**

TOMAHAWK LIVE TRAP CO.
P.O. Box 323
Tomahawk, WI 54487
(715) 453-3550

Honest Injun, palefaced animal lovers can snare savings without having the bite put on their four-footed friends. This company has humane traps and box-type cages for catching, holding, and/or transporting wild and not-so-wild beasts like mice, chipmunks, beavers, raccoons, skunks, rabbits, cats, dogs, squirrels, turtles, pigeons, fish, and rats. A 30-by-16-by-20-inch dog cage with sliding doors was $41.10 (retail $61.64), and if you buy six or more, the cost drops to $35.38 apiece. All traps are built to last and are sold factory direct so you won't get boxed in by high prices. If your pet agrees, he'll say, "Trap it up, we'll take it." (So, get set to spring into action!)
B

UNITED PHARMACAL CO., INC.
306 Cherokee St.
St. Joseph, MO 64504
(816) 238-3366

We wanted to throw rice when we saw all the bridle and grooming supplies United Pharmacal Company had to offer. They ushered us into 20% to 40% discounts on antibiotics, vitamins, insecticides, horse tack—everything we needed for dog, cat, or horse care. "I do, I do" with do-it-yourself vaccines for 80% savings off vet's fees (you must send your vet's prescription). Fall specials included the famous Barbara Woodhouse choke chains at $2.50, $27.50 per dozen and her book, *No Bad Dogs,* was $9.95 ($13.95 retail). Pin-striped sweaters for dogs were $2.15 each. Shipping costs $1.75 to $2.25 and there is a $5 minimum. Special premiums for cash orders and up to 10% additional discounts for quantity purchases make this more than a puppy love affair. **C**

THE WHOLESALE VETERINARY SUPPLY, INC.
P.O. Box 2256
Rockford, IL 61131
(800) 435-6940
(800) 892-6996: IL residents
(815) 877-0209

From hair clippers to hoof trimmers, everything you need in vitamins, supplements, prescriptions, medical supplies, shampoos, and insecticides for your Flicka, Benji, or Morris at 25% to 30% discount. Wonder wormers, anti-mating spray (works only on four-legged animals), spray cologne and deodorant, tick bombs, Jim Dandy horse treats, Pet-a-Go-Go (not a poodle punk club but a collapsible carrying case for a dog or cat), plus a conversation piece fit for shooting the bull: cow chip penholder for $8. Full-time veterinarian answers your questions at no charge. Add $2 shipping charge for orders under $20; otherwise, no charge. **C**

Tobacco

Modern literature has elevated smoking to an art form. Who can imagine Ashenden without an Indian cheroot, Lady Brett without a Gauloise, or Hercule Poirot without his pensive pipe. But even if you're not in somebody's book, smoking may still be a hobby—a pursuit of pleasure and relaxation. From the mundane to the exotic, from corncob pipes to handmade cigars—order your supplies by mail. The selection offered by the merchants in our book is great. And the savings are even greater.

FAMOUS SMOKE SHOP
1450 Broadway
New York, NY 10018
(800) 847-4062
(212) 221-1408: NY residents

Handmade, all-tobacco cigars are shipped anywhere in the world within a few days ($1 for the first box, 50 cents each additional box). You can't use your Visa for a Te-Amo Presidente, but you may open up an account and charge all you like. Send Partagas to your papa or Macanudos to your mama. The largest selection we've found of name-brand cigars and tobaccos discounted as much as 30%. Their catalog is free and informative so why don't you pick one up and . . . read it sometime. Minimum order: one box of cigars. **C**

HAYIM PINHAS
P.O. Box 500
Istanbul, Turkey
Phone: 011-90-11-229302-286951 (dial direct)

They're your pipe-line for hand-carved meerschaum pipes and their prices (20% lower) blow smoke rings around the competition. Order a lion's head pipe, Lincoln, Cleopatra, Shakespeare, Socrates, sea girl mermaid, skull head, Viking, or even Mickey Mouse. Match that with a carved cigar and cigarette holder ($1.50). Minimum order is two pipes, insurance is extra. Put that in your pipe and smoke it. **C** (issued every three years)

IWAN RIES & CO.
17 S. Wabash Ave.
Chicago, IL 60603
(800) 621-1457
(800) 972-1087: IL residents

Inhale, inhale the gang's all here. Your dollars will go up in smoke at this tobacconist—and you'll love it. Their discount prices, some to as much as 40% lower, are not just another pipe dream. Imported pipes, private label tobaccos and cigars, unlacquered corncobs, leathered briars, and hand-carved meerschaum heads got us fired up, while butane accessories added fuel to that fire. Cigar humidors, ashtrays, pipe racks, and cleaners showed no signs of smoke damage, but had low prices nonetheless. Old-fashioned, homemade fudge and chocolates were also offered to complete the evening's relaxation. Customer satisfaction guaranteed. **C**

J-R TOBACCO CO.
Tuxedo Square
Tuxedo, NY 10987
(800) 431-2380
(914) 753-2745 or 364-4600: NY residents

When in Dallas, JR likes ch-Ewing his tobacco, but in New York, he joins the fogies in puffing stogies at 30% to 60% off. JR carries handmade cigars (every quality brand offered) from such exotic lands as the Dominican Republic, Jamaica, the Phillipines, Honduras, Brazil, Costa Rica, Nicaragua, and Mexico. He also has non-tobacco cigars, as well as the JR Alternative cigars, which are discounted reproductions (40% to 60% savings) of such renowned smokes as El Caudillo, Flamenco, Creme de Jamaica, Don Tomas, Don Diego, Montecruz, Hoyo Excalibur, Hoyo de Monterrey, Macanudo, Partagas, Ramon Allones, Rey del Mundo, Romeo y Julieta, Royal Jamaica, Joya de Nicaragua, Flor del Caribe, and Cuesta Rey. JR carries Thomas Crown and Rothman cigars, too. To go with their alternative cigars, you'll enjoy their offbeat catalog. There's a $10 minimum order and satisfaction's guaranteed. If you're huffin' and puffin' to smoke your house up, the mail's your trail to this Southfork of New York cigars. **C**

4.

BACK TO BASICS

Fabrics

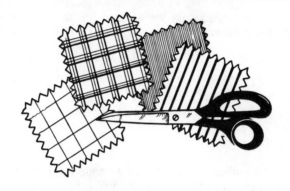

Whether you're shopping for designer fabrics like Oriental silk, camel's hair wool, natural cottons, and linens, or whether you're in the market for drapery and wall fabrics, shop these pages first. Fabric clubs offer excellent bargains for seamstresses who have special interests such as "haute couture" fabrics. When ordering specific fabrics, be sure to include a recent sample for color match and fabric details, like widths, etc. It's always a good idea to order a little more than you actually need, especially exotic fabrics from international sources. You can always make a quilt or a pillow from your elegant extras.

ALL AMERICAN FABRICS
636 S. Lafayette St.
Shelby, NC 28150
(704) 482-3271

We bet Betsy Ross came away from this store with flying colors. They sent a handful of tapestries, early American prints, and in-stock velvets based on a brief statement we supplied about the type of room, furniture, and color of walls, carpet, and drapes. They had absalutely the best discounts we've seen (up to 75%) on closeouts, overruns, seconds, and millends. Shipped UPS. **PQ** (samples)

BEE LEE CO.
P.O. Box 20558
2714 Bomar Ave.
Dallas, TX 75235
(214) 351-2091

Bee Lee-ve us when we say this is *the* source for "sewing supplies with a Western accent." With 191 different colors and styles of Western snap fasteners and trims, you'll have the C&W crowd sewn up in no time. Trims, threads, buttons, interfacings, and zippers from the finest manufacturers were represented in the color catalog. Brands included Wiss scissors, Dritz notions, White sewing machine needles priced well below retail. Shipping charge on orders up to $5 is $1.25; over $20, maximum charge is $2.50 **C**

BRITEX-BY-MAIL
146 Geary St.
Dept. US-83
San Francisco, CA 94108
(415) 392-2910

Designer domestic and imported fabrics to Brighton your days. Even if you're far from their San Francisco shop, you can sew with the best of them when you have access to four floors of beautiful fabrics. Fabrics include domestic and imported wools, silks, knits, cottons, and super synthetics, as well as American and European designer fabrics. This 33-year-old company's personalized swatch service can help you find the fabric you've been looking for. Send for complete information on getting better fabrics for less money. One yard minimum. **B $2**

BUFFALO BATT AND FELT CORP.
3307 Walden Ave.
Depew, NY 14043
(716) 683-4100

These big leaguers have been in the batter's box since 1919 (when mighty Casey was at batt?). While we struck out on craft felt (which they don't sell), the batting averages about 30% off—definitely a hit with us. We dugout this source for home sewers and groups who need team-ing quantities of pillow inserts, quilt batts, and fiberfill. BB&F only sells by the case, with a minimum order of two cases. They also include a sample card of "Superfluff" products, which they manufacture, and which (along with their other items) are in the same ballpark as other top-of-the-line quality retail products. Make your pitch for a $1 brochure and samples, and then make out your batting order. **B $1, PQ**

CASCADE WOOLEN MILL, INC.
P.O. Box 157
Oakland, ME 04963
(207) 465-2511

Bagpipes and whiskey are all you'll need to feel authentic after being outfitted in Scottish tartans, Welsh wools, and Shetlands offered by this 100-year-old New England company. Fabric and blankets available. The savings are 40% to 50% below retail. No minimum order; no restocking charge; exchange or refund only if the fabric is faulty so all sales are final. When in the area, visit their mill store located off Route 137, two miles from Interstate 95. Samples on request, $1.50 **B**

CLEARBROOK WOOLEN SHOP
P.O. Box 8
Clearbrook, VA 22624
(703) 662-3442

Is the big bad wool-f of high fabric prices keeping you wide awake? Instead of counting sheep, dream of saving up to 25% on attractive solid, tweed, and plaid patterns in 100% wool. We received some beautiful swatches in maroon, navy blue, charcoal, and cerulean blue. All 58 inches wide and $13.60 per yard. Add 60 cents per yard UPS charges. Paul revered this savings when he ordered, "One if by lamb, two if by sheep." **PQ**

CROMPTON CO., INC.
400 Race St.
Fabric Shop
Waynesboro, VA 22980
(703) 943-5000

We asked for velvet and we got it. Thirty-five samples of beautiful first-quality velvet, smooth velveteen, and knubby wide-wale corduroy in classic colors came tabbed with style names and prices. Prices were about 30% to 40% less than retail. The lines were their own (Crompton's). "Frenze," perfect for corduroy pants or skirts, was 44 to 45 inches wide, $4.85 per yard. They carry all types of fabric and prefer you send a sample or specific requests first. No minimum order. Additional charges, $2 postage; $3 over 5 pounds. **PQ**

DESIGNER FABRIC CLUB
2 Penn Plaza, Suite 1500
Dept. 1
New York, NY 10121

Exclusive fabrics from Albert Nipon, Evan Picone, Liz Claiborne, Mollie Parnis, and many other celebrated design houses are discounted 20% to 50%. This newly formed club offers only the finest quality fabrics as seen in such magazines as *Vogue* and *Elle*. Four seasonal swatch samplings and special promotions are included in the $10 annual membership fee. **B**

D. MACGILLIVRAY & COY
Muir of Aird
Benbecula
Western Isles, Scotland, PA 88 5NA
Phone: Benbecula 0870 2204 (dial "01" for operator assistance with this call)

Here's the Harris tweed and Shetland knitwear specialist "patronized by royalty and nobility." Even Her Majesty the queen and Princess Margaret own one of their hand-knit Shetland shawls 54 inches-by-54 inches, $40. For the materialistic, hand-woven Harris tweed was a good buy at $10 a yard ($19.98 locally), as well as Scotch tweed at $6.40 per yard. They have Scotch tweeds and Donegals, Scottish clan tartans, Shetland tweeds, mohair and camel's hair, sweaters, socks, bedspreads, caps, ties, rugs, and hand-blended Hebridean perfume. We were intrigued by their "real grouse claw brooches" for $10. There's no minimum order, no restocking charge, and an unconditional exchange or refund policy if not satisfied. **C $1; $4 with swatches**

DONCASTER-TANNER FABRIC SHOP
Oak Springs Road
Rutherfordton, NC 28139
(704) 287-3573

She don't cast 'er eyes down when this outlet sends out a price quote on their fabrics at wholesale prices (30% to 50% off). Specify the type of fabric you want and they'll send you small samples with width, price, and fiber content. Return the one you like with your check for fabric plus $2.50 postage. They ship promptly and will not exchange or refund on fabric. **PQ**

FABRIC CUT-AWAYS
P.O. Box 292BC1
100 Chafen St.
Glendale, SC 29346
(803) 579-2033

Sew, you need a source to cut away the high cost of keeping warm? Quilters can quintuple their supply of print and solid scraps, 6 pounds for $6.50; quilting weight cotton blends, 6 pounds for $6.95; and denim, 4 pounds for $6.25. A variety of other yard goods (1 yard or more) was offered at 3 pounds for $7.98. Cuddle up, too, to their quilts, doll clothes, and novelty items only a cut above wholesale. **C**

HARRY ZARIN CO.
292 Grand St.
New York, NY 10002
(212) 925-6134 or 925-6112

Harry Zarin Co. has been a direct importer for 50 years and has a reputation for carrying a very large and diverse selection of drapery and upholstery fabrics. This includes both imported and domestic goods at prices generally 25% to 33⅓% off department store *sale* prices. In addition to a long list of famous brands such as Schumacher, Robert Allen, Riverdale, and Covington, they are one of the largest distributors of French embroidered tergal sheers and Kirsch and Levolor blinds (including ready-mades) all at least 50%

off. *Free* shipping, which could save you as much as $30 to $40. No mail orders to Hawaii, Alaska, or Canada. Visit their warehouse store across the street at 72 Allen. **PQ**

HOME FABRIC MILLS, INC.
882 S. Main St. (Route 10)
P.O. Box 888
Cheshire, CT 06410
(203) 272-3529

Where there's a mill there's a way to save up to 50% on velvets, antique satins, sheer and textured patterns, and all of the "newly designed" fabrics listed in their brochure. Accessories, like drapery rods, trim, foam, upholstery supplies, thread, and pillows are also available. Send your descriptions. Although they have no catalog, swatches will be "cheerfully sent." Visit their other stores in Belchertown, Massachusetts, and Scotia, New York, if in the area. **PQ**

HOMESTEAD WOOLEN MILLS, INC.
The Mill Store
P.O. Box 30
West Swanzey, NH 03469
(603) 352-2023

Tweed'll de-light. Tweed'll dumbfound. Alice doesn't wonder where to land 33% to 75% savings on herringbone anymore. She doesn't have to Ches-hire priced Cat-alogs all over the place either to find classic wool and wool-blend fabrics for blazers and suits. In fact, now that she knows about Homestead, she's the Queen of Tartans. This 70-year-old Dartmouth division offers full exchanges or refunds and no restocking charges. **C**

INTERCOASTAL TEXTILE CORP.
480 Broadway
New York, NY 10013
(212) 925-9235

Haitian makes waste is not the slogan at this wholesale jobber's warehouse. They carry only first-quality slipcovers, upholstery, drapery, and curtain fabrics including attractive white weave Haitian cotton from $5 to $7.50 a yard. Prices were around 50% to 75% less than retail. A company representative sent a nice note with swatches, but no catalog is available. You must send for samples and wait for reply. Exchanges only if fabric was not cut. **PQ**

JANTZEN FABRIC OUTLET
605 N.E. 21st Ave.
Portland, OR 97232
(503) 238-5396

The other fish in the sea may turn green around the gills with envy when they see swimsuits for men, women, and children made from this famous manufacturer's distinctive fabrics sold at six stores in Nebraska, Washington, California, and Oregon. Save 25% off regular price by buying end-of-bolt precuts. Remnants by the pound started at $3.20. If you like the Jantzen line of swimsuits or sportswear and if you're sew inclined, find the fabrics here and you won't be caught without a stitch on. **PQ**

KNIGHT'S
74 State St., Suite 305
Albany, NY 12207
(518) 436-1822

Knight's into white satin, silk, and other designer fabrics, as well as Bernina sewing machines, and sewing machine repairs. Savings on sewing machines and service were feu-dal and far between at 5% to 10% and 10% to 20% respectively (we're not jesting), but prices on fabrics jousted us into a hearty appetite with 25% to 40% savings off retail. One of our ladies-in-waiting inquired about blue silk, and could hardly wait for sample mailings of light blue palace silk, 45 inches wide at $14.80 per yard; navy blue, 36 inches wide at $11.60 per yard; medium blue, 45 inches wide at $13.98 per yard; and silk jacquard in cornflower blue, 45 inches wide at $10.49 per yard. We found most 36-inch wide silk at $25 per yard averaging $45 a yard locally. Knight's not errant: They proved chivalry's not dead by slaying the dreaded Dragon of Retail, and by keeping our office damsels from distress. Pick up your telephone and give Knight's a (heraldic) ring, all you Middle Aged types—we've tested the waters and "Serf's up!" **PQ**

MARY JO'S CLOTH STORE, INC.
Highway 321 North
Dallas, NC 28034
(704) 922-3171

By Jo, they're fabric-ating cloth of all kinds: first-quality dress goods, calico, gingham, bridal, laces, eyelets, drapery, and upholstery. They carry most name-brands and there is a minimum charge for samples. They also carry notions and accessories at shear savings. Once fabric has been cut, it's yours. No refunds or exchanges unless defective or a hardship case. Catalogs were lost in a recent fire so you must inquire about their inventory. **PQ**

NATURAL FIBER FABRIC CLUB
521 Fifth Ave., Dept. 1
New York, NY 10175

For those purists who want all-natural silk, wool, cotton, and linen fabrics of the finest quality, join the club. You receive 20% discounts from four seasonal mailings, a complete sewing aids catalog, additional savings on 24 "basic fabrics," and unscheduled special offers. Membership is $10 a year. **C**

NEWARK DRESSMAKER SUPPLY
7284 Park Drive
P.O. Box 95
Bath, PA 18014
(215) 837-7500

Sew you're looking for oceans of notions, materials, and supplies. Find needles, hand and sewing machine thread in bulk. They carry basic fabrics such as muslin, crinoline, and buckram. Elastic, zippers, ribbons, bindings, bobbins, and much more. Best buy is ruffled lace, 50 yards for $7.75. Discounts 70%. **C**

SEVENTH AVENUE FABRIC CLUB
450 Seventh Ave., Suite 602
New York, NY 10123

It's easy to get Hook-ed, J.G. that is, since this is one of the best bets we found for famous designer fabrics at 20% to 50% savings. For $10 a year membership, we received four seasonal swatch mailings including Jones of New York herringbone tweed, Dior worsted wool challis, Don Sayre's silk pinstripe, and J.G. Hook's lamb's wool jacquard. The ample pack of swatches made it easy to coordinate fabrics for unique outfits, too. **C**

TESTFABRICS INC.
P.O. Drawer O
200 Blackford Ave.
Middlesex, NJ 08846
Attn: Finley Klaas
(201) 469-6446

The luxury of a pure silk blouse or dress can be yours if you or someone you know has seamstress talents. Silk crepe de chine, $12.75 a yard (retail $22); silk shantung, $9.75 a yard (retail $20); or silk voile, $7.75 a yard (retail $13). Save up to 50% on 44-inch widths; with larger orders, save even more. Wools, linens, and poly/cottons available also. All fabric is in its natural state (not printed or dyed) making it a desirable source for those allergic to fabric dyes. The samples we ordered were not only lower in price but higher in quality than full retail yardage. This 40-year-old company requires a $25 minimum order, accepts exchanges or refunds with verbal discussion, and has a 15% restocking charge if not their fault. For $8, you'll receive a swatch booklet ($6.50 with an order). Occasionally, they will have seconds on cottons available at your risk. They cut it, you've bought it. **C $8 ($6.50 with order), B, PQ (SASE)**

THAI SILKS
252 State St.
Los Altos, CA 94022
(415) 948-8611

Marco didn't trek to the Far East looking for Polo shirts—he wanted silk. Likewise, we were lured westward by *Vogue Patterns'* ads for 40 kinds of silks. These "'pillars" of the community "catered" to our expedition, and wormed their way into our hearts with shantung silk in 10 colors, $9.80 a yard. Natural and bleached raw silk priced from $4 to $13 a yard. Scarves for $4. Send $2.80 for a sample packet of closeout silks. Savings average 40% off. They also sold cotton poplin ($2.20) and batik ($6.20). See what they've been "cocoon" up for you. There's a money-back guarantee if you aren't satisfied with the worm work. **B**

TRIBLEND MILLS
4004 Anaconda Road
Tarboro, NC 27886
(800) 334-5620
(919) 823-1355: NC residents

Try buying direct from the mill at Triblend for a satisfying blend of price, service, and quality. Millie Grackin and her staff are helpful in sending samples, telling you what's on special, and giving advice to do-it-yourselfers. Prices average at least 50% lower than retail. Sample swatches and a variety of materials will come to you free. Try new insulating fabrics, decorator sheers, or fabrics to drape your windows and get the free booklet "How to Sew Draperies" with your order. You've got 10 days to return for a refund or replacement if not satisfied, and there's no restocking charge. There's also an outlet store in Rocky Mountain, North Carolina. Triblend is tried and tru-ly tremendous. **B, PQ**

UTEX TRADING CO.
710 Ninth St., Suite 5
Niagara Falls, NY 14301
(416) 596-7565

Utex-ans can cow-nt on big discounts from this Trading Company. We found a wide variety of 100% pure Chinese silks, including crepe de chine, Fuji silk, dupionni (called Italian linen for its texture), and more at savings of 30% to 40%. There's a $20 minimum order with no exchanges or refunds unless merchandise is defective. **C**

WOOLRICH OUTLET STORE
Woolrich, PA 17779
(717) 769-7009

From "the outdoor store for outdoor people" come the richest wools perfect for mountain life. Do what you wool—purists know to go for the golden fleece in outdoor clothing. The fabric of Woolrich's life is over 150 years old. Their woolens are sold at mill prices and remnants are sold by the pound. Wool less than 1 yard is $1.50 per pound, more than 1 yard is $2.50 per pound. Gain a pound of tartan or plaid or solid wool by sending an SASE for samples and information. And if you're in the neighborhood (three miles off Route 220 between Lock Haven and Williamsport), you're invited for a nickel cup of coffee, a walk in the park, and a tour of their outdoor hall of fame. **B**

Food

Who says there's no such thing as a free lunch? Happy hours at local bars feature tacos, cheeses, chicken wings, maybe even shrimp or oysters for the patrons. (Who's going to notice a few missing eggrolls?) Gallery and store openings are a dandy way to fill up on pâté, salmon, and imported cheeses washed down with a glass of wine. Show up for any demonstration of food processors, blenders, etc. (Always something cooking here.) Watch for those nice ladies giving out samples of the latest pizza flavors in the supermarket. (Get extras—for mother.) There's a bowl of caviar dip over in the deli. Go for it. Finally, if you're a schoolteacher, confiscate all the gum and candy before class. (Ummmm, a Cadbury bar!) If you must pay for your food, check the following pages for some fantastic deals.

ACE PECAN CO.
Ninth & Harris Streets
P.O. Box 65
Cordele, GA 31015
(800) 323-0593
(800) 323-9754: IL residents

Get more than you ca-shew, and soon you will be singing, "Almond the money." Introduce your friends to the niceties of nuts so that they may walk the hallowed halls of macadamia. Selling direct and packing in bulk cuts the costs of these tasty pecans. Restocking charge is 10%. Add a $1.95 shipping fee; $8 to Alaska, Hawaii, or Canada. **B**

CACHE VALLEY DAIRY ASSOCIATION
Smithfield, UT 84335
(801) 563-6262

No cheesey trap here, cheese lovers. They've nibbled away the ratty retail to sell at factory direct prices. Save at least 10% on bulk and gift boxes with Utah bee clover honey, summer sausage, smoked oysters. Cheese flavors include common Swiss, cheddar, Monterey Jack, and mozzarella, as well as taco, green onion, smoki, Swiss 'n salami, hot pepper, kuminost. Taste tours through the cheese factory, Swiss chalet, and country store are offered free. Comparing their bulk sales with Hickory Farms of Ohio: sharp and medium cheddar sliced off at $13.75 for 5 pounds here ($29.95 at HF); Swiss at $11.45 for 4 pounds (HF $14.76); Monterey Jack $12.20 for 5 pounds (HF $18.45). Any way you slice it, Cache is where your cash will spread farther. All packages postpaid anywhere in the continental U.S. **B, PQ**

CHARLES LOEB
615 Palmer Road
Yonkers, NY 10701
(914) 961-7776

Charles Loeb might define the changing of the seasons as spices that get stale and rancid as thyme goes by. Mr. Spiceman, as he's called, offers 131 spices and seasonings to specialty stores, ethnic restaurants, and *now* to the public at wholesale prices. Everything is carefully sealed in air-tight pouches to insure freshness. Says who? Sesame. He's also got saffron, charcoal salt, cinnamon, juniper berries, star anise, pignolia nuts, crab boil, kelp, shallots, instant herbal flash tea—at up to 90% below supermarket prices. Minimum order is $10. No shipping charges on orders over 75 pounds. Do yourself a flavor, seasoned shoppers, curry up—order a catalog now. **C**

CHEESELOVERS INTERNATIONAL
P.O. Box 1200
Westbury, NY 11590
(800) 645-3197: credit card orders only
(516) 997-7045: NY residents

To brie or not to brie? Pay a $6 membership fee to receive a monthly color newsletter that features domestic and imported cheeses and $6 worth of gift certificates toward your first purchase. Tasting authentic, nonmechanically-aged cheddars, havarti, port salut, the scarce cheshire cheese, and new twists such as fromaggio d'amaretto makes us smile and say cheese. Monthly sales enable cheese gourmets to sample at lower prices (usually about 10 cents a pound above wholesale). Never an obligation to purchase anything. **C**

CHEESES OF ALL NATIONS
153 Chambers St.
New York, NY 10007
(212) 732-0752

What a friend we have in cheeses! Since the summer of '42, this nationally acclaimed wholesale cheese source has been supplying New York restaurants with some of the finest deals in wheels. Now shoppers can take the bite out of both the Big Apple and some cheeses. Wisconsin sharp, $2.49 a pound; French imported Swiss, $2.69 a pound; French brie, $2 a pound; Danish Fontina, $2.98 a pound; and French goat cheese, $3.98 a pound. Minimum order, 1 pound. They guarantee products to arrive in gouda condition. Muenster up a dollar for their catalog. **C $1**

CONCEPTS IN CANDY
7823 Pencross St.
Dallas, TX 75248
(214) 233-4023

Who can take a rainbow, sprinkle it with delicious chocolates, wrap it up in fancy paper (at no extra charge), add a silk ribbon or two? The candy lady can. She sells gourmet candies like Dutch mints, mocha beans, strawberries-and-cream candies, amaretto cordials, pineapple and raspberry hard candy, and snow almonds packaged in unusual, reusable containers at low prices. Children's candy machines (including candy) are $6.50; half-litre wine carafe filled with pastel mints, $5.50. Other containers available include Lucite jars; a Texas boot; one-half-, three-quarter-, and one-litre Mason jars; and tins from England. There's a 10% discount given on all orders. No minimum order. The delivery charge is a minimum of $3.50, but don't expect bonbons in the middle of July. **B, PQ**

GOURMÉ NUTS
P.O. Box 795501
Dallas, TX 75379
(214) 733-1422

Who says bargains don't grow on trees? Say "nuts" to high prices, and get cracking without shelling out a lot of cash. This company offers delicious natural, dry-roasted California pistachio nuts with no preservatives, artificial flavoring or coloring (hence all nuts are natural white in coloration). A 5-pound bag of pistachios costs $29.90 (postage paid) and a 2½-pound bag packaged in a decorative can (a perfect gift) is $18.10 (postage paid). Sold at a small percent over cost, these nuts are cheaper than other pistachios-by-mail we checked. Nuts are shipped direct from California (truly, the Land of Nuts!) so with a check or money order, you should be happily munching on your purchase in two weeks. **PQ**

GOURMET FRANCE
10754 Stemmons Freeway
Dallas, TX 75220
(214) 350-7737

Roe, roe, roe yourself gently down this price list. Merrily, this company supplies all the fine restaurants in Dallas with their caviar and now offers the same elitist eggs under a different label to the public at wholesale prices. Beluga, which comes from Russia, sells for $17.50 an ounce, 3½ ounces for $61, 7 ounces for $119, 14 ounces for $232, and 4 pounds (have a roe-man orgy) for $1,000. Free delivery anywhere in Dallas for orders over $100. Also sells golden and black American caviar. Black: 7 ounces for $32.50, 2½ ounces for $13.25, 1 ounce for $7. Golden: 2½ pounds for $55.82, 14 ounces for $23, 7 ounces for $12.25, 3½ ounces for $6.50. Shipped frozen within 24 hours anywhere in the continental U.S. Contact them directly for accurate and up-to-the-minute prices and freight conditions since they fluctuate. **PQ**

JAFFE BROS.
P.O. Box 636
Valley Center, CA 92082-0636
(714) 749-1133

Jaffe's ranch puts a healthy squeeze on high-priced organic dried fruits, nuts, grains, and vegetarian food supplements. Picky people will go nuts over their organic unsalted peanut butter at $3.95 per quart. Unrefined olive oil made us Pop-eyes at $15.25 a gallon and nuts in the whole shell cracked up to $5.25 for 5 pounds of raw unbleached walnuts. A-loe prices on bee pollen, honey, brown rice, rolled oats, soy and mung beans. Down-to-earth prices would make Holden Caulfield a real "Catcher in the Organic Rye." Save up to 50%. Write before returning merchandise. **B**

MEXICAN CHILE SUPPLY
304 E. Belknap
Fort Worth, TX 76102
(817) 332-3871

There'll be a hot time in the Cowtown, tonight. Bag your pod-don, chiliheads know where to go for their supplies. This 92-year-old business vends a wide variety of seasonings and spices. Their custom-blended chile powder will bring tears of joy to your eyes and leave you crying for more. They save you 50% to 75% or more off the price of those little cans and bottles of spices (from allspice to pepper corns) in the stores by sending loose bulk packages under their own label, Penderley's. No returns on food products but they will refund if your request is reasonable. No matter if it's chile today or hot tamale, you'll get a taste for the flavor of the Southwest. **B, PQ**

S.A.V.E.
65 E. South Water St.
Chicago, IL 60601
(312) 977-3700

S.A.V.E. is the N.A.M.E. of the G.A.M.E. Join the Shopper's Association for Value and Economy and save on family household products. Begin with $30 worth of goodies for only $1, plus a free $20 gift. Approximately every four to six weeks, you will pay

$7.98 plus shipping for subsequent packages. Also receive a buying guide and cents-off coupons. In the box of bargains, we got Band-aids, Dixie cups, Nyquil, a toothbrush, deodorant, Murine, a razor, and Diet Dr Pepper. No losers in this game. **PQ**

WILBUR CHOCOLATE CANDY OUTLET
48 N. Broad St.
Lititz, PA 17543
(717) 626-1131

While my conscience, and Richard Simmons, and Jackie Sorenson "talk a lot," I find I am swayed by a small piece of "chocolate." This company can save "consumers" 20% on their own brand (and many other national brands) of chocolate and confectionary items. As any dedicated addict immediately will realize, this doesn't mean you save 20% of your money—it means you can get 20% more chocolate to binge on for the same price. (Like any addict, existence is hand-to-mouth.) Wilbur also has dietetic candies and a selection of chocolate and confectioner's coatings in white, pink, green, yellow, and orange sunlight. Beware of summer shipping, and chocolate that "melts in the mail, and not in your hand." **PQ**

ZABAR'S
2245 Broadway
New York, NY 10024
(800) 221-3347
(212) 787-2000: NY residents

Concerning Zabar's, the famous New York gourmet food store, there is good news and bad news. First, the good news—they have a fascinating little catalog that's crammed with gourmet goodies such as Russian coffee cake, milk-fed white veal, and more. Just reading the names of the foods is enough to make your mouth water. Now the bad news—we can't list all the discounted housewares because, as the company's spokesman said, "It'll take all year!" Glamorize your kitchen with names like Osterizer, Waring, GE, Sunbeam, Kitchen-Aid, Hamilton Beach, Krups, and Sanyo at savings of 20% to 40%. Choose from a large inventory of French copperware. You'll save a buck or two on gourmet and hard-to-find coffees such as Jamaican Blue Mountain Style, Kenya, Hawaiian Kona, Mocha Style, Costa Rican, and Columbian. Brew, too, through their selection of decaffeinated blends including expresso and water-processed. All coffees are roasted on Zabar's premises twice a week. If your palate exceeds your pocketbook, call for this catalog immediately. **C, PQ**

Gardens

Grow your own fruits and vegetables, raise chickens, repair your tractor, landscape your yard, and reap the benefits of a healthier lifestyle and a heartier bank account. Start with high-quality seeds, add good soil and weather, fertilize with tender loving care, and you'll have everything from apples to zucchini all during the growing season. When ordering live plants or seeds, be sure to consider your native soil conditions and local weather. If you're not sure a white flowering dogwood will make it through your winter, consult a local nursery or the mail-order supplier before you order. Happy growing!

BIO-CONTROL
13451 Highway 174
P.O. Box 247
Cedar Ridge, CA 95924
(916) 272-1997

Question: What winged wonder fearlessly fights for your garden's glory, risking life and limb in a never-ending struggle against those horticultural hell-raisers, insects that feast on your foliage? It's Ladybug! (No, this is not some flipped-out refugee from a religious cult, or a six-legged feminist cartoon crusader of the insect world—the Green Hornet doesn't have a wife.) Ladybugs are insects that brunch on the bugs that munch on your flowers, shrubs, and trees. They make gourmet meals of mealy bugs (mealy bugs Bourguignonne), leafhoppers (hoppers au gratin, with bay leaf), and aphids (aphids a la mode). If beetles in your beans, and crawlies in your clover are driving you buggy, write Bio-Control for a price listing of their beneficial bugs. Approximately 18,000 ladybugs per quart, $12. Biological warfare can be cheaper and safer than insecticides, and all these antennaed mercenaries ask for is a free lunch. C

CAPRILANDS HERB FARM
Silver Street
Coventry, CT 06238
(203) 742-7244

Travelers will be glad to know owner Adelma Simmons conducts tours through the farm from April 1 to October 31 for a small fee. But the next best thing is a copy of their very concise brochure including a healthy selection of medicinal and decorative herbs ranging from rosebuds and lavender to musk, clove, and orange blossoms. Books, postcards, incense, potpourri, coat hangers, notepaper, necklaces, spinning wheels are also available. Many herbal wreaths are too fragile to ship. B

CENTRAL MICHIGAN TRACTOR AND PARTS
2713 North U.S. 2
St. Johns, MI 48879
(800) 248-9263
(800) 292-9233: MI residents
(517) 224-6802

Till we meet again, here's a source for 50% savings on "good used tractor and combine parts" for the farm. When they answer the phone, expect them to identify themselves as Tractor Salvage. Parts for all makes and models, rebuilt starters, reground crankshafts, reconditioned cylinder heads, plus cylinder blocks. Thirty-day guarantee on all parts. Also discount diesel and gas engines for tractors and combines. **PQ**

COUNTRYSIDE HERB FARM
Conneautville, PA 16406
(814) 587-2736

Countryside is the largest herb farm in the northeastern part of the country supplying all of the retail herb industry. They grow 125 varieties of herbs for craft use and sell ready-made potpourris with fragrant names such as Holiday Spice and Summer Garden. Also ready-made wreaths in combinations such as strawflower, gray artemisia, and thyme are only $20 each. Compare that with the artificial plastic cheapies in stores that get tossed after Christmas. Substantial importer of spices, too. **B 50 cents**

DAIRY ASSOCIATION COMPANY, INC.
Lyndonville, VT 05851
(802) 626-3610

Hay, a horse is a horse, of course of course, and it behooves him to have, what else, soft hooves. After all, no hoof, no horse! Along with the Green Mountain Hoof Softener, get a supply of Bag Balm dilators to keep your Elsie from uddering sounds of distress during milking. Kow Kare and Tackmaster products are also available at considerable savings. Credit issued on receipt of returned merchandise, which they accept on a prepaid postage basis upon their authorization. **C, B, PQ**

DUTCH GARDENS
P.O. Box 400
Montvale, NJ 07645
(201) 391-4366

Go Dutch. This company deals exclusively in narcissus, iris, tulip bulbs, and more from Holland at 30% below retail (though some prices were comparable to retail). An exceptionally attractive catalog and each flower is pictured in full bloom with growing time, bloom size, and other pertinent information sprouting alongside. They will replace bulbs that do not grow the first year planted. Free delivery offered if order totals $40 or more; additional cash discounts offered if order totals $70 or more and though they appreciate payment with orders, they will extend credit 30 days after receipt of bulbs. Credit card purchases, $20 minimum. **C**

FLICKINGER'S NURSERY
Sagamore, PA 16250
(412) 783-6528

Is the little woman pining for some firs? You don't have to think mink to spruce up your love life! For 36 years Flickinger's has been needling their customers, and providing a hedge against inflation. Selling small trees primarily, prices are generally 50% to 75% lower than available in a nursery. We saw seedlings and transplants of Bristlecone pine, Colorado blue spruce, Douglas fir, Canadian hemlock, European white birch, and white flowering dogwood. There's a $30 minimum order, so you'll likely need to branch out and divide your order with friends. How does 100 Japanese black pine seedlings 5 inches to 9 inches tall sound? Stumped? Don't beat around the bush (or go barking up the wrong tree) —write for a free catalog. **C**

FRANS ROOZEN
214 BB
Vogelenzang, Holland

For over 50 years, this family has been tiptoeing through the tulips and singing a song of savings on over a thousand different varieties of bulbs. Prices are comparable to other discount bulb importers from Holland with savings planted in the 10% range. Minimum order $20 with a money-back guarantee if your complaint is reasonable. **C**

GREENLAND FLOWER SHOP
R.D. 1 Box 52
Port Matilda, PA 16870
(814) 692-8308

This business has been barking up the family tree since 1969. They offer perennial discounts (50% to 75%) on their flowers and plants according to the amount of purchase. Blooming in the background were dog tail cacti for $1; dwarf purple kalanchoes, 50 cents; shrimp plants, $1; green wandering Jew, 50 cents; and plants with exotic names such as Oakleaf Velvet, Mexican Stone Crop, Black Magic, Cub's Paw, Devil's Backbone. Their catalog offers photographs of small growths. Orders placed in January for spring planting receive an additional 10% off. Rooted in the village of Stormstown in Half-Moon Valley, visitors are welcome. Live delivery guaranteed, be-leaf it or not. **C 50 cents** (refundable)

GURNEY'S SEED AND NURSERY CO.
Yankton, SD 57079
(605) 665-1671

If the grass is literally always greener on your neighbor's side of the fence, try Gurney's. You've never seen so many hybrid plants, bulbs, trees, seeds, and gardening supplies. Over 4,000 items from African violets to zucchini are bursting out all over their colorful catalog. We've grown fond of their 1-cent sale, too. Plus their crop of novelty items: grow-your-own bird seed, yard-long cucumbers, loofah sponges, tobacco, horseradish, even praying mantises. Gurney's "Complete Growing Guide" sent with all orders. **C**

HICKORY HILL NURSERY
Route 1, Box 390A
Fisherville, VA 22939
(703) 942-3871

These Hickory Hillbillies aren't afraid to turn over a new leaf, or an entire layer of topsoil, with their Troy-Bilt Rototiller Power Composters manufactured by the Garden Way Manufacturing Company. Their price list showed 10 models of rototillers ranging in price from $535 to $1,231, with most discounted 10% to 20%. Prices on various attachments are also discounted. (Discounts vary with the season.) Our experience with rototillers has been akin to plowing behind a bucking Brahma bull while gripping a jackhammer, but at least here the prices won't shake you up. **PQ**

J.E. MILLER NURSERIES, INC.
5060 W. Lake Road
Canandaigua, NY 14424
(800) 828-9630
(800) 462-9601: NY residents
(716) 396-2647

No need to be a John E. Appleseed with John E. Miller's catalog including 11 pages of apple strains such as the "old-fashioned" favorites along with many other quality fruit trees. Request special catalog for Miller Nurseries' annual one-half off sale in late fall. First-class merchandise and one-year guarantees against failure. Replacements offered at no charge ($1 handling fee only) until August 1 on items ordered from their spring catalog; after that, they will replace at one-half the purchase price. Minimum charge-card orders of $10; catalog packed with facts and tips on all aspects of growing. **C**

NOWETA GARDENS
900 Whitewater Ave.
St. Charles, MN 55972
(507) 932-4859 or 932-3210

We were feelin' glad all over with all the varieties of gladiola bulbs pictured throughout this beautiful color catalog. Names like Lime Fizz, Peppermint Cane, Plum Tart, Chocolate Ripple, Sugar Maple, and Seventh Heaven sounded more like flavors of ice cream. Owner Carl Fischer's been growing 'em for 53 years. Minimum bulb order is $15 but you only receive a 20% discount with large orders of $250 or more. Usual shipping season runs from March to June 1. **C**

PINETREE SEED CO.
P.O. Box 1399
Portland, ME 04104
(207) 772-7403

Want to squash those produce prices? Grow your own, pumpkin! (This leek is bigger than Watergate.) And look at that film critic-turned-gardener, Pauline Kale. You don't have to work like a dog to grow collie-flower. You can still beet inflation. Why move to Oklahoma when you can garden on the windowsill in New York. This catalog offers small packages of vegetable, flower, herb, and house-plant seeds at greatly reduced prices. Receive a 10% discount for orders placed during the "slow season" —between May 1 and October 31. **C**

PONY CREEK NURSERY
Tilleda, WI 54978
(715) 787-3889

Visions of sugarplums and cherries? Aiming for an organic diet? Or, maybe you're just a flower-fancier. Fill your greenhouse for a year with seeds, fertilizers, insect repellents, and more. Learn gardening tips to get your little project off the ground. We priced sugar snap peas and other hybrids at 65 cents (65 cents to $1.05 at retail stores); Hummingbird Starter packs, $3.95; Plant-Rite Row Seeder, $11.95; Mugho pines, 5 inches to 8 inches, $2.98 each; a full assortment of Ortho garden products, plus tree seedlings of all varieties. Get on your way to healthier eating, beautiful landscaping, and saving $500 to $600 a year for your efforts. Become food self-sufficient with their canning, drying, and freezing supplies. They will replace *once* any shrub, tree, and evergreen that dies in the first growing season and is returned with the guarantee slip by November 1 of the year it was purchased. **C**

REICH POULTRY FARMS, INC.
R.F.D. 1
Marietta, PA 17547
(717) 426-3411

If you've been down on your cluck lately and your poultry's looking paltry, you've come to the Reich place. Lay in a fresh supply of straight run (100 unsexed baby chicks) for $31.95 compared to a competitor's price of $46.95 or all-breed pullets for $55.95 compared to $69.95. These prices are F.O.B. so you must add postage, too. Mr. Reich's been in the poultry biz for 38 years and ships baby chicks from February through October to any part of the country through the postal system. Add 4 cents per chick when ordering for debeaking. Also carries poultry equipment and health products. Savings come with volume. If you buy only 15 or so chickens, we found the price better in a local feed store. Hens-forth, we'll order in large quantities to get the better price. Minimum order: eight baby turkeys, 15 baby chicks, or 10 baby ducks. **B**

Get It Free!

Did you know you could learn the strategies of winning at chess for free? Or send an anniversary card to your grandparents from the president, cook from old New England recipes, or give a braille cookbook to a blind friend—all for free? Here are a few tips on how to ask for these "freebies." Ask for only one. Put in writing what you enclose in your request, i.e., "I have enclosed a stamped self-addressed envelope." SASE means a 9½-inch long, stamped business envelope addressed to yourself. If you need to send coins, mail as few as possible and tape them inside. Write your name, address, and zip code on both your letter and the envelope. Expect to wait a month or two before your request is answered.

AMERICAN BABY MAGAZINE
American Baby, Inc.
575 Lexington Ave.
New York, NY 10022
(212) 752-0775

Who says babies are no bargains? Get an issue free of the *American Baby Magazine* for expectant new parents. What can you expect to be delivered in your free issue? Ours contained features such as "Dear Doctor" (answered by Ralph Gause, M.D.), a parent's personal story, "Medical Update," nutrition advice, job sharing information, and a photo essay of a baby's birth. Yearly subscription is $9.87 with the first six months free.

AMERICAN FOUNDATION FOR THE BLIND
15 W. 16th St.
New York, NY 10011
(212) 620-2000

This helpful packet will increase understanding of students and friends who are visually impaired. Included is a card with raised braille alphabet and numerals, the life story of Louis Braille, and suggestions for teachers when dealing with visually handicapped children in the classroom. Publications, aids, and appliances for the visually impaired are their specialty, and their catalog of publications dealing with the blind could be very useful. **C**

AMERICAN PAINT HORSE ASSN.
General Store
P.O. Box 18519
Fort Worth, TX 76118
(817) 439-3400

This is the mane source for information on the American Paint Horse. Free information includes two color pictures, six brochures on the history and anatomy of the breed, horse shows, etc. This comes from a city "where the West begins" and there's a high interest in horses. (Did you know a Paint is not the same as a Pinto, even though the colors may be the same?) **B**

AMERICAN PHYSICAL THERAPY ASSN.
1156 15th St. N.W., Suite 500
Washington, DC 20005

Free folder prepared by physical therapists is titled "How to Prevent Jogging Injury, Backache, and Stiffness of Arthritis." Clear illustrations on stretching exercises, the right way to lift and carry, and exercises to stay flexible as the birthdays tempt inactivity. You'll learn such useful tips as "tail tucking" to prevent lower-back pain.

THE CAR BOOK
Consumer Information Center
Pueblo, CO 81009
(800) 424-9393: Auto Safety Hotline
(303) 948-3334

Call the Auto Safety Hotline Monday through Friday, 8 a.m. to 4 p.m. EST and order *The Car Book*. The Consumer Information Center (see write-up below) will then send you this beautifully prepared booklet explaining car purchasing (with comparison ratings on safety, fuel economy, maintenance, and insurance costs) including a closing chapter on buying a used car. Buyer's checklist and further reading section in back.

CONSUMER INFORMATION CATALOG
Consumer Information Center
Dept. DD
Pueblo, CO 81009
(303) 948-3334

What's on your mind lately? Savings, suntans, sensible child raising? Request free information booklets from about 30 federal agencies. We saw such best-selling titles as: "The Confusing World of Health Foods"; "Roughage"; "Storing Vegetables and Fruits"; "Baldness Treatments"; "Cockroaches"; "How Not to Get Conned"; "How to Adopt a Wild Horse or Burro"; and "Cholesterol, Fat, and Your Health." Booklet junkies in this office have also ordered: "Job Openings," "Plain Talk about Raising Children," and "Know Your Pension Plan." This catalog's like your very own mail-order bookstore. **C**

DEAK-PERERA
29 Broadway
New York, NY 10006

The firm that brings you commission-free foreign and U.S. traveler's checks will also send you a free packet including helpful booklets and folders, a foreign money converter, and a guide to their international currency and precious metals investment services. They deal in currencies from over 120 countries, keep constant watch on the markets, and claim they charge less than banks for collections and payments.

DOVER PUBLICATIONS, INC.
Free Chess Booklet Offer
180 Varick St.
New York, NY 10014
(212) 255-3755

This free booklet, "How Do You Play Chess?" guides players through the fundamentals. Dover also carries a free catalog of inexpensive chess paperbacks (over 100) to advance a player. Prices start at $1.50 (formerly priced at $8 in hardback). They'll take a check, mate. **C**

FOREST SERVICE USDA
Woodsy Owl Package
12th and Independence, S.W.
P.O. Box 2417
Washington, DC 20013

Whoooooooo . . . are you to question Woodsy Owl when he says, "Give a hoot! Don't pollute." Listen, this owl is no birdbrain: Woodsy's no fooooool. When was the last time you saw an owl hopping around on the ground at the crack of dawn looking for worms? You're darn right! Owls sleep in, and leave the worms to the early birds—they're not stupid. When we wrote to these people, we received a colorful packet including a color pin-up poster of Woodsy Owl (no, he was not wearing a feather boa, wise guy), a coloring page, a bookmark, sticker, and the music and words to "The Ballad of Woodsy Owl." The minimum orders tend to be reasonable in price but high-flying in quantity, so if you want patches, posters, pencils, or balloons you may need a class of kids, too.

HOLLYWOOD BREAD BLDG.
P.O. Box H
Hollywood, FL 33022
(305) 920-7666

Get a handy purse-size calorie and carbohydrate guide to take along to cafes and restaurants (it will even slide into wallets). Good advice is given in the introductory pages: "Forget the fad diets, keep this book handy and get to know the foods you eat." About 630 foods are listed and the guide won't cost you any dough at all.

JOHNSON & JOHNSON
O.B. Purse Pack Request
Fulfillment Center
P.O. Box 76P
Baltimore, MD 21230
(800) 631-5294
(800) 352-4719: MD residents

You will be sent a purse-size plastic box about 2 inches square. It is slightly textured outside with no lettering. Inside is stamped the O.B. trademark, but not too ob-viously.

L'OREAL GUIDELINE
(800) 631-7358
(201) 499-2954: NJ residents call collect

Why be hair-ried by the hassles of a permanently depressing perm? If you're frazzled by the frizzies or tainted by the tone of your tints, call the experts for free advice weekdays from 9 a.m. to 5 p.m. Eastern time.

MARCH OF DIMES BIRTH DEFECTS FOUNDATION
1275 Mamaroneck Ave.
White Plains, NY 10605

For a real tree-t, request a copy of "The March of Dimes Family Health Tree." You'll receive a colorful fold-out with maternal and paternal branches (mom and pop always were ab-stem-ious), flowers, and fruits (Fruits! . . . On my family tree?) on a tree large enough to record quite a bit of health history in your family. Instructions on how to fill it out or identify genetic disorders are given. Plus, there's a helpful list of sources for genealogical research on the back cover. Order your family tree today. P.S.—they don't list saps.

MODERN PRODUCTS INC.
Gayelord Hauser Offer
P.O. Box 09398
Milwaukee, WI 53209
(414) 352-3333

Enclose an SASE and receive one sample each of Spike, Vege-Sal, and low-salt Vegit seasonings. Enough comes in each packet to flavor several soup pots. Ingredients are natural salt-of-the-earth seasonings.

MORTON SALT CO.
Salt Dough Brochure
Department of Consumer Affairs
110 N. Wacker Drive
Chicago, IL 60606

"Dough-It-Yourself Christmas Decorations" is a small foldout of directions for salt sculptures. Everything you knead to know to sculpt with dough: basic recipe, tool selection, hardening methods, finishing, and ideas for Christmas ornaments.

NEW BEDFORD SEAFOOD COUNCIL
Promotion Department CDAU
P.O. Box 307
Fairhaven, MA 02719

Sea the items they offer free, graphically illustrated with the company's nautical logo. Includes iron-on transfer for T-shirts, 4-inch blue and gold round sticker, plastic litterbag, blue and gold bumper sticker, recipe folder of seafood dishes, brochure about New Bedford and the fishing fleets. Limit your requests to three items. The logo's a young man with nautical rope and nets about him. Makes you consider seafood for your next meal.

OFFICE OF METRIC PROGRAMS
U.S. Department of Commerce
Washington, DC 20230
(202) 377-0944

Give us an inch and we'll take a kilometer. Like it or not, it's coming: the metric system. The OMP helps those of us who long ago worked with inches, pounds, and gallons exclusively. Your request is answered with an information sheet and conversion cards. While we could probably cope with the change, imagine the turmoil faced by the lowly inchworm. Talk about an identity crisis!

PENNZOIL COMPANY
Gumout Division, Dept. L
4 Gateway Center, Suite 410
Pittsburgh, PA 15222

"How to Keep Your Choke Working Automatically" was the title of the small booklet we received, a reprint from *Popular Mechanics* magazine. Illustrations showed types of automatic chokes and how to test and adjust vacuum units. The other service bulletins available are "Rough Idling" and "How to Clean Your PCV Valve."

PRESIDENTIAL GREETINGS OFFICE
The White House
Washington, DC 20500

Want to give someone a really impressive Prez-ent? A note of congratulations will arrive from the president of the United States for couples celebrating their golden anniversary (or beyond) and those whose birthdays number 80 or more years. You need to write six weeks in advance, giving the occasion, the name(s), and address for the greeting to be sent.

RADIO SHACK (any retail store)
Battery-A-Month Card
Your Town, USA
Your Telephone Directory

Is this what is meant by a charge card? Once a month, you can get one free battery of your choice from Radio Shack brand bins: AA, C, D, or 9-volt. No purchase required for card. Bring it in person anytime during the month to pick out your battery and present your card for validation.

RICE COUNCIL OF AMERICA
P.O. Box 740121
Houston, TX 77274

Rice-cipes and pamphlets about menu planning and basic cooking methods using rice. "International Favorites," a color recipe booklet on everything from chicken and peas pilaf to chicken Cantonese, won't go against the grain. Recipes for the blind or visually impaired make excellent gifts. A new offering in their brochure was a pamphlet entitled, "Frugal Feasts," telling how to stretch menus with rice. **B**

ROMAN MEAL COMPANY
Dept. U
2101 S. Tacoma Way
Tacoma, WA 98409
(206) 475-0964

Receive any combination or all three of these publications: "Diet and Nutrition Plan," "Hamburger Extender Recipes," and "Roman Meal Cereal Recipes." The diet folders give menus and calorie counts for a 1,200 calorie low-fat plan. Did you know hamburger can be helped at least seven ways? An SASE is required.

SCOTT LAWN PRODUCTS
Marysville, OH 43040
(800) 543-8873
(800) 762-4010: OH residents

Call 543-TURF and receive two years of quarterly mailings of "Lawn Care" literature on taking care of landscapes and gardens and coupons good on all their products. Publications consider regional differences such as rainfall, soil types, and temperatures and tailor them to your area. Great Scott, you can also put your tu-lips together and ask for free horticultural advice on their toll-free line.

U.S. DEPARTMENT OF EDUCATION
Bureau of Financial Assistance
P.O. Box 84
Washington, DC 20044
(800) 638-6700

To receive a free copy of "Five Federal Financial Aid Programs, A Student's Consumer Guide," you may call toll-free from 9 a.m. to 5:30 p.m. EST. Our copy arrived with an addendum page of changes in the Guaranteed Student Loan (GSL) program. Other programs described were National Direct Student Loans, College Work-Study, Supplemental Educational Opportunity Grants, and Basic Educational Opportunity Grants. Restrictions are tightening and you can't take financial assistance for grant-ed anymore. It pays to keep current.

WALLCOVERING INFORMATION BUREAU INC.
66 Morris Ave.
Springfield, NJ 07081
(201) 379-1100

Are you climbing the walls? When your walls are singing the glues, hang it up and write for a free information booklet, "Wallcoverings How-To Handbook," put out by this nonprofit organization providing educational materials for consumers. Illustrations are large and help you understand the basics such as measuring, tools needed, cutting, hanging, rolling, and working around tricky places like windows, switchplates, and ceilings. With this booklet, you may get a new wrinkle on wallpaper (and avoid the same).

W.J. HAGGERTY & SONS
P.O. Box 1496
South Bend, IN 46624
(800) 348-5162
(219) 288-4991: IN residents

We took a shine to their 5-gram sample of Haggerty silversmiths' polish (European formula with tarnish preventative). Included was a color brochure of their products to care for metals, pearls, and wood finishes.

WOMEN'S SPORTS FOUNDATION
195 Moulton St.
San Francisco, CA 94123
(800) 227-3988
(415) 563-6266: CA residents

This nonprofit organization encourages women to be involved in sports. They publish guides, posters, and pamphlets. Their Women in Sports films list is available to schools and community groups and the foundation publishes a guide listing scholarships to American colleges and universities. Scholarships ranged from under $100 to "full ride."

5.

BUSINESS AND PLEASURE

Art and Collectibles

Are you the type who takes delight in finding truly unusual collectibles that don't cost as much as the Smithsonian Institute itself? Or have you been looking to Degas-rate your posh pad ever since you turned to lofty living? Maybe there's a room in your house that needs a little something to jazz it up—like a hand-loomed rug from Tibet, perhaps? Whether it's a vintage Georgia O'Keeffe poster or a signed silkscreen from a Texas artist, there will be prints among paupers at these low prices, so hang in there.

ANTIQUE IMPORTS UNLIMITED
Dept. US
P.O. Box 2345
Carson City, NV 89701
(702) 882-0520

You can avoid the frantic antics of antique shopping if you let your fingers do the walking through the yellowed pages of old legal documents, maps, prints, and paintings listed in their catalog. This company, formerly Gand Ltd. of England, offers great buys on ancient items from Egypt, Greece, Rome, and Persia, as well as antiques from Ireland and England. They have five catalogs ($1 each) and carry fine lines of antiques, with antique jewelry a specialty. Old news is good news: Timeless collectibles are offered at prices that time has passed by—40% to 80% less than in antique shops. Minimum order, $30. Full refund, less postage and packing charges on all items found unsuitable, if posted for return within 10 days of receipt. **C $1** (also annual subscription rate)

DECOR PRINTS
Box 502
227 Main St.
Noel, MO 64854
(417) 475-6367

Stop waiting for Prints Charming to arrive at your doorstep. Shop without waiting very long for art prints and reproduction antique classics at a savings of 30% or more at Decor. Immediate refund issued if not completely satisfied. Smile with the Mona Lisa, turn green with envy at Blue Boy, or kick up your heels with a Degas for as little as $2. **B**

FRONT ROW PHOTOS
Box 484-U
Nesconset, NY 11767

If you can't get front row seats, get Front Row Photos. David Mortensen and his partner offer a wide variety of rock music acts in their catalog, which comes with two sample snapshots. Hard-core rock fans will scream over thousands of photos of heavy rock and New Wave performers from the past 20 years. Don't say "I can't get no satisfaction" since refunds or exchanges are accepted within 10 days. One dollar restocking charge and a minimum order of $5. **C $2** (includes two samples)

METROPOLITAN GALLERY OF FINE ART
215 Lexington Ave.
New York, NY 10016
(212) 683-0220

Fine prints by artists such as Pierre Bayle, Alexander Calder, and Antonio Rivera. Intent on bringing limited editions into homes everywhere with a no-frills, no-nonsense approach. Framed prints, not reproductions (artists work directly on the plates used for printing) of lithographs, serigraphs, etchings, etc., are priced anywhere from $115 to $2,000 (with an average price of $250). The gallery contracts for entire editions and is a high-volume operator. You may order a print on a trial basis and decide within 30 days. Each print comes with a signed certificate of authenticity for insurance and estate appraisal purposes. **C**

MURRAY'S POTTERY, INC.
802 Kings Highway
Brooklyn, NY 11223
(212) 376-6002

Remember rock promoter, Murray the Clay? Well, this Murray offers a 117-page catalog filled with sculptured replicas of famous as well as contemporary works from ancient Chinese pieces to cowboys and horses at very reasonable prices. In addition to the familiar (Rodin, Michelangelo) he carries many lesser known works by even lesser known artists. Shipping by UPS. **C**

MUSEUM EDITIONS NEW YORK, LTD.
105 Hudson St.
New York, NY 10013
(800) 221-9576
(212) 431-1913: NY residents

One of the best sources we found for fine art posters, this young company recently consolidated their California office and moved to the City. They'll keep you posted (new catalog sheets five or six times a year) with classic posters such as Man Ray's "Peaches" for $30 ($45 elsewhere) and John Wesa's "Orchid" for $25 ($35 elsewhere). Even with a $5 shipping fee for up to 20 posters, the savings is still enough to purchase your very own "Poverty Sucks" poster for $8. Museum Editions supplies posters from the Guggenheim Museum, the New

York Philharmonic, the Phoenix Art Museum, the Corcoran Gallery, the Boston Symphony Orchestra, and independent artists. **C**

NEPAL CRAFT EMPORIUM
G.P.O. Box 1443
Kathmandu, Nepal
Phone: 12500-21220 (dial "01" for operator assistance in making this call)

Nepal Craft Emporium's handsome handicrafts should be featured in "Home Buddha-ful." Thirty Buddha gods and goddesses ranging in price from $2 (for children of a lesser god) to $99 (Oh God) are cast by the ancient "lost wax process" making them a sought-after collector's item. Turquoise-and-coral-studded filigree boxes, birds, animals, and jewelry make unique, inexpensive gifts from $1 to $8. Minimum order, $300 (F.O.B. Kathmandu). **C $3**

RYNO PRYNTS
P.O. Box 4071
Temple, TX 76501
(817) 778-6299

Decorate with art. Original signed serigraph (silk screen print) on 100% cotton paper comes ready to frame. An 8-by-10 print is $40, 11-by-14 is $75, and 20-by-30 is $100. You just send samples of your room colors and they will send you two sample coordinating sketches. Decide which one you'd like, send the appropriate amount of money plus $5 for handling, and you will receive a completed print by return mail. Guaranteed 30-day delivery won't leave you thinking "someday my prints will come." **Samples**

SI DANLIN ORIGINALS
1705 Live Oak
Longview, TX 75601
(214) 758-5188

The quiet serenity of the Far East is here in the far South at the studio/home of Si Danlin. She has mastered the ancient technique of Oriental brush strokes including the difficult lettering and special mounting processes. We particularly liked her calligraphy and paintings on rice paper and silk—art we could afford to splurge on. Custom orders welcomed. **B**

TIBETAN REFUGEE SELF-HELP CENTRE
Havelock Villa 65, Gandhi Road
Darjeeling, West Bengal
India
Phone: 2346-DE: office (dial "01" for operator assistance in making this call)

For $1 you can learn about the "courageous flight of the Tibetan people who were forced out of their homeland by invaders in 1959." The center was created to enable refugees not only to earn a living but also to keep their cultural heritage and craftmanship alive. Using wools and vegetable dyes imported from Nepal, they specialize in making a beautiful assortment of rugs. Complicated designs sell for about $9.70 per square foot and simple designs for about $9 per square foot. Add 10% for carpets larger than 50 square feet and 5% if it is a custom-made carpet. Sweaters, woolen half-boots, Tibetan soldier's hats, greeting cards, and stationery may also be of interest. The black-and-white catalog also mentions making reservations to purchase the rare Tibetan Apso puppy. Either bank transfers to the Grindlays Bank Ltd., Darjeeling, or checks are acceptable payment. C $1

WORKS OF MAX LEVINE
19-18 Saddle River Road
Fair Lawn, NJ 07410
(201) 797-7216

Max Levine's three-dimensional wall sculptures are made from heavy gauge steel finished with patina of gold leaf and solid brass accents. Many of these "limited edition" contemporary works are specially designed to mix with the business or home atmosphere. Prices range from $65 to $325. Since this is the only outlet for his work, it's hard to compare prices. Full refund in 10 days. C

WURTSBORO WHOLESALE ANTIQUES
P.O. Box 386
Wurtsboro, NY 12790
(914) 888-4411

These folks aren't afraid to peddle their wares (accessories and smaller items only) through the mail, Wurts and all. This company sells European primitive antiques 100 years old or older. (American primitive pieces are sold in the store only.) Their hottest selling items are butter churns, $40 to $65, and wooden hay forks (so when it's butter up, you can keep on pitching). Bloomingdale's buys from them for resale but you can buy-pass the middleman, and go directly to Wurtsboro. Shipment by UPS. **C**

Investments

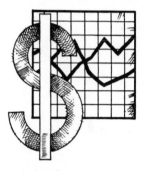

The financial investment market is currently undergoing radical changes. This has opened up many opportunities to the smaller investor for saving money on sales commissions by investing through the mail. People capable of making their own investment decisions can utilize discount brokers for their stock trades or invest in mutual funds with no sales commissions. In this way, they can avoid the commissions paid to the major brokerage houses, which are charged in order to provide investment "advice" to their clients. We have also listed several Swiss banks suitable for smaller investors. They welcome mail accounts and have officers fluent in English.

DISCOUNT BROKERS

Discount brokers do not provide investment advice but they will execute your buy and sell orders at rates significantly below those of "full service" brokerage houses. Among discount brokers, there is a range of transaction costs depending on the manner of payment and extent of services. Most set up credit accounts for their clients and that is reflected in the rates. Check around and find one that offers only what you need for the lowest cost. Discount brokers have become very popular, but remember, their clients must get their own investment information.

BROWN & CO.
7 Water St.
Boston, MA 02109
(800) 225-6707
(617) 392-6077: MA residents

This company charges $25 for the first share traded, and 4 cents to 8 cents for each remaining share. Customers must have a minimum of five years' trading experience. There's a $5,000 minimum order. Margin accounts available.

CHARLES SCHWAB & CO., INC.
1 Second St.
San Francisco, CA 94105
(800) 648-5300
(415) 546-1000: CA residents

Charles Schwab is one of the largest discount brokers with offices around the country. They have added many services like a money market fund for ease of trading, long business hours, cheap term insurance, and 24-hour price quotation. Minimum commission is $18.

OVEST SECURITIES, INC.
76 Beaver St.
New York, NY 10005
(800) 221-5713
(212) 425-3003: NY residents

When it comes to trading stocks, you can "share" the wealth or play your cards close to the Ovest. This discount commission stock brokerage firm charges up to 90% less than other brokerage firms. Active traders can find what are perhaps the lowest commissions in the industry. Under this company's "Premier Status" program, traders can pay an annual fee of $1,000 and trade New York Stock Exchange (NYSE) and American Stock Exchange (ASE) for $25 plus 3 cents or 4 cents per share, per trade. Lower charges are available for over-the-counter (OTC) trades, and margin accounts are welcome. They're members of the NYSE, National Association of Securities Dealers (NASD), and Securities Investors Protection Corporation (SIPC).

ROYAL INVESTORS GROUPS, INC.
120 Wall St.
New York, NY 10005
(800) 221-9900
(212) 635-0880: NY residents

Royal Investors will give free stock reports and a comprehensive 10-year history on earnings, dividends, payout ratio book values, etc., to their clients. Savings can range from 50% to 80% over transactions from regular brokers. Minimum commission per trade, $30. They will trade listed and over-the-counter stocks, put and call options on corporate, government, and municipal bonds. Cash balances of $1,000 or more automatically receive interest. Member NYSE and access to all principal exchanges and OTC markets.

TEXAS SECURITIES
Texas Securities Building
Fort Worth, TX 76102
(800) 433-5658
(800) 772-5974: TX residents

Fort Worth may bill itself as "Cowtown," but you won't find these stockbrokers at the stockyards. This 5-year-old company is Fort Worth's oldest and largest discount brokerage firm, and they've expanded into such new frontiers as Amarillo, El Paso, and Wichita Falls. Commissions average 50% to 80% lower than elsewhere, and there's only a $25 minimum order. They're members of the NASD and SIPC. They'll sell blue chip stocks, but for cow chips, you'll have to find a more "bullish" company.

TRADEX BROKERAGE SERVICE, INC.
82 Beaver St.
New York, NY 10005
(800) 221-7874
(800) 522-3000: NY residents
(212) 425-7800

Margin accounts available. No service fee charged for opening an account and no commission advance required. Members of NASD, SIPC. Minimum trade commission is $25. They also execute stocks, bonds, options, and commodities on all exchanges.

NO-LOAD MUTUAL FUNDS

A mutual fund is an organization through which investors pool their money and have it professionally managed. This can be quite helpful to those who either don't have much money to invest or don't know much about investing. Most mutual funds invest in the stock market, but may pick something like tax exempt bonds, Treasury bills, gold, or new companies. All your deposits and withdrawals are handled through the mail. You need to find a "no-load" mutual fund, meaning that there is no sales commission attached to your transactions. Some no-load funds advertise in the financial sections of major newspapers. You can also get a list of no-load funds by writing to: The No-Load Mutual Fund Association, 475 Park Ave. S., New York, NY 10016. Or, you can call any of the following companies for information on their mutual funds:

Alliance Capital Reserves:
     (800) 221-5672, 8:30 a.m. to 6 p.m. EST
     (212) 902-4126, NY residents call collect
Delaware Cash Reserves:
     (800) 523-1918
     (215) 988-1333, PA residents
Dreyfus Liquid Assets & Dreyfus Group:
     (800) 645-6561, 8 a.m. to 8 p.m. EST
     (212) 223-0743, NY residents
Fidelity Daily Income:
     (800) 225-6190, 8:30 a.m. to 5 p.m. EST
     (617) 523-1919, MA residents
Financial Programs:
     (800) 525-9831, 7 a.m. to 4 p.m. MST
     (303) 779-1233, CO residents

Penn Square:
>(800) 523-8440, 9 a.m. to 5 p.m. EST
>(215) 376-6771, PA residents

Permanent Portfolio:
>(800) 531-5142, 9 a.m. to 5 p.m. CST
>(512) 453-7558, TX residents and outside continental U.S.

Scudder, Stevens & Clark Investment Council:
>(800) 225-2470, 9 a.m. to 5 p.m. EST
>(617) 328-5000, MA residents

T. Rowe Price:
>(800) 638-1527, 8 a.m. to 6 p.m. EST
>(301) 547-2000, MD residents

Vanguard Group:
>(800) 523-7910, 8:30 a.m. to 5:30 p.m. EST
>(215) 648-6000, PA residents

Many investment institutions accept collect calls from shareholders or those requesting information.

TREASURY NOTES, BONDS, AND BILLS

Buying direct from the Federal Reserve Banks' Securities Department can save you the $25 to $40 commission you pay at the bank. You can enter a noncompetitive bid by mail for the next auction, which means you are going to pay the average price of the competitive tenders. Ask for the next mailing and carefully note the deadline. There are Federal Reserve branches in Atlanta, Boston, Chicago, Dallas, Cleveland, Kansas City (Missouri), Minneapolis, New York City, Philadelphia, Richmond, San Franciso, and St. Louis.

SWISS BANK ACCOUNTS

Swiss banks hold a unique position in worldwide banking. The stable economic characteristics of Switzerland combined with their traditions of privacy in banking matters could offer advantages not found in federally regulated American banks. The following list has three such Swiss banks willing to open up mail accounts for smaller American investors. They all have officers fluent in English. Our original source for this information was *Inflation Proofing Your Investments* by Harry Browne and Terry Coxon (New York: William Morrow & Co., 1981).

BANQUE INDIANA (SUISSE) SA
50 Avenue de la Gare
CH-1001 Lausanne, Switzerland
Phone: 20-4741 (dial "01" for operator assistance in making this call)

Minimum to open account is approximately $600. Contact Mrs. Francine Misrahi or William Strub.

FOREIGN COMMERCE BANK
Bellariastrasse 82
CH-8038 Zurich, Schweiz/Switzerland
Phone: 482-66-88 (dial "01" for operator assistance in making this call)

Minimum to open account is $10,000. Contact Bruno Brodbeck, Roger Badet, Andre Rufer, Frank Bachmann, or Jakob Baumgartner.

UEBERSEEBANK AG ZURICH
Limmatquai 2
CH-8024 Zurich, Switzerland
Phone: 252-0304 (dial "01" for operator assistance in making this call)

There is no minimum to open an account. Contact Bruno Mattie, Siegfried Herzog, or Kurt Kamber.

Novelties

"Novelty" means "new thing" and these companies will make a new person (or gorilla or Hawaiian dancing girl) out of you. You can twist balloons into dachshunds, set off some star-spangled noisemakers, give the kid a hand-carved gift with a life-time guarantee, or dig into a tin of delicious fortune cookies—plus hundreds of fun-loving and novel treasures. If you've been feeling that there's nothing new under the sun (or under the water) check here—but watch out for motorized shark fins.

ACE FIREWORKS
P.O. Box 221
Conneaut, OH 44030
(216) 593-4751

These bang robbers steal the show. "Class C common fireworks" including "happy lamps" at $3 each, "baby magic blooms" for $10 a gross, and other noisemakers for celebrating Chinese or American New Year's. Save 10% to 15%, though you must be 18 or over to order. Minimum order, $25. **PQ $1**

BALLOONS OF THE UNIVERSE
24715 Butler Road
Junction City, OR 97448
(503) 998-8233

Buy balloons without paying inflated prices! If people tell you you're full of hot air, you'll breathe easier when in the company of little windbags. This company sells balloons, kits, accessory supplies, many how-to books, and even erotic books. Prices are wholesale and below (at least 50% less than retail). There's a $75 minimum order on balloons and kits but no minimum on books. There's a 100% return policy on books and balloon accessories; latex and mylar balloons are not refundable unless there is factory error. Entertainment balloons, which can be twisted to make animals, are a specialty. **C, B, PQ**

BILL MULLER'S TOYS
P.O. Box 1838
Oak Hall, VA 23416
(804) 824-4373

So, you don't believe in Santa Claus? Well, don't tell Bill. He's one of Santa's commissioned craftsman, carving all sorts of cars, trains, pull toys, boats that float, puzzles, and knickknacks out of sugar pine and white pine with the idea that they are "smooth, soft, and safe." Toys are guaranteed for life against faulty craftsmanship and will be replaced or repaired at no extra charge. As we Muller-ed over the prices, we toyed with the idea that they were very reasonable for the effort expended. You won't be able to say, "Oh, no" to Mr. Bill when you see his toy catalog. **C**

B.J. ALAN
P.O. Box 3
12900 Columbiana-Carfield Road
Columbiana, OH 44408
(800) 321-9071
(800) 362-1034: OH residents
(216) 482-5595

Dyno-mite! Well, not really, but you can at least have a blast if you're the type who likes to pop off. This fireworks company offers a wide range of firecrackers at prices up to 50% lower than usual. They've got Roman candles, fountains, ground spinners, missiles, rockets, parachutes, sparklers, bottle rockets, smoke items, snakes, as well as many other bang-up bargains. There's a $25 minimum order, an offer of gift certificates or refunds for "valid reasons," and a 20% charge for restocking. Stock up for New Year's, July 4th, or even add a little drama to the night you "pop the question." (She can't refuse!) You must be 18 to buy. **C** $2 (refundable)

CARRIAGE TRADE CREATIONS
P.O. Box 116
Lincoln, RI 02865
(401) 724-4655

Call Robert Reuter, that's the name, and away go troubles down the drain. His company is offering readers of *The Underground Shopper* a 33% discount off already low-priced personalized gifts. Monogrammed acrylic keyholders were clearly a buy at $4. Solid brass G.I. dog tags on an 18-inch chain were another interesting item at $8. Their write-it-yourself desk markers are tempting for anyone who's ever wanted to put a sign on his desk that says, "You Have Reached A Nonworking Person." **C** $1 (refundable)

CURRENT
The Current Building
Colorado Springs, CO 80941
(303) 593-5990

In the high country of Colorado, Current carries stationery and gift items, and if you go with the flow, it's hard to go wrong. The current Current catalog is over 70 pages and displays calendars, all-occasion cards, memo boards, date books, stationery, wrapping paper, recipe cards, and birthday party kits in many attractive designs. Discounts are based on the number of items ordered: Significant savings occur with price breaks starting with the eighth and 16th items ordered. (It's another way to save some Current-cy.) Their guarantee's a good one: The customer must be totally satisfied or they'll replace the order or refund the money. It's comforting to know you won't have to fight against the Current. **C**

FAIR AND SQUARE
22 Huron St.
Port Jefferson Station, NY 11776
(516) 928-8707

Fair they are, but square? Not likely, since they circle the globe looking for out-of-this-world bargains in rock 'n' roll collectibles, posters, T-shirts, hats, bumper stickers, patches (all sizes up to jacket-size), wall hangings, tapestries, smoking paraphernalia, and more. Save 10% to 70% (attention flea marketers: the more you buy, the bigger the deal). Hot items this year include the imported cloisonné enamel pins with logos like the Doors and a line of imported records and tapes including the picture discs with each group emblazened on the record itself. **C $5** (refundable)

LA PIÑATA
No. 2 Patio Market
Old Town
Albuquerque, NM 87104
(505) 242-2400

Need a piñata for your next bash? Vent your frustrations on small $2.25 (regularly $3.50), medium $5.50 (regularly $6.98), and large $8.25 (regularly $12) piñatas in characters like a burro, frog, bear, bull, Spiderman, Big Bird, or the Cookie Monster. (Sorry, they do not carry a Howard Cosell piñata.) The minimum order is 25 piñatas; they'll refund if not satisfied. **B, PQ**

LAURENCE CORNER
62/64 Hampstead Road
London N.W.1 2NU, England
Phone: 011-44-1-01-388-6811 (dial direct)

Forget the lampshade at your next party and make your grand entrance in checkered trousers, prison pj's, oxygen mask, and fez hat. Laurence Corner sells new and used theatrical costumes, light-erweight party costumes, inexpensive props, government surplus, medical lab instruments, and much more at "ridiculous" prices. If you want to get ahead with a hat that's different, check out their huge selection of unusual headgear from Civil War caps to Quaker hats. **B**

THE LETTER BOX
Box 371
Woodbury, NY 11797
(516) 367-4234

Is your creative self expressed best in traditionally elegant or con-temporarily bold writing papers? Does your pen whirl through Vic-torian swirls or dance across art deco-rations? The Letter Box will sign, seal, and deliver you fine designer stationery—all sealed with savings of 15% to 50%. The more you order, the more you'll save. The rage in personalized pages these days is the mini-pad (legal looks, graph paper with your name etched in art deco type, gingham and woodgrain prints)—all 25% less than the likes at the Drawing Board. Postage is determined by the total dollar amount of your order. **B,** samples $1

LINCOLN HOUSE
2015 Grand Ave.
P.O. Box 19836
Kansas City, MO 64141
(816) 842-3225

Gift-giving ideas just seem to multiply in this house undivided against itself. Honest, Abe, Lincoln logs in fine candles, inexpensive gifts, and stationery in an attractive catalog. We found cookie tins and other kitchen knickknacks, magazine holders, Muppet enve-lopes, Sesame Street playmates, and a small army of other items including a spaghetti measurer (so you won't have to use your noo-dle?). Prices were 20% to 40% off retail, and satisfaction is guaran-teed, so they ain't just whistlin' Dixie. Do you suppose everything bears the Union label? **C**

PARADISE PRODUCTS
P.O. Box 568
El Cerrito, CA 94530
(415) 524-8300

We thought Paradise Products consisted of apples, fig leaves, and serpents until we looked through their catalog and discovered nothing was lost. Party goods for 23 international and nine seasonal themes with tempting discounts of 25% on an assortment of favors, posters, crepe paper, hats, banners, flags, and masks, all in their own Party Host line. Say "Aloha!" to Hawaiian orchids and packets of beach sand, "How!" to an Indian peace pipe, or save a fortune on cookies for your next Chinese party. There's a $30 minimum order (if order is less than $30, enclose a $3 service charge). All items are guaranteed to be as represented in the catalog with shipments guaranteed to arrive on time (not fashionably late) for the party and in perfect condition or your money cheerfully refunded. **C $2**

STEVE'S DISCOUNT UNIVERSITY T-SHIRTS
P.O. Box 253
Denton, TX 76201

"If you think it's time for a Discount University . . . think no more." Steve's Discount University proclaims the virtues of bargain basement education through its line of T-shirts. The designs vary from the Red Tag Sale shirts announcing reduced course prices to the more formal School Seal version depicting a flaming cuspidor and university motto, "Education Is All In Your Mind." Send $9.50 for sizes small through extra-large.

SUNSET HOUSE
800 S. Broadway
C.S. 6000
Hicksville, NY 11802
(516) 576-9000

Seventy-seven Sunset tricks! Here's an innovative catalog that won't let the sun set without the assistance of a gadget or gizmo to make your life easier. Some of the more bizarre items we found included a "wrist pen," which doubles as a rubbery piece of jewelry, for $1.99, a nifty "pop top lifter" for $1.49, a banana harmonica also $1.49, and a beer mug shaped in the form of the female anatomy. Don't leave foam without it, $2.99. Save up to 65% over prices found on similar items at airport gift shops. A division of Unity Buying Service. Full refund if not completely satisfied. **C**

Office Supplies

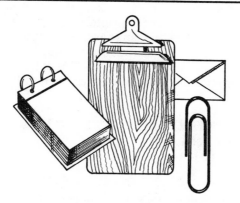

High prices often contribute to the demise of a small company. A good place to start cutting corners is right at the bottom line: office supplies and equipment. Buying them from a discounter will free you up to concentrate on some luxuries. Discount typewriters, computers, word processors, dictaphones, and floppy discs will keep you from sloppy invoices. Shop around and let the salesmen do the talking. Continue to do the walking till you've located what you want. Compare the prices before you place your order by mail. Though it may come off your taxes, remember, it's still out-of-pocket.

ALLIED BUSINESS MACHINES
9281 Earl St.
La Mesa, CA 92041
(619) 461-6361

The ABM system we encountered here was far from hit-or-missile. Their 78-page catalog listed items from reconditioned IBM typewriters to computer paper, with shredders, binders, tape recorders, answering machines, calculators, and desk files filed in between. Their selection of ribbons for printers really threw us for a loop. Prices were up to 50% less than conventional office suppliers, which is good, but they do not accept returns, which is not-so-good. We hadn't expected such an explosion of office options, and we have to admit we were caught with our defenses down. **C $1.50**

AMERICAN INTERNATIONAL TYPEWRITERS
745 Alexander Road
Princeton, NJ 08540
(606) 452-7500

American International sells typewriters by such striking manufacturers as Brother, Olivetti, SCM, Royal, Olympia, and Smith-Corona. Besides catering to the carriage trade, they also carry Cross pens at 30% off list price and have a small selection of Sony and Sanyo "walking" stereos. Discounts are about 30% to 50% off retail. There are no refunds or exchanges except for freight damaged and defective merchandise. **C, B**

AMITY HALLMARK LTD.
P.O. Box 929: first class orders
Linden Hall Station
40-09 149th Place: special delivery orders
Flushing, NY 11534
(212) 939-2323

They don't need red trucks, hoses, and loud sirens to put out the fliers down at the station. Amity Hallmark offers a wide variety of computerized typesetting and offset printing services for letterheads, envelopes, booklets, and business cards and offers "extra services" such as padding, punching, and stapling all at nominal prices. They are a large facility and because of technology and the latest in printing equipment, can pass their savings in efficiency on to the consumer. Most orders shipped within 24 to 48 hours after receipt. Certain jobs take longer—such as cards, carbonless forms, booklets, envelopes, and colored ink. Shipping is free in all the New England states and Washington, DC. **B**

B & I FURNITURE CO.
611 N. Broadway
Milwaukee, WI 53202
(800) 558-8662
(800) 242-7200: WI residents
(414) 272-6082

B & I has a full-color catalog displaying such furniture lines as La-Z-Boy and Rubbermaid at up to 30% off (just above wholesale prices) plus larger discounts on quantity orders. Another 84-page catalog is available for the industrial market with listings for cabinets, shelvings, hoists, safety, and dock equipment. There's a 100% guarantee on these first-quality products, which are shipped directly from the plant to the customer in four to six weeks (normal ship) or 10 to 15 days (quick ship). Minimum freight charge, $31.50. **C**

BUSINESS ENVELOPE MANUFACTURERS
900 Grand Blvd.
Deer Park, NY 11729
(800) 645-5235
(516) 667-8500: NY residents

Parton us, but nobody's Fonda working 9 to 5. And puttin' all that Tomlin can be a drag if you don't have the right equipment. BEM will "envelope" you in business statements, invoices, stationery, ledgers, labels, ribbons, jumbo markers, and more at factory-direct prices. Imprinted business envelopes were $23.90 for 1,000 (up to $60.45 elsewhere). **C**

BUY DIRECT, INC.
216 W. 18th St.
New York, NY 10011
(800) 221-5332
(212) 255-4424: NY residents

Bye, bye, blackboard; hello word processors that need their own set of supplies. This company carries all types of business forms (snap-out and computer forms), labels, and assorted printing items in addition to their latest stock of computer, minicomputer, and word processing supplies like special binders, disc cartridges, storage systems, and print wheels. Prices are consistently 15% to 30% below retail from this wholesale distributor. There are different minimum orders for different products and there's a 10% restocking charge on returns. Send for a free catalog that will give a partial listing of items carried. **C, PQ**

COMMERCIAL OFFICE PRODUCTS
1000 E. Higgins Road
Elk Grove Village, IL 60007
(800) 323-0662
(312) 364-7544: IL residents

Time for a Commercial: "There are over 8 million stories in the Naked City. This is just one of them. It was a dark, dreary night. I had just come from Joe's Bar when I responded to an 852—typing without a ribbon. I'd dealt with this type before. The victim was named Smith-Corona, the suspect, Mike Masher. I let him go once and he promised not to return. Now he had two strikes against him. I dusted the keys for fingerprints. I guessed this guy Corona to be a big ticket item, but I was 35% off. Masher had a record of cold, calculating assaults with a battery in the TI and HP cases. Masher was trying to save the $4.95 shipping, but now he'd be shipped up the river. At 10:15, I received a call on my Record-O-Call ($249, $349 elsewhere) from the chief: Get some milk on the way home. Case closed." **C**

FIDELITY PRODUCTS CO.
5601 International Parkway
P.O. Box 155
Minneapolis, MN 55440
(800) 328-3034
(612) 536-6500: MN residents

Fidelity's own brand of opaque correction fluid was incorrigible at 39 cents per bottle, but the corrigated modular storage systems ranked even higher in our files. We didn't see the writing on the wall with their anti-graffiti urethane, $26.95 a gallon, which protects against aerosol spray paint, felt pen, and most other visual pollutants. Over 1,800 products for office, factory, or warehouse including temporary files, packaging tapes and containers, first aid kits (OSHA approved). This 21-year-old company offers 15% to 20% savings across the board and up to 40% savings on quantity purchases.

Thirty-day free trial with a full refund during that time. **C**

FRANK EASTERN CO.
625 Broadway
New York, NY 10012
(800) 221-4914
(212) 677-9100: NY residents call collect

Message from the boss: Keep this company on file—under "M" for memo-rable. Savings up to 50% off retail on business and institutional equipment. They've got folders, file cabinets, Bics, binders, desks, diskettes, lockers, library shelves, typewriters, tables. There's a $40 minimum order, money-back guarantee, and no restocking charge. Their catalog's free, touting lines like High Point, Vangard, Nightingale, and La-Z-Boy. They've got everything a business needs but has no business paying retail for. **C**

JILOR DISCOUNTS
1178 Broadway
New York, NY 10001
(212) 683-1590

Getting through the daily grind is easy with the right office machines. We brewed a bargain on calculators reduced 20% and more especially by makers like Sony, Toshiba, Sharp, and Victor. Get keyed up on typewriters by Smith-Corona, Olympia, Silver-Reed, and Olivetti. Get the message? Answering machines by Sanyo, Code-A-Phone, and Panasonic recorded record savings. Dial away the hours on a cordless, refurbished, or new decorator-style telephone. Call if you require service on calculators, answering machines, or dictation equipment. Shipping charges extra, but very reasonable. **PQ**

LANDMARK SPECIALTIES, INC.
8549 Sunset Ave.
Fair Oaks, CA 95628
(916) 961-2896

Looking for a computer that won't spindle, fold, and mutilate the company budget? Check the lineup of computers on-line here. This company serves as a broker and will ship or drop ship computers bearing such esoteric names as Alspa, Altos, Atari, Cromemco,

Dynabyte, Eagle, Godbout, Kaycomp (Kaypro), NEC, North Star, Televideo, Texas Instruments, VIC 20, Xerox, and Zenith. (Computer names always sound to us like the babblings of an electronic baby.) Besides computers, Landmark has CRTs, terminals, monitors, printers, boards, and accessories, software, modems, and supplies from a wide range of manufacturers. Prices indicate about 20% to 40% savings off list. Write or call for a price quote and tell 'em the Underground sent ya. **PQ**

NATIONAL BUSINESS FURNITURE, INC.
222 E. Michigan St.
Milwaukee, WI 53202
(800) 558-1010
(800) 558-9803: customer service
(800) 242-0030: WI residents

One of America's leading distributors of discount office furniture offers many opportunities for BBB (Better Business Bargains). Shop for top-drawer brands without leaving your desk. Names like Cole, Hon, Jefsteel, Globe/Cosco, and Samsonite all available direct from the manufacturer. Three to five weeks delivery for drop shipment with reasonable freight charges tacked on. Restocking charge of 25%. **C**

NEBS
500 Main St.
Groton, MA 01471
(800) 225-6380
(800) 252-9226: MA residents

NEBS (New England Business Services) will make your office feel all-write by taking care of business with discounts on carbonless business forms, sales slips, envelopes, invoices, labels, files, and check-writing systems. Prices won't put you out of business: 12 large (600 sheets) legal pads for $9.50 ($10.50 elsewhere), raised print business cards, $19.95 for 1,000 ($27 elsewhere). No shipping charges on prepaid orders. **C**

OLYMPIC SALES
216 S. Oxford Ave.
Los Angeles, CA 90004
(800) 421-8045: orders only
(800) 252-2153: CA residents
(213) 739-1130

No gold medals awarded here with their rather abrupt response to our inquiry: "The prices in the catalog are what we charge and no, we don't take requests for catalogs over the phone!" Still, you may want to pole-vault over their large assortment of computers and printers, calculators, typewriters, cassette recorders, VCRs, stereo equipment, and video games from Apple, Atari, and more. When you cross the finish line, you will track definite savings. Bronze through their catalog for $2. C $2

PEARL BROTHERS TYPEWRITERS
476 Smith St.
Brooklyn, NY 11231
(212) 875-3024

Net one, Pearl two, and save up to 50% on typewriters that have more than a few years shell-f life. The retail oyster was shucked open to reveal lustrous 10% to 40% discounts on name brands like the Adler-Royal Satellite I for $325 (regularly $575). They also have a service department that will repair any make of typewriter. Write for more information and wait for good tide-ings. PQ

S-100 INC.
Division of 696 Corp.
14425 N. 79th St., Suite B
Scottsdale, AZ 85260
(800) 528-3138
(602) 991-7870: AZ residents

In this computer age, Barnum & Bailey would say life is a circuit. S-100 has the high-wire on microcomputers and peripheral devices: floppy discs, "Morrow" memory boards, alphanumeric line printers, video boards, music synthesizer boards, and terminals you'd die for. Over 60 brands like Cromemco, Godbout, North Star, Seattle, SSM, Televideo, Qume, and Epson. Their two-tier pricing system helps out in these days of double-digital inflation. A 10% discount for C.O.D. or credit card holders, a 14.5% discount when cash payment (in the form of a check of money order) accompanies order. Usually a 10% restocking charge with exchanges accepted on defective merchandise only. **C**

THRIFTY PRINTS, INC.
103 Hotel St.
Brooklyn, WI 53521

Send them your copy-ready work and get back 1,000 sheets (one side printed) size 8½-by-11, black and white, for $14 ($21.80 elsewhere). Choose from many paper colors like buff, canary, pink, blue, etc. Thrifty typesetting, too: 1-inch display ads, $1; and 20 proofs for 50 cents. An 8½-by-11 circular was $16, 20 proofs were $2.50 extra. Prices include UPS delivery. Turnaround time is usually seven days on camera-ready printing, two weeks on typesetting. Minimum order is 250 copies. Sorry Canada, due to duties, they can't ship to you. **B, SASE**

TYPEX BUSINESS MACHINES INC.
119 W. 23rd St.
New York, NY 10011
(800) 221-9332
(212) 243-8086: NY residents

Typex doesn't sell Brand X: only Royal, SCM, Silver-Reed, Olivetti, Olympia, IBM, Adler, and Brother typewriters including the foreign language varieties not available elsewhere. Key into savings from 30% to 50%. They also have an X-cellent service department to repair any make of typewriter. Now is the time for all good shoppers to come to the aid of this company. **PQ**

VIP PAYMASTER SALES
7879 Riverfalls, Suite 144
Dallas, TX 75230
(214) 750-7940

Protect all your checking accounts from fraud and alteration by purchasing a Paymaster Checkprotector from VIP (Very Inexpensive Paymasters) and save 10%. They have a wide variety of models to suit all needs and budgets. The Paymaster Corporation also issues a manufacturer's certificate of warranty against forgery and alteration up to $40,000. VIP pays shipping costs and 100% reimbursement for parts and labor. **PQ, B**

WOLFF OFFICE EQUIPMENT
1841 Broadway
New York, NY 10023
(212) 581-9080

Shepherding the company finances? "Cry Wolff" for savings on typewriters, computers, and office equipment as these folks flock to your rescue. Savings run 20% on names like Olympia, Olivetti, Smith-Corona, Osborne, Commodore, SCM, IBM, and others. Check out the electric checkwriters, dictating machines, and office furniture, too. Their minimum order is $100, with a 15% restocking charge on returns. Not Baaaa-d. **PQ**

Romance

Remember the first love letter you ever wrote? Ours got confiscated by the fourth-grade teacher as it sailed past her nose. Well, romance is in the airwaves and the air mail once again. Long distance love affairs have taken on an even greater element of interest for single men and women in our 50 states. Finding the perfect match has come full circle from the days of tossing around one-liners at singles bars to composing beautiful missives. You may meet your match through one of the special interest clubs for gourmet food and classical music lovers. From bachelors to book lovers, here's a practical and inexpensive link to love.

THE ARTS WORLD
P.O. Box 833
Amityville, NY 11701
(516) 454-0673

Don't be single, be singular. If you're a classy classics lover, you won't find a soulmate in a C & W saloon. If you're too shy to talk to the guy in the next seat at the symphony, try The Arts World, an organization of people who like art, crafts, theater, ballet, poetry, photography, literature, etc. An $18 membership fee (six months) circulates your three-line profile to other art lovers. Choose from over 500 members. Now in its fifth year. Owner Ms. Jens Jurgen Wegscheider also operates the Travel Companion Exchange. (See Travel) **B**

BIBLIOBUFFS
Box 995
Ingram, TX 78025

If you've been wondering who wrote the book of love, perhaps one of these bibliophiles can answer your question. Besides craving pointed dialogue, members' interests include backpacking, mountain climbing, flying, and many other climactic experiences. For $20 a year, you will receive a monthly newsletter and the opportunity to purchase for 65 cents each, a descriptive profile of your intended pen-fatale. Stamp out lonely Saturday nights. **B $20**

CLASSICAL MUSIC LOVERS EXCHANGE
Box 31
Pelham, NY 10803

Maybe you've never used the line, "We could make beautiful music together" to get a date. But here is a group that capitalizes on helping single classical music lovers find dates to attend concerts. Founder Tamara Monique Conroy of Pelham, New York, says she has already orchestrated two marriages. A six-month membership costs $22 and includes short sketches of fellow music lovers. Then for $1 each, you receive the names and addresses to begin a harmonious relationship. Membership currently includes about 1,300 music lovers who know the score, but look for a crescendo from Ms. Conroy's advertising efforts. **B**

THE GREATEST LITTLE BACHELOR BOOK IN LA
Carolyne Nolen Publications
6110 Nevada, Suite 309 D
Woodland Hills, CA 91367
(213) 710-0114

Hollywood and di-Vine! Here they come: actors, models, doctors, directors, and everyone else you've dreamed of, all parading through these pages. There are 187 bachelors of all sizes, shapes, and backgrounds to ogle over. This sensational book is an indispensable source for every single, or single-again woman. For a man-size bargain, this book is man-datory reading for the marriage-minded. The price is $3.49 (half price), plus $1 for postage and handling. **C $4.49**

THE GREATEST LITTLE BACHELOR BOOK IN TEXAS
SusAnn Publications, Inc.
3110 N. Fitzhugh
Dallas, TX 75204
(214) 528-8940

Lonely in the Lone Star state? Try this book on for sighs. The *original* bachelor book complete with photographs and biographies of Texas' most eligible men. They've got looks. They've got money. Honey, they've got it all! Want to meet a cardiologist who's a man after your own heart? How about building a relationship with a millionaire real estate developer as your next project? We know a handsome travel editor who isn't flighty. They're all ready, willing, and written-up so you can contact them. (Each subject is pictured, too.) Send $2.95 (half price), plus $1 (shipping and handling) for your male orders today. **C $3.95**

JAY LARSEN
10640 Steppington, Suite 2148
Dallas, TX 75230
(214) 691-5734

Don't write this man off. Jay Larsen has 15 years' experience analyzing handwriting. He does everything from dating service work to prescreening for employment agencies and corporations. According to Larsen, success may be only a dotted "i" away. Send Jay a sample of your belle's letters, and for $10 to $25, he'll advise you of your compatibility or combat-ability. **B**

SINGLE BOOK LOVERS
Box AE
Swarthmore, PA 19081
(215) 566-2132

Want to turn up the volume on your love life, or maybe find someone who's stacked? Single Book Lovers offers a novel approach to meeting people that's long overdue. If you're too reserved to check out the library patrons, but want a binding relationship with another bibliophile, this outfit offers an encyclopedic listing of other similarly inclined book lovers anxious to get off the shelf and into circulation. For a $32 cover charge, you get 12 months of newsletters with hundreds of two-line biographies touting age, height, hometown, profession, and interests (including favorite books) of members, plus one free detailed profile sheet on one of them. Buy extra profiles for 60 cents each for the first six, 45 cents each thereafter. When we telephoned and said we were from Dallas, the man we spoke with asked us "You mean you people read books down there?" We do, of course (having been a member of SBL for several years). Perhaps he needs to read, *How to Win Friends and Influence People* 'cause without it, customers are going to be *Gone with the Wind.* **B**

SINGLE GOURMET
5415 Bellaire Ave., Suite 135
Bellaire, TX 77401
(713) 665-0505

Why spend your salad days trying to get a date? This group knows what's cooking among single gourmet food lovers. For $35 a year, you can join one of the chapters (presently in Houston, New York, Los Angeles, and eight cities in Canada) and explore the pleasures of pâté, the ecstasies of escargot, or the glee of glacés. Join other affluent professionals who pay their own way at local restaurants and maybe the tab won't be all you pick up. **B**

XANDRIA COLLECTION
Lawrence Research Group
P.O. Box 31039
San Francisco, CA 94131
(415) 864-5406

In love with the wizardry of 20th-century technology? Then thrill to the chill of becoming one with a mechanical manipulator. Sink back, and relax to the quiet conversational hum of your lover. At last you can choreograph your most intimate of encounters, achieve the ideal of passion without involvement, ecstasy without emotion. Xandria offers all this and more at prices 20% to 30% lower than at adult bookstores. Orders of Motion Lotion, Joy Jelly, sexual treasures for earthly pleasures, gadgetry, and assorted paraphernalia are all discreetly packaged and promptly shipped. **C $3**

Telephone Services

Southern Belles have come a long way from the place they held in the days of Alex Bell. So have telephones. They now come in all shapes, sizes, and colors with features like video displays, speaker phones, cordless models, and computer hook-ups. If you leave home without one, you haven't read our Electronics section for car telephones. Today, more business is conducted over the wire than ever before, creating the need for WATS time-sharing and other cost-cutting services. Check these listings for other alternative ways to reach out and touch someone for less.

AMERICAN DISCOUNT DIALING SYSTEM
2641 N. Main St.
Walnut Creek, CA 94596
(800) 227-1617
(800) 772-3545: CA residents
(415) 932-5600

Where else but California would you find a commune for corporations? This enterprising young company is basically a corporate
secretarial, answering service, and order department all tolled into
one. Companies too small to afford their own WATS line, but who
nevertheless would benefit from such service, use this number for a
nominal all-American fee. **PQ**

MCI TELECOMMUNICATIONS CORP.
1275 Summer St.
Stamford, CT 06905
(800) 772-0126
(203) 324-7781: customer service, CT residents
(203) 324-1975: business office, CT residents

For across-the-switchboard savings that are far from phony, MCI
offers a long-distance alternative to calling Ma by way of the Bell. If
your monthly long-distance telephone bill is $25 or more and you
have a touchtone phone, savings per call can range from 15% to 50%,
depending on when you call. For a $5 or $10 monthly charge (no
deposit or installation fees) and then a per call charge similar to Bell's
(only cheaper), you're hooked up. People in many parts of the country
now have access to calling anywhere in the U.S. and installation time
averages only a two-week wait. **PQ**

SATELCO
1 Satelco Plaza
San Antonio, TX 78205
(800) 292-1007

If this name doesn't ring a Bell, ma guess is, it soon will. They're
getting the busy signal from price-conscious ding-a-lings all over.
Many customers can dial long distance to anywhere in the U.S. at
savings of 10% to 20% during business hours, and up to 50% from 11
p.m. to 8 a.m. and on weekends. You pay a $10 fee to start, then $5
monthly plus your long-distance charges. Depending on the number
of long-distance calls made, savings can be considerable. **PQ**

SP COMMUNICATIONS
1 Adrian Court
P.O. Box 974
Burlingame, CA 94010
(800) 521-4949
(415) 692-5600: CA residents

These folks should get the no-Bell prize for cheapness. If you tend to talk till you're blue in the face, Bell's bill could put you in the red. SPC's service is called "Sprint" and is a godsend for those who run at the mouth. Savings per call vary depending on time and distance, but run 22% to 44% less than Bell during the day, 45% to 50% less in the evening (5 p.m. to 11 p.m.) and 56% less at night (11 p.m. to 8 a.m.). One significant advantage is that "Sprint" has an extensive "travel call" network that is available to those frequently on the road. Travelers can use "Sprint" from many cities that are not available on other telephone systems, and at no extra charge. As with other systems, a touchtone phone is required, or at least a touchtone adapter. **B, PQ**

U.S. TELEPHONE, INC.
108 S. Akard
Dallas, TX 75202
(800) 527-4105

Do high phone bills put your cash flow on hold? U.S. Telephone can get you off the hook. They're the only discount phone service that reaches out to every city in the continental U.S., Hawaii, Puerto Rico, and the Virgin Islands. Though they can't give an exact discount, they tell us they are "much lower" than Bell (probably ranging to about 40% lower for residential customers on full-time service). Choose from two basic services: one operates on a 24-hour daily basis, the other runs after 5 p.m., before 8 a.m., and all day on weekends. "Cost cutter" calls made during special daytime hours earn a bonus discount up to 20%. They also offer business service for large and small companies, and they will customize services for individual businesses. Give them a call and tell them we tolled ya. **PQ**

U.S. TRANSMISSIONS SYSTEMS
ITT Longer Distance
333 Meadowland Parkway
Secaucus, NJ 07094
(800) 221-7267
(800) 652-2871: NJ residents
(201) 866-5700

If you've been spending long green on long distance, don't let your long-windedness put you in the red, dial ITT for some fast relief. Their long-distance rates can save you plenty of wampum without sending smoke signals. We thought about IT&T-remendous was what we decided were the savings. **PQ**

Travel

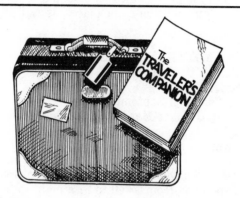

You don't have to be rich to travel first-class. Try an airline broker. Or, contact one of the travel clubs who provide country club atmosphere, group travel rates, and comraderie to world ports-of-call. Pack your bags at a discount (see Luggage and Handbags) and have your "Travel America at Half Price" coupon book on hand. Have no reservations about a room through the many bed & breakfast programs available—all confirm reservations in advance. See the countryside on your bicycle or trade your Pacific condo for a bungalow in Kennebunk.

ADVENTURES IN LIVING HOME EXCHANGE SERVICE
P.O. Box 278
Winnetka, IL 60093

Whether you're interested in a castle, treehouse, villa, igloo, cabin in the woods, or an everyday condo, rondo with this service that lists hundreds of swapable sites to stay in. A directory of locations in 34 states and 14 foreign countries, two supplements during the year, and a helpful "guideline for going places" is available for $35.

AMERICAN YOUTH HOSTELS, INC.
1332 "I" St., N.W., Suite 800-UF
Washington, DC 20005
(800) 424-9426: April-September only
(202) 783-6161: October-March; DC residents year-round

Students who want to see the USA or foreign countries have resorted to this inexpensive housing alternative for years. With over 5,000 hostels worldwide, AYH also appeals to travelers of all ages who think spending from $3.50 to $7 a night for a "delightful surprise" is the best deal in the land. Dorm rooms are the norm. And, if you are going to San Francisco, be sure to wear flowers in your hair and call ahead for reservations. Fees: Junior Pass (17 years and under), $7; Senior Pass (18 to 59 years), $14; Senior Citizen Pass (60 years and over), $7. Members receive a book of friendly hostel facilities available to nonmembers for $3 including postage. Hostel-la vista! **C, $3 for nonmembers, free to members; B**

BED & BREAKFAST LEAGUE, LTD.
2855 29th St., N.W.
Washington, DC 20008
(202) 232-8718

Get lodged without getting stuck. This service provides an expanded "bed & breakfast" concept in lodging available exclusively through full-service travel agencies. Travelers stay with families in their homes, sometimes even sharing bathing facilities. Breakfast is generally in the continental tradition (juice, toast, and coffee), although varying with location and regional customs. This service's advantages include affordability (since rates for their hotels, inns, motels, condos, and residential rooms are usually about half as expensive as ordinary lodging), greater freedom (since one can stay in the city, country, or an attractive vacation spot), atmosphere (since one stays

with local inhabitants), and breakfast (since there's no extra charge).
Every facility is inspected for comfort, cleanliness, and convenience.
The annual membership fee is $25 and reservations are confirmed.
Write for a list of cities and start living it up to the Hilt-on a bed &
breakfast budget. **B**

BEST WESTERN INTERNATIONAL TRAVEL GUIDE
Best Western Way
P.O. Box 10203
Phoenix, AZ 85064
(602) 957-4200

Best Western: *High Noon* starring Gary Cooper. Best Travel Log:
Travel Guide by Best Western International. The free 300-page
guide has a foldout cover with key to travel symbols in five languages.
Atlas-style road maps are threaded though the first 50 pages, fol-
lowed by room listings with full-color photographs from Alberta,
Canada, through Wyoming. An international index to their lodgings
is in the back.

BIKE VERMONT, INC.
P.O. Box 75-LF
Grafton, VT 05146
(802) 843-2259

Roll across the rolling hills of Vermont as you tour the verdant
countryside, quaint towns, and historic inns of one of the most scenic
states. Weekend bike tours are $145 for adults and $130 for children,
which includes spending two nights in a historic Vermont inn. Midweek tours begin with a Sunday dinner and end Friday evening,
costing $365 for adults and $335 for kids. Midweek tour patrons
receive lodging in a different inn each evening. Tours are leisurely
and are suitable for beginning to advanced cyclists. Reservations
require a deposit of $50 per person for weekend tours, and $100 for
midweek tours. BYOB, or rent a bicycle from them. As a nice touch,
the tour director will write a personal note of acknowledgment to
signees. **B**

COUNCIL ON INTERNATIONAL EDUCATIONAL EXCHANGE (CIEE)
205 E. 42nd St.
New York, NY 10017
(212) 661-1414

The free *Student Work/Study/Travel Catalog* lists all kinds of travel bargains and study abroad opportunities available to high school and university students. The International Student ID Card, for example, can save up to 50% on air fares, rail tickets (international and domestic), bus tickets, ship and ferry tickets, tours, accommodations, and even department stores and boutiques. In addition, the council offers work programs in Great Britain, Ireland, France, New Zealand, and other countries. Language programs for all levels are offered year round for anyone over 17. Tuition and accommodations with meals in a French household were $561 for three weeks. Write for their catalog and discover a whole new world open to everyone. Several other offices are located throughout the U.S. and in Paris and Tokyo. **C**

THE COUPON BROKER
1780 S. Bellaire St., Suite 135
Denver, CO 80222
(303) 757-8144

In business since 1979, David Kenny goes for broke. As a buyer and seller of discount airline and hotel coupons, vouchers, and certificates, Mr. Kenny can help consumers fly first class at prices lower than coach. Coupons can be used at national hotel chains to save 25% to 35% (more if a group). The closer to expiration date, the lower the price. This service is offered for both short- and long-haul distances. You can fly standby on any Continental Airlines flight and receive an additional 15% off the quoted fare. Newsletter to customers. **B**

THE EAST WOODS PRESS
429 East Boulevard
Charlotte, NC 28203
(704) 334-0897

A number of well-written guides to inexpensive travel are available from this publisher. *The Best Bed & Breakfast in the World* ($9.95 paperback) describes hundreds of accommodations in Great Britain and Ireland plus brief listings in major cities in Austria, Belgium,

Denmark, Finland, France, Germany, Holland, Norway, and Sweden. *The Mid-Atlantic Guest House Book* ($7.95) lists guest houses in New York, Pennsylvania, New Jersey, Delaware, Maryland, and West Virginia with accommodating hosts. Other books are available for New England and the South. *Hosteling USA* ($7.95) described the more than 280 American Youth Hostels all over the country. Another book, *Free Campgrounds*, included more than 6,000 free campgrounds in the USA including Alaska and Hawaii ($9.95). Shipping is free to readers of *The Underground Shopper*, so mention us. Shipping is free to noncommercial accounts only. **C**

ELKIN TRAVEL, INC.
25950 Greenfield Road
Oak Park, MI 48237
(800) 445-1666
(800) 423-5355: 24-hour service
(313) 968-7800: MI residents

Now you can trip the flights fantastic, have a wingding and not create a flap. If your travel plans are up in the air, Elkin can bring the expenses down to earth. This agency offers free gifts (up to $100 per couple) just for booking cruises or tours to Mexico, Europe, Hawaii, the Caribbean, or vibrant Las Vegas. They offer 24-hour service to implement any flight of fancy or to book any cruise, tour, or flight you fancy.

ENTERTAINMENT PUBLICATIONS
1400 N. Woodward
Birmingham, MI
(800) 521-9640
(313) 642-8300: MI residents

Remember *A Tale of Two Cities?* Well, here's a tale about cities and two-fers. *Entertainment 83*, a thick coupon travel book published for 30 cities, enabled us to get 50% discounts on hotel rooms, gourmet dinners, football games, jazz concerts—everything from submarine sandwiches to symphony seats. The price of the books varies from city to city ($16.95 for Cincinnati up to $30 for Seattle). These attractive books include menus, reviews, and glossy photos of participating restaurants. According to one travel writer, "If one were to use all of the coupons in the new Manhattan book, there would be a cumulative savings of more than $4,000." Another book, *Travel America at Half Price*, includes 400 half-price hotel coupons around the country. That beats the Dickens out of paying full price. Call for more information.

FORD'S FREIGHTER GUIDE
P.O. Box 505
22151 Clarendon St.
Woodland Hills, CA 91365

Some people have to get away come hull or high water. Freight travel can cut costs way down, and from what some salty dog adventurers say, "It isn't bad!" Oftentimes you'll have access to the passenger lounges, dining rooms, studies, and outdoor decks. The food is excellent, the ride is smooth, and the boat's not as crowded as they claim. To find out more about the 46 cargo/passenger lines, send $6.95.

NEW AGE TRAVEL/THE INTERNATIONAL SPAREROOM
839 Second St., Suite 3
Encinitas, CA 92024
(619) 436-9977

Pam Davis is the organizer of this economical, personalized style of travel. Send for a list of worldwide accommodations in North America, Canada, Mexico, Hawaii, the Caribbean, Europe, Australia, and New Zealand for $4. From this directory, the traveler is able to select his first, second, and third choices and send a request back to The Spareroom with the appropriate deposit (usually 50% plus $5 for less than a four-night stay). This organization will then act as the liaison between the hosts and travelers and confirm reservations. A listing of home exchanges is also available. Related travel services such as charter flights, European rail passes, currency exchange, and travel insurance also offered. C $4

ODYSSEY AIR ONE
2965 N. Airfield Drive, Suite 223
DFW Airport
Dallas, TX 75261
(214) 574-6376

If you're set to jet into the wild blue yonder but don't want your wings (or wallet) clipped, this charter travel club can send you soaring. Trips are planned regularly to such places as Panama, Peru, Puerto Vallarta, Hong Kong, Hawaii, Las Vegas, Costa Rica, the

Caribbean, and Salzburg, Innsbruck, and Munich for the Oktober-fest, so you won't have to wing it on your own. Annual dues are $150 for individuals, $250 for families. Terminal-types can trip out without feeling Ill-iad on Odyssey. **B**

Some other travel clubs include: Ambassadair, Inc., 2410 Executive Drive, P.O. Box 41619, Indianapolis, IN 46241, (317) 247-5141; Atlanta Skylarks, 789 Oak St., Hapeville, GA 30354, (404) 763-8100; Jet Set Travel Club, P.O. Box 80443, Seattle, WA 98108, (206) 762-6300; Nomads, Inc., 10100 Middle Belt Road, Detroit Airport, Detroit, MI 48242, (313) 861-3604; Ports-of-Call, 2121 Valentia St., Denver, CO 80220, (303) 321-6767; Shillelagh Air Travel Club, 152 Hillwood Ave., Falls Church, VA 22046, (703) 241-7595.

P.T. INTERNATIONAL
1318 S.W. Troy St.
Portland, OR 97219
(800) 547-1463
(503) 245-0440: OR residents

P.T. Barnum may have housed his traveling entourage under the Big Top, but these folks are a lot more accommodating. This is a whole-sale room reservation service, worldwide, for bed & breakfast, with specialized lodging for individual and group travelers. Use of PTI allows one access to more than 25,000 B&B rooms with a toll-free call, and thus to reserve accommodations in such intimate and affordable places as private homes, country inns, and small B&B hotels in 10 foreign countries and more than 40 states. PTI also has access to some house and/or apartment rentals available in Australia, England, France, and the U.S. The properties represented are generally low in visibility and are difficult for travelers to locate and reserve without assistance. All properties are inspected to insure quality. To avoid overpriced hotels and a three-ring circus while arranging your own accommodations, let these folks swing your trip-ease. **B, PQ**

STAND-BUYS LTD.
26711 Northwestern Highway, Suite 310
Southfield, MI 48034
(313) 352-4876

While Tammy Wynette stands by her man, you can stand for savings with Stand-Buys. By phoning these innocent buy-standers up to three weeks in advance, you can find yourself winging your way to some far off and exotic land. Savings run 15% to 67% off the price of charter flights, tours, and cruises, with always a confirmed reservation. A one-week package tour from Cleveland to Ireland (talk about culture shock!) on 14 days' notice last summer cost $499 (retail $799). Subscribers pay a $45 fee each year and receive newsletters about pending trips and access to a toll-free number that gives information on the status of excursions. Trips originate from all parts of the country. We know a couple who has five sets of luggage (discount, of course) packed with clothes for different climates and we can under-Stand, Bye. **PQ**

TANGLEPOINT TRAVEL, INC.
1551 Avenue K
Plano, TX 75074
(214) 423-6555

A full retail and wholesale travel agency specializing in international travel (Middle East and Europe) that also brokers for all airline frequent-flier vouchers. Call and ask for Bob Bullard for travel savings savvy, par excellence. **PQ**

TRAVEL COMPANION EXCHANGE
P.O. Box 833
Amityville, NY 11701
(516) 454-0673

While the Travel Companion Exchange is a relatively new organization (founded in 1982), it is affiliated with The Arts World, a well-established 5-year-old matching service for cultured singles. Run by Jens Jurgen Wegscheider, a veteran consumer-oriented travel writer, TCE has mostly single and unattached members (the never-married, divorced, separated, and widowed). Couples or perhaps two females or two males may utilize the organization also. "It's a great way to make new and interesting friends and save money at the same time," says Jens. She also helps members find reduced rates in exchange for their services as translators, secretaries, babysitters, etc. Membership is $36 for one year, $18 for six months. Visit their office at 44 County Line Road, Farmingdale, NY 11735. **B**

URBAN VENTURES, INC.
P.O. Box 426
New York, NY 10024
(212) 662-1234

We'll venture that urbane urbanites (or others) venturing to the Big Apple aren't after some seedy, slice-of-life slum as an abode to abide in. Fortunately, Urban Ventures can be very accommodating. They offer single rooms, private suites, and elegant apartments right in the core of the Apple. Prices range from $23 to $55 for single rooms, and $32 to $70 for a double. Apartment prices (they're the only place in New York where short stays in apartments can be booked) range from $55 to $100 a night. Urban Ventures also offers additional services such as securing theater tickets, steering you to moderately priced restaurants, and guiding you to top tourist attractions. If you opt out, there's a $15 cancellation fee, which is applied to any future booking, and no-shows and same-day cancellations must pay for that night. **B**

THE Y'S WAY
356 W. 34th St.
New York, NY 10001
(212) 760-5856/57/92/40

Y spend? The expanded network of YMCA overnight centers spans coast to coast in 68 cities in the USA and Canada and 24 overnight centers in 13 overseas countries. Family vacation centers, located in the Blue Ridge, Adirondack, and Rocky Mountains and the foothills of the Berkshires are also available. Low-cost package tours to New York, San Francisco, Seattle, and upstate New York are perfect for those who don't give a hoot for fancy hotels and just want to travel the Y's Way. **B**

Budget Hotels with Toll-Free Numbers

"Budget hotels" is a term for the alternative to the luxury hotels or the chains with cocktail lounges and conference rooms. They are chain operated, no-frills lodging offering a clean room with the basic comforts, but inexpensively. Different parts of the country feature chains such as these with toll-free numbers. (Hint: Have paper, pencil, and major credit card available when calling 800 lines for reservations.) For a national directory of budget bunks write: Motel 6, 51 Hitchcock Way, Santa Barbara, CA 93105.

NAME	NUMBER	HOME OFFICE
Chalet Suisse	(800) 258-1980 (800) 572-1880, NH residents	Nashua, NH
Days Inns	(800) 325-2525 (404) 325-4000, GA residents	Atlanta, GA
Econo Travel Motor Hotels	(800) 446-8134 (800) 582-5882, VA residents	Norfolk, VA
Family Inns of America	(800) 251-9752 (800) 332-9902, TN residents	Knoxville, TN
Red Roof Inns	(800) 848-7878 (800) 282-7990, OH residents	Columbus, OH
Scottish Inns of America	(800) 251-1962	Brentwood, TN

6.

HOME ENTERTAINMENT

Appliances and TVs

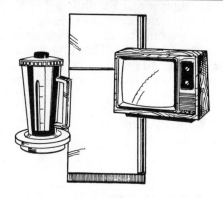

If your video game is on the blink or your vacuum cleaner is spitting out more than it's sucking in, don't despair. First, write to the manufacturer and give him the opportunity to respond. If satisfaction is not achieved, write the Major Appliance Consumer Action Panel (MACAP), 20 N. Wacker Drive, Chicago, IL 60606 or call their toll-free recording (800) 621-0477 or office (312) 984-5858. The recording gives a step-by-step summary of what to do if your major appliance problem is not resolved by the dealer. Supply them with manufacturer's name, type of appliance, model number, date purchased, a description of the problem, and copies of all correspondence and receipts.

AAA ALL FACTORY FANS AND VACUUMS
241 Cedar
Abilene, TX 79601
(915) 677-1311

Here's a vac-cination against the disease of high prices. First-quality, brand names like Kirby, Rainbow, Filter Queen, Hoover, etc., are discounted as much as 50%. The best price breaks are on door-to-door sold brands. Maxam and Satellite ceiling fans were also an antidote to feverish prices. Parts and vacuum bags are discounted but you need to buy in volume to offset mailing costs. They issue their own parts and service contracts. They give factory-authorized service for Hoover, Regina, and some others. If your local dealer will not honor your service contract, send it back to AAA for repairs. **C $1**

ABC VACUUM WAREHOUSE
7021 Burnet Road
Austin, TX 78757
(512) 459-7643

There's a sucker borne every minute. That's why ABC doesn't want you to be taken in or get left holding the bag. Business is picking up for owner Ralph Baccus who told us he's been in business since 1977. Although science tells us there is no such thing as a perfect vacuum, we found some of the best brands (Rainbow, Kirby, Filter Queen, and Compact) discounted 40%. Kirby cleaners are warrantied for parts and service for two years. All others have a one-year warranty for parts and service. Full refunds within 15 days, excluding shipping charges. **B, PQ**

BONDY EXPORT CO.
40 Canal St.
New York, NY 10002
(212) 925-7785

The stock at Bondy's is available over-the-counter or by mail. They trade in name-brand small appliances discounted 30% to 50% and this pays off in big dividends. They had the best prices of any store we shopped for Krups coffee grinders, $18 (retail $32). Irons, toasters, hair dryers, coffee makers, can openers . . . perfect for wedding presents. Their portfolio includes stock from such companies as GE, Oster, Hamilton Beach, Clairol, Hoover, Sanyo, Sony, Zenith, Corning, Farberware, Smith-Corona, and Samsonite. Ray Ban sunglasses and Bushnell binoculars were also discounted. Bondy's specializes in products for use overseas (220 volts). Cameras by Canon, Minolta, Pentax, Sankyo, plus all kinds of film make getting a price quote first from Bondy's a wise investment. **PQ**

COMP-U-CARD
777 Summer St.
Stamford, CT 06901
(800) 243-0266
(800) 942-3315: CT residents
(203) 324-9261

She'll be Comp-in' round the mountain when she comes, she'll be savin' time and money, she'll be shoppin' for her honey, she'll be Comp-in' round the mountain when she comes. For $25 a year, she'll receive unlimited toll-free price quotes on over 30,000 major brands (appliances, furniture, jewelry, etc.) available to subscribers of this "electronic shopping service." A late-breaking entry in *Best Buys*, their publication issued six times a year, listed a Litton Microwave #1590 for $366 ($498 at a discount store). If you've been waiting for the big brake in buying a new car, Comp-U-Card claims they can get it for you from their dealers or yours for $125 over dealer cost plus destination charges from Detroit to your door. **B, PQ/$25**

DIAL-A-BRAND
110 Bedford Ave.
Bellmore, NY 11710
(212) 978-4400
(516) 783-8220
(201) 653-6727

One ringy-dingy, two ringy-dingies . . . well, you won't get Ernestine, but you can get the low price lowdown on TVs, air conditioners, major appliances, videotape recorders, or microwaves. Used by major airlines, universities, and banks in an effort to save some cash as well as recommended by national consumer groups. Just call and give the model number of the item desired, and lo and behold, it's whisked C.O.D. to your door in the factory-sealed carton (complete with full warranty and service). Will exchange at no cost if damaged or defective on delivery. **PQ**

EBA WHOLESALE
2329 Nostrand Ave.
Brooklyn, NY 11210
(212) 252-3400

They voted to pass this EBA (Equal Bargains Amendment) and give up to 60% discounts on all major and small appliances, TVs, and video equipment. Liberate yourself from high-priced air conditioners. It's a g-ratifying experience to find dozens of products from manufacturers including Admiral, Panasonic, Litton, KitchenAid, Westinghouse, General Electric, and many more. Send a description of the item to EBA and they'll quote a price. If you decide you want to exchange for another model, they will be glad to make amends but a 20% restocking charge is required on returned merchandise. **PQ**

HUNTER AUDIO-PHOTO LTD.
507 Fifth Ave.
New York, NY 10017
(212) 986-1540

Watch out for these a-wrist-tocrats: Seiko, Bulova, Bulova Caravelle, and Casio watches up to 50% off. Take a few cheap shots at cameras by Canon, Pentax, Yashica, Fujica, and Nikon. Space out with Atari and Intellivision cartridges. Take a walk on the wild side with Sony, Sanyo, Panasonic, and Toshiba personal stereos. Write your own ticket with pens by Parker and Cross. Your days are numbered with adding machines by Canon, Sanyo, TI, and HP. Run that by us one more time, video movies at $10 below list like *Jane Fonda's Workout*, $49.95 (retail $59.95). Tally ho, this hunter's a fox. **PQ**

INTERNATIONAL SOLGO, INC.
1745 Hempstead Turnpike
Elmont, L.I., NY 11003
(800) 645-8162
(212) 675-3555 or 895-6996
(516) 354-8815

They mark the merchandise down Solgo faster. Major and small appliances, washers, dryers, air conditioners, televisions, camera equipment, jewelry, dishes, silverware, clocks, radios, luggage, and more are Sol-idly discounted, up to 40%. Sol-diers of your good fortune include: General Electric, Zenith, Magnavox, RCA, Sony, Sanyo, Polaroid, Toshiba, and Kodak. You can't say no to Seiko watches at a 40% discount. This firm has been around since 1933 with a lot of buying clout in the industry. They also carry a large selection of all voltage merchandise for export. They can arrange shipments to include prepaid charges for preparing the proper documentation, insurance, etc., for shipments either to pier or airport. **C** $5 (refundable with $100 first purchase)

LVT PRICE QUOTE HOT LINE
P.O. Box 444
Commack, NY 11725-0444
(800) 645-5010
(516) 234-8884: NY residents

No, LVT is not E.T.'s big brother, even though a lot of people do phone, and even though some prices they quote are "out of this world." Given the model number of an item carried by one of the 235 big-name manufacturers they do business with, LVT will quote a price to you, often as much as 40% lower than retail. Major appliances, televisions, microwave ovens, kerosene heaters, video recorders, video discs, telephone answering machines, computers, calculators, digital watches, office equipment, cash registers, and air conditioners are all items they regularly handle. There's free nationwide UPS delivery, with all merchandise covered by manufacturer's warranties. You must be sure of your selection—merchandise is not sent on approval. Write for the brands list, find out those model numbers, and phone home to LVT. They'll give you the Spiel, no matter your burg. **B, PQ**

MODERNAGE TV AND APPLIANCE
417 Casa Linda Plaza
Dallas, TX 75218
(214) 320-8914

With the flip of a switch you can mash, crumble, crush, slosh, wash, slurp, gurgle, churn, chill, sizzle, bake, freeze, irradiate, dehydrate, refrigerate, or just quietly vegetate in this ModernAge of TV and appliances. These folks sell trash compactors, air conditioners, microwaves, dishwashers, washer-dryers, refrigerators, TVs, and video stuff in such brand names as GE, Whirlpool, Amana, Zenith, RCA, Hitachi, Sony, Sharp, Sylvania, Litton, Friedrich, and Fedders at generally 10% to 20% (although occasionally more) off retail. Super deals can also be had in the top names in video cassette recorders, color cameras, and portable TVs. Shop your local area to determine what you want, and then call to describe your desired brand, features, size, and color. They'll quote a price and either ship your order themselves (generally within five working days), or drop ship from the factory. Everything's first-quality merchandise and has a factory warranty, but there are no exchanges or refunds. Ask for Wayne or Chuck. **PQ**

SEWIN' IN VERMONT
84 Concord Ave.
St. Johnsbury, VT 05819
(800) 451-5124
(802) 748-3803: VT residents

They're Sewin' in Vermont and their motto is: "Why pay through the nose when you can save through the mail?" Excellent values on many domestic and foreign brands of sewing machines, including the top-selling Singer Touch-Tronic 2010 Memory machine. The prestigious Viking and Pfaff brands were discounted 25% to 30% proving that a stitch in time saves, period. The price of the Viking 190 kept us in stitches at $549 ($799 retail). Write for manufacturers' brochures and price lists. **B, PQ**

SEW 'N' VAC
82 E. Main St.
Newark, DE 19711
(302) 368-2292

The swami says: "It is easier for a camel to pass through the eye of a needle, than for a rich man to be sucked into the dustbag of an Eureka." This company carries a good selection of foreign and domestic sewing machines, accessories, cabinets, and vacuum cleaners in such names as Viking, Elna, White, Pfaff, New Home, Eureka, and Panasonic. Their prices tend to be around 30% to 40% less, with some as much as 50% off retail. Their warranty is one year's labor on sewing machines; the exchange or refund period is 30 days. There's no restocking charge on returns and the catalog's free. Forget the swami, he doesn't have his act toga-ther! **C**

S & S DISCOUNT SERVICE
P.O. Box 76
Bedford Hills, NY 10507
(914) 666-4641: call collect

Ah, Sew! Confucius say: Man who needles wife wake up with hemorrhage. This company sells the Singer and Elna brands at 25% to 35% below retail. The most expensive Singer they carry costs $789; bought in a store at suggested list price it would cost $1,300. A-hem, we don't want to needle you into writing or calling for a price quote on the model you want. **PQ**

WISAN TV AND APPLIANCES
4085 Hylan Blvd.
Staten Island, NY 10308
(212) 356-7700

Wisan up and stop paying retail because this company has been saving people money on name-brand appliances, TVs, audio equipment, and a wide selection of TV and video screens for over 40 years. The savings coming over from this island were "ferry" good from 10% to 40%. We'd have to be Quas-y to pass up the Quasars, zany to leave Zeniths, silly to skip the Sylvanias, luny to leave the Littons, the Speed Queens, the Amanas, the world! They also take special orders. **PQ**

Cameras

Before deciding to order a camera by mail, visit several camera shops to look over the selection and get some professional assistance. When you have narrowed your choice down to a few, contact the mail-order sources to see if they have the equipment you want in stock. Resist the impulse to order over the phone. Always order in writing and keep copies of correspondence. If anything goes wrong, you'll have records. When the camera arrives, unpack carefully and save packing materials, in case you need to return it. Don't fill in the warranty cards until you're sure everything is working perfectly. Follow these tips and with the money you save, you can buy an extra lens!

AAA CAMERA EXCHANGE
43 Seventh Ave.
New York, NY 10011
(800) 221-9521: orders only
(212) 242-5800: NY residents; inquiries

Strictly a mail-order house, AAA features triple-good discounts on optics, many from famous makers. We found many discounted zoom lenses. A Nikon 80mm—200mm f/4.5 zoom retails for $540. But AAA has a comparable range and speed Cambron 70mm-210mm f/3.8 macro for only $180 and an un-named 75mm-205mm f/4.5 for only $140. That's a lot of money saved and this is only one of the many bargains. If you know what you Leica, but you're not a name snob, you'll get the picture fast. Contact Mr. Swede for information. **PQ**

B & H FOTO ELECTRONICS
119 W. 17th St.
New York, NY 10011
(800) 221-5662: orders only
(212) 807-7474: NY residents, inquiries

B & H has caught the light on photographic specialty equipment. Light meters by Gossen, Calculight, Sekonic, and Vivitar, tripods by Bogen, Velbon, Slik, Stitz. Even the strange and exotic Novoflex follow-focus systems that allow you to keep a subject in focus even as it moves. They've got Cokin's and Tokina's and Osaw's and Kiron's. The prices are hard to beat (15% to 20% lower) and the equipment is built to take it. There is a 14-day exchange or refund policy and no restocking charges. **PQ**

CAMBRIDGE CAMERA EXCHANGE, INC.
Seventh Avenue and 13th Street
New York NY 10011
(212) 675-8600

You'll find some of the sharpest students of camera equipment at Cambridge. While Cambridge isn't in England, or even in a suburb of Boston, discounts are in the vicinity of 30% to 50% on cameras, lenses, and lights. We found Nikons, Pentaxes, and Canons present and accounted for at far below retail prices, as well as less expensive, less well known equipment on the roll. Cambridge is one of the few stores handling European cameras like Hanimex, Praktica, and Exacta—these offered the greatest savings. This company has a 20-

day exchange or refund policy, no restocking charge on returns, and their merchandise is fully guaranteed. While they don't quote Shakespeare, they will quote prices. **PQ**

CAMERAS WEST OF SEATTLE
1908 Fourth Ave.
Seattle, WA 98101
(800) 626-1111: orders only
(206) 622-0066: WA residents, inquiries

West Coast prices compared favorably with their East Coast dis-counterparts. They specialize in the top five: Nikon, Pentax, Canon, Minolta, and Olympus. A Nikon FE was $277 ($400 list). All "full pack" (everything included from manufacturer). They ship in 24 hours, have a camera repair department, and carry all the major lines with a one-year warranty. Shipping costs about $8. Trades accepted. These folks are an f-stop above anyone within 1,000 miles. **PQ**

EXECUTIVE PHOTO AND SUPPLY CORP.
120 W. 31st St.
New York, NY 10001
(800) 223-7327: orders only
(212) 947-5290: NY, AK, HI residents, inquiries

We always thought executives were known more for flashing rolls of bills than rolls of film, but then again, how else can they see the Big Picture? Executive Photo is a midtown photo dealer with a less buttoned-down, traditional outlook. Besides cameras, lenses, film, paper, and photographic accessories in names like Nikon, Minolta, and Canon, they sell computers, calculators, and electronic gadgetry as well. They have a very wide range of equipment. Prices tend to be 40% to 50% lower than retail competition and in line with other NYC photo mail-order companies. (Executive sells at dealer's net.) Whether you're the Big Cheese, or just someone who gets chewed out a lot, you'll like this place. **PQ**

FLASH PHOTO
1206 Avenue J
Brooklyn, NY 11230
(212) 253-7121

Quick as a flash, you can capture top-name photo equipment from

Pentax, Minolta, and Nikon at 10% to 30% off. They also sell kitchen-ware and appliances by Westinghouse and Maytag, and sound equipment by Sony, Panasonic, and more. If they don't stock it, they can special order it. Stop down and see them sometime. **PQ**

FOCUS ELECTRONICS, INC.
4523 13th Ave.
Brooklyn, NY 11219
(800) 221-0828: orders only
(212) 871-7600: NY residents, inquiries

Focus is no hocus-pocus place even though they juggle cameras, computers, video and stereo equipment, large and small appliances, and even film in their store. They've been in business for 15 years, so they won't do a disappearing act, either. They can pull most cameras out of their hat (Nikon, Kodak, Canon, Pentax, Vivitar, Minolta, Kiron, Tokina, even the prestigious Leica) at prices "lower" than full-price retail stores. It's still a mystery as to how they do it, but then again, maybe we just weren't focusing. Returns accepted within 14 days if in original mint condition as shipped. Restocking charge 10%. **C $2** (refundable)

47TH ST. PHOTO
36 E. 19th St.
New York, NY 10003
(800) 221-7774
(800) 221-5858
(212) 260-4410: AK, HI, NY residents

Since 47th St. Photo is located at 36 E. 19th St., we can only conclude that either somebody's heavily into numerology or else they've got it in for the postman. We'll forgive them if they don't "address" this issue, because while these people may not know where they're at, they definitely know what they're doing. A broad selection of top brands, efficient service, 15-day return/exchange policy, and discounts of 20% to 75% off retail on cameras, watches, audio video, computers, TV games, computing typewriters, dictation equipment, answering machines, and cordless phones make this company a top name in mail-order. Their selection of electronics is so broad they have a whole catalog devoted just to video products. If you say you read about them in *The Underground Shopper*, they'll only charge you a buck (regular, $2) for their catalog. Minimum order, $35. Closes early Friday, all day Saturday, but open Sunday to Friday. Toll-free inquiries handled by a well-trained and well-versed sales force. **C $2** (see special offer in write up), **B, PQ**

GARDEN CAMERA
345 Seventh Ave.
New York, NY 10001
(800) 223-5830: orders only
(800) 223-0595: orders only
(212) 868-1420: NY residents, inquiries

Not long ago we heard of a man who accidentally locked himself in a darkroom. He died of exposure. Needless to say, it was not a pretty picture. But here's a story that won't make you shutter: good prices, good service, good selection, and ads that tell you exactly what you're getting. This company has a large darkroom equipment center with such items as enlargers, meters, Cibachrome paper and chemicals, color drums, and analyzers. In fact, you can find cameras, videos, calculators, electronic games, watches, computers, and telephones in such names as Nikon, Minolta, Canon, Pentax, Olympus, Kodak, Polaroid, Hasselblad, Cibachrome, Seiko, Sony, Panasonic, RCA, Atari, Coleco, Phone-Mate, Code-A-Phone, Freedom Phone, and others at 30% to 50% below retail. There's a $50 minimum order and a 10-day limit on returns. Film and mailers are discounted over your local drugstore. Ordering's a snap, so see what develops. **C**

HIRSCH PHOTO
699 Third Ave.
New York, NY 10017
(212) 557-1150

No "Judd-heads" need to Taxi in to this Hirsch outlet. With a no-questions-asked service policy, years of reliable customer recommendations and bargain prices, you'll cross the photo finish line without the meter running. No hidden surprises and name-brand camera equipment puts you in the driver's seat. **PQ**

JERSEY CAMERA
540 Cedar Lane
Teaneck, NJ 07666
(201) 836-8863

Jersey Camera has a lot of stores and even more equipment. If you live in Jersey, you might just want to stop into one of their four stores. They feature camera specials, where you not only get a camera, but a flash and some other accessories as well. In addition to cameras, they also sell calculators and video recorders. **PQ**

MASTER COLOR LAB
G.P.O. Box 30M
Newark, NJ 07101

Yes, master, color labs *aren't* camera stores, they're film processing labs. High volume and high-quality business can save you money. It takes a little longer to go through the mail, but Master processes it the day they get it. Processing and prints for a 24-exposure roll of Kodacolor (using only Kodak chemicals and paper) was only $4.45 (compared to local drugstores, $9 to $15). Multiply that times your vacation pix and you've already saved enough to buy a new strobe. Being in business 30 years means somebody finds their prints charming. **PQ**

MINIFILM PHOTO
44 W. 44th St.
New York, NY 10036
(212) 869-7820

Minifilm's prices are as low as prices get, their ads are easy to read, there are no attempts at confusion or deception, and they carry a wide range of cameras, accessories, and equipment from Olympus, Canon, Polaroid, Pentax, and others at a 10% to 30% discount. Return for credit within ten days. **C 50 cents**

OLDEN CAMERA
1265 Broadway
New York, NY 10001
(800) 223-6312: orders only
(212) C-A-M-E-R-A-S: NY residents, inquiries

Olden is one of the granddaddies of the mail-order camera business. They've got ordering down to a science and selection down to an art. From new Nikons to old Minoltas, if it's photographic, they sell it. They carry known and not-so-known meters and motors, stereo cameras (how about a used Viewmaster personal stereo camera for only $198.95?), and slide projectors. Leasing plans available for purchases of $3,000 or more. Buyer protection plan allows you to return equipment, no questions asked, in 30 days as long as it is returned in its original condition. They even take trade-ins through the mail. Olden is a top-notch organization. You won't expose yourself to any dangers dealing with them. **C $2** (credited toward first purchase)

SAVERITE PHOTO AND ELECTRONICS
46 Canal St.
New York, NY 10002
(800) 223-4212
(212) 966-6655: NY residents

Remember the hunchback of Notre Dame, Quasi Photo? Well, if the name of this company doesn't ring a bell, we have a hunch it will soon. He took pictures of the belfry with a camera bought from Saverite. They also carry small appliances, silver, stereo and video equipment, TV screens, Casio keyboards, calculators, and watches discounted 40% to 45%. Minimum of $25 for charge orders and a 20% deposit is required on all orders (unless sent C.O.D.). Don't cut out this middleman (Mr. Martin Mittleman, owner), he's pulling for you. **C, PQ**

SHARP PHOTO
1225 Broadway, Suite 501
New York, NY 10001
(800) 223-7633: orders only
(212) 532-1733: NY residents, inquiries

Sharp is a midtown mail-order photo store that features name-brand, high-volume equipment at good discounts. They don't advertise much darkroom equipment, but they are strong, strong, strong in 35mm cameras and lenses. Their catalog is helpful in making decisions. A special department sells electronics like watches and Sony Walkmans. And, unlike many mail-order houses, they sell film at big discounts. If you're going on vacation and need 20 rolls of Kodachrome, you could get it at Sharp for only $130 including Kodak processing. Get sharp and save some cool green this summer. **C**

SOLAR CINE PRODUCTS, INC.
4247 S. Kedzie Ave.
Chicago, IL 60632
(800) 621-8796: orders only
(312) 254-8310: IL residents, inquiries

Get variety in your mailbox and focus on the star performers. All the cameras and lenses you could possibly consider buying are carefully described in the catalog. Film and processing, wedding albums, movie gear, darkroom clips, video movies, rear projection screens, film handling gloves, calculators, and pocket slide viewers. A veritable warehouse of photographic products, situated right in the middle of the country. They spell out in detail what they have to sell. **C**

SPIRATONE
135-06 Northern Blvd.
Flushing, NY 11354
(800) 221-9695: orders only
(212) 886-2000: NY residents, inquiries

Spiratone is *the* camera specialty equipment store. They don't sell Nikons or Canons, but they pioneered the field of accessories over 40 years ago to make your cameras do things you never thought possible. Their catalog alone is the source for exciting ideas for the creative photographer. Some of their special lenses are simply unmatched values. The Spiratone 400mm "Sharpshooter" telephoto, $70, is one of the finest bargains in all of photodom. They have more special filters than Kodiak has bears. Exchanges only, subject to prior authorization. **C 75 cents**

T.M. CHAN & CO.
P.O. Box 33881
Sheung Wan Post Office
Hong Kong

Ever wonder what happened to Charlie Chan's heirs? The great sleuth's namesakes have cracked the case of the overpriced piece of electronic equipment. We grew suspicious when we priced the Asahi Pentax ME camera with a 50mm f/1.7 lens and case at $277 (about what the catalog distributors offer on a regular basis without across-the-ocean anxiety). However, the watch selection clued us into a Seiko Sports 100 watch for only $99 (retail $215) and Rolex watches in the sub-$1,000 category. We detected similar bargains (savings of 30% to 50%) on their high-quality clothing tailored from the finest British and Italian fabrics. Bank check, money order, certified check, or cashier check (no credit cards) must accompany every order before shipping. All goods come with a one-year warranty and insurance is extra. **C**

WESTSIDE CAMERA INC.
2400 Broadway
New York, NY 10024
(212) 877-8760

"Maria! I just bought a camera for Maria!" Cool your Jets and stop fighting for the lowest price. This gang's got it, man. There's a place for us, and it's here. Westside's story is selling all photographic equipment and supplies at 25% to 30% lower than retail. Don't walk the streets after dark, stay in the darkroom since all the equipment and chemicals are also discounted. They have a $10 minimum, can you handle it? Be tough, write to Barry Glick and ask for a brochure or price quote. That love affair you're having with a Nikon doesn't have to be just a dream. Make it real, man. **B, PQ, SASE**

Electronics

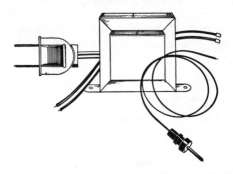

The thing to remember in purchasing electronics is that technology updates itself almost daily. Prices on electronics generally drop from year to year. If there is something you're dying for, but think you can last a few more months without, wait a bit and see if the price drops. If you've just got to have some nickel cadmium batteries or the latest Apple computer, shop around. Prices are extremely competitive.

AEROCOMP INC.
Redbird Airport, Building 8
P.O. Box 24829
Dallas, TX 75224
(800) 824-7888 operator 24
(214) 337-4346: TX residents

Jettison your overloaded file cabinets and get into the computer age at a discount. You can order Aerocomp's 5¼-inch and 8-inch floppy disc drive or a complete line of Radio Shack's TRS-80 hardware and software discounted 10% to 15%. If you're a budding novelist, you can get a Starwriter printer and become a star. The Epson or Okidata lines are OK, too. **C**

ALLIED ELECTRONICS
401 E. Eighth St.
Fort Worth, TX 76102
(800) 331-9106
(800) 523-3925: TX residents
(817) 336-5401: TX residents

Earth-bound space invaders order their mix & match mechanical components from this company by mail or at one of the 21 allied stores across the country. They get a charge out of nickel cadmium batteries, two packages of two for $5.95. They attribute their long life to the myriad of parts in their 258-page catalog featuring the oldest and newest styles in plugboards, memory circuits, rectifiers, neon indicator lights, adapters, and connectors. Prices don't compute as "wholesale to the public" for the small-volume buyer. Get on their mailing list and become allies for special small-quantity sales. **C**

COMPUTER SPECIALTIES
1251 Broadway
El Cajon, CA 92021
(800) 854-2833: orders only
(714) 579-0330: CA residents

Nearly everything for Apple, IBM, and Atari computers at "exciting discounts" including software (cassette demos, "Applebug Debugger," "Fastgammon"—even the "Asteroids in Space" program), hardware, interface cards, and accessories like the Apple Joystick (whatever that is) as well as printers and monitors discounted 35%. Manufacturers' catalogs are available. **C**

COMPUTIQUE
3211 S. Harbor Blvd.
Santa Anna, CA 92704
(800) 854-0523
(800) 432-7066: CA residents
(714) 549-7373: inquiries

Computique is a boutique for computers, calculators, musical key-boards, answering machines, microcassette recorders, and computer games. Brands read like a "who's who" in electronics: Atari, Texas Instruments, Hewlett-Packard, Toshiba, Casio, Sharp, Seiko, GTE, ITT, Apple—all at calculated discounts. They promise to meet or beat the Asteroids off of any competitor's price on most items if merchandise is in stock. Minimum order is $15. Some items, like the Osborne Personal Computer, were not discounted. **PQ**

ELEK-TEK
6557 N. Lincoln Ave.
Chicago, IL 60645
(800) 621-1269
(312) 631-7800: IL residents

As one might expect, Elek-Tek elects to offer high-tech consumer electronics direct to the customer. Major manufacturers such as Hewlett-Packard, Texas Instruments, Canon, Sharp, Casio, Mattel Intellivision, and Atari are carried with percentage discounts varying but often being quite substantial, particularly on more expensive items. The HP-38C calculator was $75 ($150 list), and Atari video game cartridges like "Asteroids" and "Berserk" were $25 ($31.95 manufacturer's suggested retail). "Defender" and "Pac-Man" were $29 ($37.95 list). All merchandise is covered by the manufacturer's warranty; Elek-Tek will replace defective merchandise within the first 30 days. Minimum order, $15. **C**

ETCO
Route 9N North Country SC
Plattsburgh, NY 12901
(518) 561-8700

From alarm parts to zeners, Etco sells a huge array of electronic equipment in their 96-page catalog. Hobbyists and electro buffs should have a field day with this one. Experimenters in unscrambling cable TV signals should tune into Etco's channel for electrifying, shocking discounts of 20% to 80%. **C**

INTERNATIONAL ELECTRONICS UNLIMITED
435 First St., Suite 19
Solvang, CA 93463
(805) 688-2747

All the accessories the mechanical brain needs are here. Who can resist this season's styles of resistors, transistors, capacitors, IC sockets, diodes, dip switches, solid state buzzers, LEDs, and project kits. Make your neighbor's electrodes light up green with envy when you can buy a lot cheaper here than at Radio Shack. Minimum order is $10. **B**

LORAIN ELECTRONICS
2307 Leavitt Road
Lorain, OH 44052-4194
(216) 835-8610
(216) 282-6116: Lorain residents

Get smart and stop talking into your shoe. A gentle $99 will buy one of the hottest two-way radios ("handy talkies") on the market today. This company carries "walkie-talkies," repeater systems, on-board (boat) paging systems, etc., even top-of-the-line car telephones that you own, not rent, all at a savings of approximately 20%. All products include a warranty. Lorain services what they sell. If you already own a marine radio, you can take advantage of their VHF ship-to-shore radio station serving the Great Lakes area. Write for their free credit card, which will save you money on your ship-to-shore calls using Lorain's VHF channel. **PQ**

MICRO MANAGEMENT SYSTEMS
2803 Thomasville Road E.
Cairo, GA 31728
(800) 841-0860
(912) 377-7120: GA residents

Micro's scoped out the competition and focused in on saving their customers 15% to 20% on a variety of computer products including the TRS-80 Model III 16K for $748 (retail $999). TV and video equipment by Radio Shack and Panasonic rounded out their inventory. **B**

PAN AMERICAN ELECTRONICS, INC.
1117 Conway
Mission, TX 78572
(800) 531-7466
(512) 581-2766: TX residents

Mission's accomplished with accomplished discounts of 10% to 20% off the price of Radio Shack products including the TRS-80 computers and software. Your prospecting will pan out and you'll also find TVs, radios, security systems, and calculators in them thar' hills of Mission, the birthplace of Dallas Cowboys' Coach Tom Landry. **B**

PHONE CONTROL SYSTEMS
92 Marcus Ave.
New Hyde Park, NY 11040
(516) 248-3636
(212) 343-1215

Does your phone control you? Put a ring around the caller with Phone Control Systems. You can get wired by choosing from a large selection of answering machines from Code-A-Phone, Panasonic, Phone-Mate, Record-A-Call, Sanyo, and others. Portable phones let you take it with you when you go. Brands include Electra, Extend-A-Phone, ITT, Fanon, Phone-Mate, Technidyne, La Phone, and Webcor. Dialers, diverters, dictaters, transcribers, and novelty telephones . . . it's one way to find out who's "phoney" among your friends. They also carry electronic games, calculators, and tape recorders. **C, B, PQ**

POLY PAKS, INC.
P.O. Box 942
South Lynnfield, MA 01940
(800) 343-3086
(617) 245-3828: MA residents

Polly want a pak-er? Polypak sells a hodgepodge of surplus electronic equipment, including such items as Opto couplers, solenoids, VU meters, and more. There are wide assortments of miscellaneous packaged items (a potpourri of diodes, a grab-bag of transistors, etc.) for those partial to pot luck. Discounts are 25% plus and during their frequent sales you save up to 75%, com-parrot to retail prices. **C**

TELEPHONES UNLIMITED
P.O. Box 1147
San Diego, CA 92112
(619) 235-8088

When it comes right down to the wire, TU is the people's voice. Speak easy and put high-pitched phone prices on hold. Listen, they plug into only newer styles from Mickey Mouse phones, music-on-hold phones, or bean bag phones with built-in doodle pads. Only a push button away is a GTE flip-phone for $59.95 (retail $65) or a standard push-button desk phone for $45.50 ($65 list). They're your hot line to savings on parts and accessories, too, from jacks to "aid-to-hearing" amplifiers and modular conversion kits. **C** $1 (refundable)

Stereo and Video

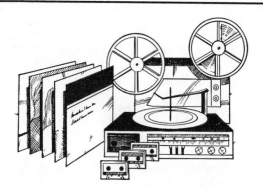

Audiophiles and video-nuts should pick up a copy of *Consumer Reports* for the facts on turntables and readouts. They can provide you with unbiased reports on advantages and disadvantages, quality, and prices of all major models of stereo and video equipment. You can save yourself a lot of trouble if you do your research before you buy. And for your listening pleasure, we've included record and tape vendors in this section.

ANDRÉ PERRAULT
73 E. Allen
Winooski, VT 05404
(800) 833-9000
(800) 462-8424: NY residents
(802) 655-1095

This fellow holds a lot of records, but you won't find him in the record books—his records are all full of holes. (What's more, while it's often said that records are made to be broken, his records are made to be played.) If you haven't guessed by now, André's into music. He has an unbelievable selection of classical records from Arthur Rubinstein to Zubin Mehta, Brahms to Strauss. If you give a Wolf(gang) whistle, you can get Amadeus Mozart; and for the price of a stamp you can quit beating the bush for Beethoven and receive their monthly newsletter. They carry all domestic records and foreign labels such as EMI, Deka, Hyperion, Argo, Chandos, Abby, Pathé Marconi, RCA France, RCA Germany, Electrola, Schwann Musica Mundi, Acanta, Telefunken, and Psallite (specializes in organ music) to name a few at very reasonable prices. Convenience of ordering under no obligation, knowledgeable salespeople versed on every level of music appreciation, and low prices . . . they're playing our song. Also in Canada at P.O. Box 2000, Bedford, Quebec, JOJ 1A0. **B**

ANNEX OUTLET LTD.
43 Warren St.
New York, NY 10007
(212) 964-8661

Annex marks the spot for savings up to 45% on video recorders, videotapes, video cameras, TVs, and home and car stereos. They carry such brands as Sony, Panasonic, Pioneer, Hitachi, RCA, TDK, and JVC. There's a $4 minimum order for shipping, no restocking charge, and they'll exchange damaged merchandise within seven days. Catalogs come out monthly—if you don't see something you want, call or write. **C, PQ**

ARCHER AVE. STORE
4193 Archer
Chicago, IL 60632
(312) 523-2323

We hit the bull's eye: Sony blank tapes at prices that have been, until now, unheard of! We broke the record and took 25% to 40% discounts on other name-brand sound and videotapes. If they don't have the tape you request in stock, a representative will return the order and show the restock date with an SASE. Minimum order is 10 to 12 tapes, but at these prices you'll break the record, too. **C, B, PQ**

AUDIO ADVISOR, INC.
Box 6202 US
Grand Rapids, MI 49506
(616) 451-3868

Dear Audy: My husband is tweeting me badly. Last month, he hit me and I slipped a disc. He still wants me to cook his tuner casserole before he gets home from work. More than that, if he woofs at me one more time, I'm going to unleash my fury. I can't take his constant needling. It's like a broken record. My head is spinning. What should I do to turn the tables? Signed, Played Out in Yonkers. Dear Out: Take my advice and get rid of the bozo who's bonkers in Yonkers, then check out this company. They are 15% to 50% lower on the average and they carry mid- to high-quality stereo and video products from over 200 manufacturers. Restocking charge of 15%. **C**

CALIFORNIA SOUND
P.O. Box A82088
San Diego, CA 92138
(800) 854-2273: U.S. & Puerto Rico residents, except CA
(800) 542-6228: CA residents, except San Diego
(619) 578-9692: San Diego, AK, HI residents

With what frequency have you searched for the perfect car stereo only to encounter amplified prices and salespeople speaking on another wavelength about tweeters, woofers, wow, and flutter? Treble yourself no further. Listen, "America's car stereo experts" pull the plug on high-priced car stereo equipment with five-year warranties and free shipping. At the top of the charts were Pioneer, Craig, Sanyo, Jensen, Sony, and Blaupunkt. Their catalog provides advice on what to consider in component systems and an easy-to-understand glossary of technical terms. All items are priced from 10% to 25% lower than retail and sometimes lower still. **C**

CHESTERFIELD MUSIC SHOPS, INC.
12 Warren St.
New York, NY 10007
(212) 964-3380

Make note of this music shop if you like to hear of sound savings (up to 80% off) on records and tapes. They've got big band, pop, folk, renaissance, classical, opera, and all that jazz. Prices sounded off from $2.99. A special "inflation busters" package offered five LPs (or tapes) for $11.96 (a $24.90 value) and put a song in our heart without taking money from our pocket. Four records went for $9.99—one of our researchers (of dubious musical taste) wanted such all-time favorites as: 1) *Bavarian Yodeling Songs and Polkas* (complete with clog dances as an added bonus), 2) *Rudy Vallee Sings Heigh-Ho Everybody,* 3) *Yugoslavian Folk Music of Macedonia,* and 4) (the incomparable) *Pidgin-English Songs of the South Seas.* Thankfully, the record player is baroque. **B**

CONSUMER ELECTRONICS
P.O. Box 550
Mt. Vernon, NY 10551
(800) 431-2932: orders only
(914) 664-2909: NY residents

While we're not big consumers of electronics (we prefer food), as hungry bargain hunters we can't resist these palatable prices. We perused their 32-page menu of products and found blank tapes by such manufacturers as TDK, Maxell, 3M, BASF, Sony, Scotch, Fuji, and Memorex. We also saw Sony and Pioneer car stereos, Pioneer and Jensen speakers, Blaupunkt, Concord, Sanyo, and Craig stereo cassette players, etc. Prices ranged to 40% off retail, depending on the type of merchandise. There's a minimum order—10 tapes, assorted, or $100. That's what we call a reel meal. **C**

THE CULTURAL GUILD
P.O. Box 5468
Richardson, TX 75080
(214) 231-0142

If you're watching a bunch of people shouting at each other, waving their arms, and cavorting to beat the band (and none of what you're seeing or hearing makes any sense), then you're either at the opera or at the state capital. The Cultural Guild has composed a series of cassette tapes expressly to help you become more familiar with some of the world's best-loved operas. You'll learn to recognize the key musical themes and arias from the operas and gain insight into their characters, plots, dialogues, and meanings. There are no intimidating overtones, just explanations in both conversational and musical language. You can bone up on *La Boheme* on the way to work or you can give your boss *Madame Butterfly.* (Fluttery will get you everywhere.) When these folks can figure a way to make government comprehensible, we'll *really* shout "Bravo!" **PQ**

DIRECT DISCOUNTS
P.O. Box 841
Cooper Station, NY 10276
(800) 221-2848: orders only
(212) 254-3125: NY residents

Direct Discounts turns tables over its retail competitors by raising the volume and turning down the treble of retail prices for famous names in stereo and video equipment. They'll fill up your senses with 10% to 30% savings on all you love to see and hear. **C**

DISCOTRONIC
713 Military Trail
West Palm Beach, FL 33406
(800) 327-7309
(305) 689-2022: FL residents

You ought'a be in pictures . . . Waiting until your celluloid favorites roll into the dollar theaters may be one ticket to cheap cinematic thrills. Buying new and used videotapes at Discotronic is another. We projected new movie releases at 10 to 50% off and four-star discounts up to 50% on reruns. Exchanges on used movies were $10. From general release to XXX, this 7-year-old video house charges a $3 fee for fast delivery. All major video equipment also shown. If the primal screen is your therapy, you can get the picture here. Defective merchandise replaced within 14 days of purchase. **C**

DISCOUNT SOUND, INC.
12200 Parklawn Drive
Rockville, MD 20852
(301) 881-8890

Just because this company calls itself Discount Sound doesn't mean it's only for those who have tin ears. They have stereo and video equipment built by such companies as Technics, Becker, Sanyo, Toshiba, and others and they'll quote prices if you tell them what you want. There are no refunds on opened merchandise, no exchanges after seven days, and there's a 10% restocking charge on returns. Give them a phone call—they're (dis)counting on it. **PQ**

GLOBAL PRODUCTS
3009 Faulkner Drive
Rowlett, TX 75088
(214) 475-4021

We thought all records were flat, but if they say they're Global, well okay. A membership/coupon book costs $30 and entitles you to order 30 albums at a retail value of $8.98 each for $1 each (plus $1.50 per album postage). Order from current charts or shop any record store for the names of albums of your choice. As long as the record is available, they can get it for you. No out-of-print or outdated records on a backlist. We could have chosen from Kenny Rogers to Pat Benatar, Eric Clapton to Waylon Jennings, or the Vienna Philharmonic sausaged in between. **B**

INTERNATIONAL WHOLESALERS
17866 Ipco Road
(N.E. Fifth Ave.)
Miami, FL 33162
(800) 327-0596
(305) 940-7542: FL residents

Savings averaged 30% on electronic games, wide-screen TVs, video recorders, and other products by leading manufacturers. We found a discontinued line of Sony Beta video recorders for $850 (retail $1,295). **B, PQ**

J & R MUSIC WORLD
23 Park Row
New York, NY 10038
(800) 221-8180: orders
(212) 732-8600: NY residents

High fidelity is a sound virtue, 'cause nobody likes a speaker that squeaks around. This maestro of music mail-order houses blends 30% to 50% discounts with a huge selection of products. Their catalog of audio, video, and electronics runs well over 200 pages (over 10,000 products) and conducts a symphony of famous-name cartridges, headphones, audio and videotapes, video electronics, computers, communications items, car stereos, calculators, and video games. Their record and tape catalog consists of 32 pages of predominantly popular and disco music, although they do have soundtracks, jazz, reggae, C&W, oldies, easy listening, etc., as well. (Classical records were fugue and far between.) The modal record price was $6.99. There's a $25 minimum order, a 15% restocking charge, and exchanges on defective merchandise within 30 days of receipt of merchandise. The A/V/E catalog's $2.95; the record and tape catalog's free. **C** ($ varies)

LYLE CARTRIDGES
365 Dahill Road
Brooklyn, NY 11218
(800) 221-0906
(212) 871-3303: NY, HI, AK residents

Lyle be seeing you in all familiar places . . . wherever there's a phonograph. Cartridges, replacement needles, and record care items from Shure, Pickering, Stanton, Audio-Technica, Empire, Grado, ADC, Sonus, Ortofon, and Micro Acoustics are all with 15% to 75% discounts. Minimum order is $15. Add $2 for handling, plus extra for shipping C.O.D. or by UPS. **C, PQ, SASE**

THE RECORD HUNTER
507 Fifth Ave.
New York, NY 10017
(212) 697-8970

Got a minuet? If you've got a bad case of Saturday Nacht Fever and have been itching for some entertainment, you can step out in style to the classical big symphony sound of Mozart, Haydn, Beethoven, Schubert, Strauss, or Mendelssohn at good discounts. Names like Dvořák, Smetana, Borodin, and Khachaturian compose a Slavonic festival of sound. Along with their classical records, TRH also has tapes and records for nonclassical music lovers. We saw *The Best of the Oak Ridge Boys* for $3.68 ($4.18 in tape) and were intrigued by the exercise record entitled, *How to Keep Your Husband Happy,* $3.68 by the legendary Debbie Drake. A five-LP set of the collected works of Simon & Garfunkel was $21.99. There's no minimum order: They'll exchange defective merchandise and give credit on returns. **C, B**

ROSE RECORDS
214 S. Wabash Ave.
Chicago, IL 60604
(312) 987-9044

Everything's coming up Rose's. Record prices can present a thorny problem, but this place can soft-petal a solution. While we never promised you a Rose bargain, albums at 20% off list smelled like a pretty sweet deal. Budding classical music lovers will find scores of selections, although folk, pop, blues, soul, and jazz albums are also there for the picking. Cutout LPs (LPs "cut out" of a record company's regular stock) started blooming at $2.99; with a list price of $4.98, their price was $3.98; and $5.98 albums were $4.75. A nice arrangement for those who like to face the music without paying the piper. **C**

SOUND REPRODUCTION, INC.
7 Industrial Road
Fairfield, NJ 07006
(201) 227-6720

"OK youse guys, sound off: Brands?" Technics! Sony! Sansui! Pioneer! Akai! ("I can't hear you!") Hitachi! Panasonic! Sharp! ("Louder!") Koss! Jensen! ("At ease, men.") For 26 years this company has taken its orders for audio components, etc., from the public and they're not about to quit after so many years of distinguished service. Prices are about 20% to 40% off retail on about 40 brands. Enlist the aid of their catalog before you march somewhere else for your next audio purchase. **C**

SOUNDS GOOD
9535 Cozycroft Ave.
Chatsworth, CA 91311
(213) 341-4359

Sounds Good, in fact, sounds almost too good to be true. This company is more than just a source for pop, classical, and jazz records— they also stock many hard-to-find imports and cutouts at up to 50% off. Their new catalog consists of over 100 pages of record listings, etc. We saw a cutout of Steve Martin's, *A Wild and Crazy Guy* for $2.99, along with lots of rock records and tapes. There's a $10 minimum order with charge cards and no restocking charge on returns. We groove on the sounds of good music when we're not in a financial hole, so if you shop underground, you'll stay above ground longer. **C $1**

S & S SOUND CITY
58 W. 45th St.
New York, NY 10036
(800) 223-0360
(212) 575-0210: NY residents

Morris coded an SOS to S & S and they dashed to our rescue with the information we requested. This company offers TVs, video equipment, electronics, appliances, air conditioners, and microwaves at 25% to 40% lower than most retail stores. Brands carried include Sony, Panasonic, RCA, Zenith, Amana, Toshiba, Litton, Hitachi, Friedrich, and Air Temp. There's a $30 minimum, a seven-day return policy (as long as the purchased item is in the factory carton with all packing material intact), and no restocking charge. Items carry a standard manufacturer's warranty. All things considered, we'd say S & S is a City built on a "sound" economic foundation. **B**

STEREO CORP. OF AMERICA
1629 Flatbush Ave.
Brooklyn, NY 11210
(800) 221-0974: orders only 9 a.m. to 5 p.m. EST
(800) 327-1531: NY, HI, AK residents, 5:30 p.m. to 10 p.m. EST
(212) 253-8888: inquiries

List-en up, and take a deep breath . . . Advent, Acutex, Alpine, AR, Aiwa, Altec, Akai, Audio Technica, Audiovox, ADC, AKG (and that's just the A's), BSR, BASF, Cannon, DBX, Dynavector, Discwasher, Dual, Empire, EPI, Fisher, GLI, Harmon Kardon, Hitachi (bored yet?), JBL, JVC, Jensen, KLH, Kenwood, Koss, Maxwell, Marantz, MXR (sounds like a roll call of sci-fi characters, doesn't it?), Nagatron, Numark, Onkyo, Optonica, Olympus, Ortofon, Osawa, O'Sullivan, Panasonic, Phase Linear, Pickering (spelling out all these names is no picnic for us, either), Pioneer, Sennheiser, Stanton, Sanyo, Sansui, Shure, Sony, Soundguard, TDK, TEAC, Technics, Visonik, and more (Whew!) are recognizable names in receivers, speakers, turntables (here we go again), cartridges, cassette decks, separate components, mini and micro components, headphones, videos, car stereos, portables (almost finished!), blank tapes, and audio furniture carried by this 31-year-old firm. Discounts of 30% off list were commonplace at this place. **C, PQ**

STEREO COST CUTTERS
Box 551 US
Dublin, OH 43017
(614) 889-2117

They can save you 30% to 50% and more. "Oh, cut it out." No, really, on stereo equipment closeouts, special purchases, and discounts. "Oh, cut it out. Ah, you're killing me, tee hee." Brands include: Dynaco, Marantz, Dual, MXR. "Wahhh, that's so funny, cut it out, stop it will ya' please." Just pick up their catalog sometime and see for yourself: receivers, turntables, cartridges, cassette decks, portables, video recorders, amps, equalizers, speakers, furniture, and kits. "That's the funniest thing I've ever heard. What's that name again?" **C**

VVV
3906 Cedar Springs
Dallas, TX 75219
(214) 522-3470

Here, here! Hard-to-find British imports aren't hard to find at VVV. New Wave has splashed down and is dreadlocked with reggae in sales. The 45s are holding up well at the cash register and the independently produced albums are standing alone. Electronic music and soundtracks were found milling around, too. Used records of every type available. Used new releases were $2.50 to $3. Periodic sales. Contact Neil Caldwell. **PQ**

WISCONSIN DISCOUNT STEREO
2417 W. Badger Road
Madison, WI 53713
(800) 356-9514
(608) 271-6889: WI residents

A friend in cheese is a friend indeed, but we'll forgo the idle cheddar and get right to the pint. In "The Dairy State," the folks churn to the beat of Pioneer, Kenwood, Sony, Marantz, and other top-line stereo components, at prices that won't make your blood curdle. Discounts of 10% to 30% are no udder disaster, when they save your hard urned cash. **B, PQ**

7.

NOT FOR JOCKS ONLY

Automotive

Over the years, we've heard so many horror stories about auto mechanics. If you can't take time to mount your own muffler or you haven't the slightest desire to adjust your own carburetor, at least you can choose a mechanic who is right for the job. For the price of a stamp, you can receive a list of local service mechanics who have been certified in specialized areas of training. Name of the company, address, and telephone are given. Write to the National Institute for Automotive Service Excellence, 1825 K. St., N.W., Washington, DC 20006 or call (202) 833-9646 for more information.

BELLE TIRE DISTRIBUTORS, INC.
Competition Division
12190 Grand River
Detroit, MI 48204
(313) 834-3880

These belles are properly at-tired by such companies as Michelin, BF Goodrich, Goodyear, Firestone, Uniroyal, Pirelli, and Trans Am priced 15% lower than some full-priced stores. Check local sources, however, before purchasing long distance to insure maximum savings. Shipping is $5 to $20 per tire. **PQ**

CAPITAL CYCLE CORP.
2328 Champlain St., N.W.
Washington, DC 20009
(202) 387-7360

Too pooped to pop a wheelie, or looking for a spokes-person for your mechanical cause? Capital Cycle got us charged up with the largest inventory of genuine and original BMW parts in the U.S.—and at 20% off retail. Frankly, we weren't too exhausted to give a muffled roar of approval because Easy Riders like us don't need any price shocks to help us get our bearings, or get us all choked up. You can rev up your classy chassis here with everything from a vacuum screw gasket to telescopic fork parts. They carry over 4,000 parts in stock and promise clutch performances on mail and telephone orders. The catalog we got could only be described as (what else?) encycle-opedic. Minimum order $15 ($25 with Visa or MasterCard). **C**

CHERRY AUTO PARTS
5650 N. Detroit Ave.
Toledo, OH 43612
(800) 537-8677
(419) 476-7222: OH residents

Repair to Cherry's on your next pit stop and say "cherry-o" to high-priced auto parts. Choose quality used parts for foreign cars from their large selection—no lemons here. They have a large selection of small electric parts. A carburetor was $50 (retail $150). We cannot tell a lie: Most parts have been removed from some poor unfortunate car that has met an untimely death. **PQ**

CLINTON CYCLE AND SALVAGE, INC.
6709 Old Branch Ave.
Camp Springs, MD 20748
(301) 449-3550

Here's something that will make you want to crack up. Clinton operates a mail-order used motorcycle parts business specializing in Japanese 250cc and larger street motorcycles in names like Kawasaki, Suzuki, Yamaha, and Honda. They offer 40% to 60% off retail parts, although the prices vary with the condition of the item. It sure sounds like a good deal—satisfaction is guaranteed or your money back upon return of merchandise within two weeks of purchase. A restocking charge is levied only when the customer changes his mind. There's no minimum order. So if new (and very expensive) parts are not needed for your bike's image, get it from Clinton and spend the savings elsewhere, and that's no joke. **B, PQ**

EDGEWOOD NATIONAL, INC.
6603 North Meridian
Puyallup, WA 98371
(206) 927-3388

Off-road, pick-up, and small truck owners (not to mention owners of small trucks) will love this catalog. It's the most complete parts inventory we've seen. On top of that, it's all up to 30% off list. Burbank Spring suspension kits at 16% off, Advance adapter transmission kits at 22% off, Bestop tops at 30% off. Rule winches and many more name brands are combined with numerous gadgets you didn't know you needed—until now. **C $2**

EXPLOSAFE GASOLINE CANS
44 County Line Road
Farmingdale, NY 11735
(516) 454-0880

Explosion-proof gasoline cans by Kidde marked down 50% are shipped UPS. "Most ordinary gas cans emit dangerous fumes and do not have anti-explosion systems," we learned from the brochure. "Explosafe cans will not explode . . . the special vent prevents escape of dangerous explosive fumes." Five gallons, $22 (retail $44); 2.5 gallons, $18 (retail $36). Shipping costs $3 per can. **B**

FINDER'S ELITE
9400 N. Central Expressway
Suite 1300
Dallas, TX 75231
(214) 739-1066

Drive an elite bargain without wrecking your budget. This company
has European automobile dealer contacts which can mean savings of
up to 10% to 20% off local dealer prices on Mercedes Benz, Audi,
Porsche, BMW, Ferrari, and other expensive, sought-after auto-
mobiles. They'll purchase your dream car in Europe, arrange to have
it altered to meet U.S. auto safety standards, and deliver it to you.
Customizing is no problem—the German dealers dealt with have
done everything from creating 24K weatherstripping for an Arab
shiek's Mercedes to creating a rainbow-colored fleet of Benzes for
another Arabian oil baron. **PQ**

GARD-A-CAR
9505 Groh Road
Grosse Ile, MI 48138
(313) 671-0478

Gard-A-Car is not a security cop or loud burglary siren. It's a 2-inch
box that prevents theft by immobilizing your car and was rated best
product for the price by *Consumer Reports,* September '82 issue.
Install it yourself, press the "on" switch when you leave your car, and
if a thief starts the car, it will stall in eight seconds by cutting off the
electric current to the distributor. The thief cannot restart the
engine and is forced to flee or be caught. Also works with boats,
motor homes, trucks, recreational vehicles. Cost: $30 for one, $53.40
for two. **B**

JAY ROBERTS TIRE CONNECTION
1313 St. Paul St.
Baltimore, MD 21202
(800) 638-4770
(301) 252-8585: call collect in MD

Jay Roberts has a wide range of tires and accessories for your car or
RV (Pirelli, Michelin, BF Goodrich, and Goodyear). They also have
lots of other goodies like Koni shocks at 30% off plus Monroe and
KYB, and a wide selection of famous-name custom wheels like
Crager. They also sell Cibie headlamps and driving lights. The pièce

de résistance is that Jay Roberts pays the freight on all but truck tires. The price you see is all you pay. **B**

J.C. WHITNEY & CO.
1917-19 Archer Ave.
P.O. Box 8410
Chicago, IL 60680
(312) 431-6102: orders only, 24 hrs.

When your car budget's been totaled, and the sum is greater than the parts, call J.C. If you have a car, RV, or motorcycle, J.C. Whitney has everything you've always wanted to put on but didn't know who to call. All sorts of customizing items from hood ornaments to fuzzy dice. Or fix up your older car with replacement parts like ball joints, convertible tops, seat covers, or new carpets. Then there are all the special tools necessary for these jobs. J.C. Whitney is chock full of parts for all cars, foreign and domestic, going back to the model T, many at really low prices (up to 60% off) though you may need a magnifying glass to see them. They even offer an across-the-running-board discount if you order promptly. Friendly order-takers 24 hours a day, seven days a week. **C**

KARZUNDPARTZ
P.O. Box 7207
1145 Silver Ave.
High Point, NC 27264
(800) 334-2749
(919) 889-2121: NC residents

Ach tune-up? Is your Gesund t-heit enough? Nein? Das ist nicht gut! European, American, and Japanese sports karz can get partz here. You can get Ricardo orthopedically designed seats, grab Momo steering wheels, stick Kamei spoilers all over, and catch sight of Cibie lights. Their specialty though is offering an extensive inventory of BMW and Porsche replacement parts at discounts up to 25%. They have 'em all from engine to muffler and wheels to roof. So mail for their catalog, macht schnell! **C**

MANUFACTURER'S SUPPLY
P.O. Box 157-US
Dorchester, WI 54425
(800) 826-8563
(800) 472-2360: WI residents
(715) 654-5821: inquiries

This party of the first part packs small engine parts, snowmobile parts, cycle parts, ATC parts, lawn mower parts, and chain saw parts to ship to parts unknown. A part of their appeal and what sets them apart is national brands like Champion, NGK, Wiseco, Remington, Gravely-Hahn, Arctic Cat, Husqvarna, Oregon, and Heli-coil at 30% to 40% less than retail. Savings like these are in our de-part-ment. **C**

MICKEY THOMPSON TIRES
P.O. Box 227
Cuyahoga Falls, OH 44222
(216) 928-3326

Next time someone tries to slip you a Mickey, take it. Tired of trying to track down wide wheels? This 20-year-old firm has on- and off-road RV and specialty tires at about 30% less than retail. Mickey Thompson carries an extensive line of such exclusive tire manufacturers as Mickey Thompson, Mickey Thompson, and of course, Mickey Thompson. No handling charge or returns. Customer pays UPS or freight charges. There's a complete material and workmanship warranty for the life of the tire. **C**

NATIONAL AUTOFINDERS
520 S. Holland St., Suite 410
Wichita, KS 67209
(800) 835-2132
(316) 721-3000: KS residents

Let National Autofinders put you in the driver's seat. Derive the benefits of a national network of franchises established through local new car dealers (call your local car dealer to see if he is a NAF broker). They will sell your current car or find a '71 Jag your dad is dreaming of. By keeping their overhead low, buyers and sellers get reasonable prices plus financing and warranties. **PQ**

RELIABLE TIRE CO.
1115 Chestnut St.
Camden, NJ 08103
(609) 365-6500
(215) 928-1450: Philadelphia residents

Reliable Tires will roll you over—the best we've seen on Michelin, BF Goodrich, Uniroyal, Firestone, Goodyear, and General. They even carry 18-wheeler and road-grade tires! Their prices are low and they include FET taxes. Use their UPS freight chart to see how much money you'll save over your local dealer. You won't be too tired treading over their reliable catalog. **C**

TEXAS VEHICLE MANAGEMENT
3504 Belt Line Road
Dallas, TX 75234
(214) 243-0007: call collect

We thought Texas Vehicles came with a set of hood horns and a six-pack of Lone Star. But over 20,000 customers (and a 70% referral rate) have proved that *price,* not promotion, sells cars. This 8-year-old, $32 million company will put you in the driver's seat of the car of your choice. Top choices: Mercedes 380SL, Datsun 280ZX, Datsun Maxima, Mazda RX7, the four-door Honda Accord—or any new or short mileage (10,000 miles or less) pre-owned car to buy or lease. They're also deep in the heart of hand-picked, pre-owned Mercedes, Porsches, and Rolls-Royces. They buy or trade cars dealer-to-dealer in the wholesale price spectrum and maintain a $2.5 million inventory on hand to select from. Company President Geoff Deasy says, "A good deal is when both parties are happy." Financing arrangements through four banks and two retail financing companies. They take trades or buy your car outright or will dispose of it for you. Call collect and ask to speak to Greg Randolph. **PQ**

Marine

If you're a seagoing type or have a seagoing friend, this section's for you. Getting ready for America's Cup? Order some new winch handles for your yacht. Planning your next cruise in the backyard? Order some rubber boots for the children. There's something for everyone and all at watered-down prices.

AMERICAN MARINE ELECTRONICS
1082 Post Road
Darien, CT 06820
(800) 243-0264
(203) 655-1409: CT residents

We harbored no resentment when we piered at the prices here. Marine electronics, navigation electronics, and communication equipment in names like Furuno, Sitex, Raytheon, Regency, Standard, Horizon, and Cybernett docked us off our feet at 25% to 40% lower than conventional retail. There's a ten-day refund-in-full policy, a 15% restocking charge after that, and no minimum order. They have their own repair facility, which is moor than most folks have. **C, B, PQ**

DEFENDER INDUSTRIES
255 Main St.
P.O. Box 820
New Rochelle, NY 10801
(914) 632-3001

Up periscope to sight in on savings! Defender torpedoes the competition with sub-marine prices—in fact, the lowest prices (35% to 65% off) we've seen on a complete line of nautical gear. Discounted items ranged from Seth Thomas clocks, to dinghies, to marine stoves, to heads. Defender also will match any competitor's advertised price. The depth of their fiberglass inventory (the largest in the U.S.) gave us a real charge. Before you Destroyer finances paying retail, bow down to their stern 40% discounts on boat and sailing supplies. Minimum order, $15 and ten-day refund policy. **C $1 (refundable)**

E&B MARINE SUPPLY
150 Jackson Ave.
P.O. Box 747
Edison, NJ 08818
(201) 442-3940

This catalog arrived just in the nick of time for all the poor-poises who pass as captains of their own fate. Savings on thousands of items soared to 60%: The latest in recorder technology, the Unimetrics Sea Hawk 422 is a high-performance white-line recorder designed for shallow water, bay, and coastal shelf fishing, list price, $749—E&B's price, $299.88; enjoy freshly made hot coffee on board or on the road with a two-chamber warming oven, list price, $40—E&B's price, $29.88. Other marine marvels such as depth sounders, CBs, boat shoes and boots, brass clocks and barometers, cushions, furniture, toilets, and pumps are all easily charged to your Visa, MasterCard, or American Express. All rates include postage, packaging, handling, and insurance. **C**

GOLDBERG'S MARINE
202 Market St.
Philadelphia, PA 19106
(800) 523-4506: orders
(215) 627-3700: PA residents

Buoy, oh buoy, this company's been afloat for 40 years! Goldberg's has really gone overboard on pleasure boating equipment and nautical clothing at sea-worthy savings of 20% to 45% below retail. We piered at such items as life vests, boat covers, pumps, and clothing in their catalog of cargo and noted that sonar fish sounders received in-depth treatment. Danforth anchors held fast at almost 50% off manufacturer's list which gives us anchors a way we want 'em—at a discount. Minimum order $25; 30-day money-back guarantee. **C**

LORAIN ELECTRONICS
2307 Leavitt Road
Lorain, OH 44052
(216) 835-8610: sales & service
(216) 282-6116: Lorain residents

"Shop Ahoy!" You'll have a mari-time saving 20% off on navigational equipment, radar detection, depth sounders, and fish finders from Lorain Electronics. Whether you're a professional deep-sea mariner, land rover, or a part-time trout hooker, they've got the top-of-the-line equipment you'll need to cruise on course and scope out that swimming school from name brands we can't mention. Marine radios and telephones were $290 to $1,400; depth sounders $225 to $5,000; marine and land mobile hand-helds $400 to $2,000; small vessel radars $2,900 to $8,000; large vessel radars $8,000 and up; Loran C $1,600 to $11,000; mobile telephones (own, not rent) ranged from $2,500 to $4,500 without installation. Call or drop them a line. **PQ**

MAST ABEAM
5859 New Peachtree Road, Suite 104
Atlanta, GA 30340
(404) 458-2213

Do you know the way to San Jose? If not, one of Mast Abeam's compasses might come in handy. A "first-come, first-served" offer included overstock and discontinued merchandise discounted 50%. A Danforth anchor went down at $60 ($120 retail), an Olin Locater flare kit sparked our interest at $15 (retail $30). Harry Whitehead started the company five years ago and, so far, sales have been buoyed by offering 20% to 30% discounts on quality items by known manufacturers. Great savings on outer wear like Sperry topsiders, raincoats, Great Wallaby hats. Returns and refunds must be made within 10 days of purchase. Cargo is normally shipped same day order is received. Minimum order, $10. **C**

M & E MARINE SUPPLY CO.
P.O. Box 601
Camden, NJ 08101
(609) 858-2307

Everything you've ever wanted to buy for your boat (over 24,000 items) all in one, 2-pound, 355-page catalog and at discount prices, right? Not so, bilge breath. They have special sale supplements four times during the year. The depth and breadth of this catalog is astounding—from power and sail equipment, marine electronics, hardware, paint, sports and fishing equipment, furniture, clothing, and gifts. They even sell toilet paper. All items were offered at 10% to 25% discounts. Use the green sheet at the back to figure out your applicable discount. Then, ship 'em out. Orders of $10 or less assessed a $2.50 surcharge. **C $2**

NATIONAL MARINE ELECTRONICS
P.O. Box 1308
263 Kelly St.
Lake City, SC 29560
(800) 845-5927
(800) 922-3618: SC residents
(803) 394-5132

This company offers the broadest line available for marine electronics and at sensational prices. Radios, telephones, depth recorders, antennas, radar, autopilots, and more at big discounts. Besides the savings, they pride themselves on offering expert product knowledge. Each section has a shopper's guide of general information. The staff is willing to assist you in selection of the best item for your particular needs. They also have a call-in special of the week. Buoy, oh, boy! **C**

THE SHIP'S STORE
Division of Performance Yacht Sales, Inc.
501 E. Boston Post Road
Mamaroneck, NY 10543

Marine merchandise including computerized steering equipment, radio telephones, battery chargers, ladders, winches, and accessories. Special bargains on blue poly/winter covers at 50% off. Hand-sewn, Maine-made footwear in the classic moccasin style was $31.89 (retail $45.95). Norcold "Islander" AC/DC refrigerator/freezer was $270 (retail $450) and the Dual Automatic Receiver with ComPuNav Steering (model 767) was reduced from $1,795 to $1,059.95. All electronics carry full factory warranties, however not all products do. The Ship's Store doesn't guarantee anything so it's sink or swim if your compass conks out. Custom goods cannot be returned. Catalog sales are seasonal and merchandise is sold on a first-come, first-served basis. C

WAREHOUSE MARINE
P.O. Box 70348
Seattle, WA 98107
(800) 426-8666
(206) 789-3296: WA residents

Set your sales at 30% to 50% off (more during seasonal catalog offerings) on marine equipment, supplies, clothing, accessories, and electronics. All major brands represented from their over 60,000 square-foot warehouse. Guaranteed customer satisfaction with a 30-day return policy and a 15% restocking charge only after the 30-day limit. Turn to their tide-y, thick 200-page catalog even if you're not into New Wave. C $2

YACHTMAIL CO., LTD
5-7 Cornwall Crescent
London W. 11 1PH
England
Phone: 727-2373 (dial "01" for operator assistance in making this call)

The wide inventory of cruiser yacht equipment available from this company is all-encompassing. Flares and foghorns, heads and hatches, pumps and pulleys, lights and logs, and on and on. We're not dinghy, just a little dizzy with discounts of 20% to 30% off U.S. prices (10% to 20% lower than UK prices), a lifesaver in today's economy. Seaworthy notables: Avon, Seafarer, Autohelm, and Zeiss Sextants. The only albatross was freight charges on the inflatable boats. We were buoyed by the tax-free export price of about $600, but shipping by surface mail nearly put us under at $140. **C**

Sporting Goods

Serious athletes and weekend jocks can get outfitted here. Everything from basketballs to bass lures can be found by mail. When ordering boots or running shoes, always send along an outline drawing of your foot. Sizes vary, even within the same brand. When telephoning for information, ask if there's a floor model for sale of whatever you might be looking for. It's a great way to save on tents, golf clubs, pool tables, weights, and gym equipment, just to name a few.

ALPINE RANGE SUPPLY CO.
Route 7, P.O. Box 356
Fort Worth, TX 76119
(817) 478-6613 or 478-2881

The owner had "gone hunting" when we visited and a follow-up call almost resulted in a shooting match with the uncooperative personnel; still we found the whole range of guns and ammunition at a 25% to 50% discount to buy, sell, or trade. Take a look at Bushnell 7x26mm binoculars for only $153.30 (retail $200 plus). Take a shot at these fantastic savings but remember you must buy through a dealer (for a small fee) and send a copy of your dealer's federal firearms license signed in ink before a gun can be shipped to you. We will continue to sing their praises since a Sunday phone call triggered such a nice response from one of their salesmen. **C**

AMERICAN TROPHY AND AWARD CO., INC.
1006 S. Michigan Ave.
Chicago, IL 60605
(312) 939-3252

Award to the wise: "This takes the prize" for savings on trophies, cups, medals, and plaques offering discounts of 50% plus free engraving, free plaques, and a 10% group bonus discount. Attention: bowlers, golfers, hockey players, pool players, riflemen, and runners. We don't want to meddle but if you need metal for your medals, this is where to turn. **C**

ANGLER'S DISCOUNT WAREHOUSE INC.
P.O. Box 158 UN
Wellsville, PA 17365
(717) 432-8611

We fell hook, line, and sinker for this warehouse stocked with rods, reels, lures, lines, and terminal tackle and accessories from Daiwa, Shimano, Penn, Fenwick, Lew Childre's, and more. Merchandise is approximately 25% to 35% less than retail. If the consumer orders the wrong merchandise, there's a 20% restocking charge; there's no charge for company mistakes; and in the case of mutual error, they split the difference. The minimum order is $10. Their catalog lists plenty of items to nibble on. **C $1**

ATHLETE'S CORNER
P.O. Box 16993
Plantation, FL 33318
(800) 327-0346
(305) 475-0327: FL residents

Been paying retail for your recreational gear? Then go stand in the Athlete's Corner. If Nike is what you like-e, this company offers six styles of basketball shoes, ranging from canvas at $19.95 to leather at $29.95 (retail $29 to $42). Good sports will find sporting goods for tennis, raquetball, running, and basketball—in fact, everything you've always wanted to know about exercise, but were afraid to ask (pricewise). Such leading brands as Nike, Adidas, New Balance, and Ektelon huddle here before making tracks to go a-courtin'. Savings were around 30% on most items and team orders are welcome. Unused merchandise can be exchanged or money refunded. **PQ**

AUSTAD
4500 E. 10th St.
P.O. Box 1428
Sioux Falls, SD 57101
(800) 843-6828
(605) 336-3135: SD, AK, HI residents

Como está, Austad? If you've been engolfed with the urge to hit a little white ball, bogie on down and putt in an order here. Austad stocks a complete line of quality golf gear (Ram, Wilson, MacGregor, and more) at 10% to 30% off retail, so they won't put a divet in your green. Their full-color catalog features clubs, bags, carts, shoes, sportswear, and accessories. Many items are made exclusively for Austad by leading golf manufacturers. If golf is your handicap, this 20-year-old company should treat you in a fairway. **C**

BOWHUNTERS DISCOUNT WAREHOUSE
P.O. Box 158
Zeigler Road
Wellsville, PA 17365
(717) 432-8611: orders
(717) 432-8651: customer service

We wanted to talk to an expert, so we asked William to Tell us where to target in on discount hunting bows. Since he aimed to please, we got the point instead of the shaft. Browning, Bear, Jennings, Martin,

and Ben Pearson hunting bows were all discounted from reta
Tree stands, targets, broadheads, camouflage clothing, and ac⸺sso-
ries were also available. Most discounts ran 20% to 30% off retail.
Even better bets for bargain hunters are during the Christmas
season. There's a customary $10 minimum order and a 20% restock-
ing charge on returns. Lastly, and as a parting shot, less discriminat-
ing single girls, a-quiver with the notion of doing a little beau-hunting
of their own, can find a selection of turkey calls to help them bag a
Tom (or Dick or Harry). **C**

CABELA'S
812 13th Ave.
Sidney, NB 69160
(308) 254-8800: orders
(308) 254-7032: customer service

Anyone for singing praises in a Cabela's choir? While we're big
believers in being in harmony with nature and in tune with the
outdoors, our voices may be a bit too corn-husky for this Nebraska
firm. They offered good prices on high-quality outdoor gear like
down jackets and vests, but while we like to "get down," we prefer to
rock to prices closer to rock bottom. Don't discount Cabela's, though,
for outdoor gear, binoculars, knives, sleeping bags, outdoor accessories, although they don't claim discount prices. **C**

CAMPMOR
810 Route 17 N.
P.O. Box 999
Paramus, NJ 07652
(800) 526-4784
(201) 445-5000: NJ residents

We camp-aigned for this cause in the Garden State: 15% off brand-
name sporting goods. Eureka tents, Camp 7 goose-down sleeping
bags, Cannondale bicycle touring accessories, Wilderness Experience and Kelty backpacks, Coleman stoves, and lots more—everything you need to survive in the outdoors was found in the pages of
this 112-page catalog. We compared the price of Victorinox, the
original Swiss army knife, with local retailers and found a 30%
savings. Refunds within six months of purchase and most items have
a flat $3 shipping fee. Worth a trip to visit their showroom for
additional savings when you're in New Jersey. **C** (three times a year)

CARLSEN IMPORT SHOES
524 Broadway
New York, NY 10012
(212) 431-5940

This is where athletes foot the bill for less. With over 10,000 pairs of shoes in stock, it must be hard to keep track of their running footgear in brands such as Puma, Spaulding, Pony, and Adidas. Order their free catalog and dash through their sports equipment including bags, balls, and track suits. We received a phone quote on a pair of discontinued Adidas Orion jogging shoes for women, size 7, at $18.95 plus $1.75 shipping. These shoes retailed for $30 three years ago. Discounts jog, sprint, run, and jump up to 70%. All orders must be prepaid. **C**

DINN BROS.
68 Winter St.
P.O. Box 111
Holyoke, MA 01041
(413) 536-3816

There's a soccer (player) born every minute. Why else would the brothers Dinn sell so many trophies and plaques, just for kicks? We saw every conceivable type of trophy, ribbon, medal, wall plaque, desk accessory, etc., in their 48-page catalog, with factory-direct wholesale prices up to 70% lower than retail. Swimmers, golfers, runners, bowlers, skiers, skaters, weight lifters, tennis-baseball-basketball-football players, as well as speakers, champion dogs, horses, bulls, and big fish are all represented in walnut and marble-based trophies. A 12½-inch tennis trophy was $8.75 (retail $26.25) and a 5½-inch track trophy was $3.50 (retail $12). Free engraving. Orders over $200 shipped free: no minimum order. **C**

EISNER BROS.
76 Orchard St.
New York, NY 10002
(212) 475-6868
(212) 431-8800

The special-T of the house is a product to "be worn on top as a T-shirt and not hidden under a button-down shirt like underwear." Sized from 6 months to adult size 60. Minimum order is a dozen in same size and color. Baseball jerseys, tank tops, sweat shirts, but T-op savings to T-eam orders. **C**

THE FACTORY OUTLET
679 Belmont St.
Brockton, MA 02401
(617) 583-3782

After 14 years as the Eaton Factory Outlet, the name changes but the bargains stay the same. Giving 20% to 50% off Etonic, Brooks, Converse, Pony, Fred Perry, Lee, Bassett and Walker, Fox River, and others keeps everyone Eaton out of their hands. Hit a long drive down the green in the "Cadillac" of golf pants. You'll look sporting in a pair of Etonic golf or running shoes or a LaCoste alligator shirt. Choose from a variety of factory irregulars of name brands offered at substantial savings. A pair of Lee jeans or corduroys will help keep you and your budget in the straight and narrow. Minimum order is $20. **B**

FOLKS ON BUCK HILL
P.O. Box 306
North Industry, OH 44707
(800) 321-0200
(800) 362-6540: OH residents

We won't take any potshots at these Folks just because they live on Buck Hill—though the only thing we've ever poached was an egg. These people offer outdoor sporting goods at 15% to 20% below retail. Their massive 300-page catalog covers such outdoor items as archery equipment, fishing lures, bullets, lanterns, guns, sights, sleeping bags, etc., in all sorts of brand names recognizable to the outdoor aficionado. Their slimmed-down catalog of Christmas gift ideas offered some especially good savings: Camel goose-down sleeping bags were $99.95 ($169.95 list), a Daisy pneumatic pellet pistol was $47.45 ($62.70 list), and Bushnell binoculars were $77.30 ($109.95 list). There's a $10 minimum order. **C**

FUNCTIONAL CLOTHING, LTD.
Wilderspool Causeway
Causeway Avenue
Warrington WA4 6QQ, England
Phone: Warrington STD 0925 53111 (dial "01" for operator assistance in making this call)

The name says it all: functional clothing for leisure and work.

Whether you're going on an Arctic fishing expedition, climbing the Himalayas, caravaning across Europe, sailing the Love Boat, or merely birdwatching in your snowy backyard, the patented Airflow construction of their all-weather wear will keep you warm in winter, cool in summer. Waterproof and windproof with removable foam liners in coats, jackets, leggings, mitts, head warmers, thermal clothing, seagoing overtrousers for men and women. Might not win you a best-dressed award, but then again, in the Arctic, who cares what the penguins next door will think? **C**

GOLF AND TENNIS WORLD
P.O. Box 668
1351 South Federal Highway
Deerfield Beach, FL 33441
(800) 327-1760
(305) 428-3780: FL residents

Pay less green for all you need on the green or on the court. They double-guarantee their name-brand equipment and promise to meet any competitor's price on any golf item. Prices you can't putt down: AGI custom woods, $46 to $59 (retail $58 to $90); deluxe 9-inch golf bags, $69.95 (retail $85); AGI golf carts, $34.95 to $89.95 (retail $45 to $100). Footwear, fuzzy headcovers, gloves, plus tennis rackets, balls, graphite string, wrist bands, and shoes. They even do golf club repairs by mail, but after adding $4 for shipping and handling and waiting two to four weeks, prices are only par for the course and you can probably do it faster locally. **C**

GOLF HAUS
700 N. Pennsylvania
Lansing, MI 48906
(517) 482-8842

Be-Fore you swing into action and get teed off, tally up the savings here! With prices slicing 40% to 60% off retail, you can make your pitch at Golf Haus and save yourself a long drive, as well as some green. Owned by two brother pros, brands carried include all those normally found on the leader board: Spalding, Dunlop, Wilson, Titleist, Lynx, Ping, etc. We saw 1983 Titleist Accu-Flo Plus clubs (Cast Metalwoods) 1, 3, 5 woods, 3 through 9 irons, and a pitching wedge listing at $640 for $280. A set of 1983 MacGregor Jack Nicklaus clubs 1, 3, 5 woods, 3 through 9 irons, and a pitching wedge was $170 ($390 retail). Foot Joy and Etonic golf shoes averaged almost 50% off retail and MacGregor, Maxfli, and Titleist golf balls also rolled in at rough-ly 50% off. Though typed price sheets are not up to par (being disorganized), they are worth scrutinizing. There's a $30 minimum order and a free set of headcovers (worth $15) to those who buy a set of clubs and mention *The Underground Shopper.* Exchanges made or full refunds. **B**

GREAT LAKES SPORTSWEAR
11371 E. State Fair
Detroit, MI 48234
(313) 372-4500

Ski-p the slopes and head for the apres ski activities in cheap chic. This factory offers their own brand of nylon jackets, vests, and arctic gear sold in their outlet store. The more you buy, the more you'll save. Their full-color, 16-page catalog displayed racing jackets, sport and mopar jackets, astronaut and bomber jackets, and even water-repellent arctic jackets and vests. Jackets came unlined, Kasha (lightweight flannel) lined, and pile lined and in a variety of bright colors. Prices were very good, about 50% off conventional retail and ranging from $9 for a lightweight unlined jacket to $23 for the pile-lined bomber-style arctic jacket. They'll exchange damaged products and there's no restocking charge. Send for their catalog to get the snow down on bargains. **C**

JOHN VERDE TENNIS CO.
P.O. Box 31249
Dallas, TX 75231
(214) 475-0888

John Verde offers all the products to start your own Forest Hills. Strokemaster brand tennis equipment from portable nets to line tapes is available at 25% lower. He also provides a tennis court contractors' referral service. Additional bargains can be netted in the used Prince and Strokemaster ball machines, which vary in price according to model and condition, and used Tournament tennis balls at $7.50 per dozen (six dozen minimum order). Love, savings. **B, PQ**

'S OUTDOOR PRODUCTS
...e St.
Salt Lake City, UT 84115
(800) 453-7756
(801) 486-4161: UT residents

After a hard day of camping and hiking, at night we like to sleep in-tents-ly. Kirkham's carries tents, backpacks, cross-country skis, backpacking equipment, and sleeping bags in such names as Kirkham's, Downers/Jansport, Wilderness Experience, and Kelty. Their refund policy is hardly tent-ative: "Any Kirkham's product will be replaced or money refunded within 30 days of purchase if not satisfied. All products are warrantied against material and work-manship defects for 10 years, and will be promptly repaired or replaced upon receipt of merchandise." There's no restocking charge. Kirkham's tents are sold factory direct, without dealers or distributors, resulting in a direct price to the consumer. Choose from many styles and sizes, from one-person pup tents (for dogged out-door buffs), to family tents sleeping six (for those who are into group sacks). **C**

LAS VEGAS DISCOUNT GOLF AND TENNIS
4813 Paradise Road
Las Vegas, NV 89109
(800) 634-6743
(702) 798-6300: NV residents

You have to know when to hold 'em and know when to sell 'em at a discount. The classic La Mode Du golf shirts for men and women were slotted at $19.95 (regularly $30 to $40), Varela slacks from $49.95 to $59.95 (regularly $80 to $90), Izod sweaters $22.50 (regu-larly $35), and $25 for the really big Macks (crocs for the XXL). Most major brands of pro-line golf clubs, shoes, bags, and accessories and tennis gear shipped almost immediately upon order. They put all their cards in their catalog and continue to come up a winner. **C**

LOMBARD'S PRO SHOP
1861 N.E. 163 St.
North Miami Beach, FL 33162
(305) 944-4499

Lombard's prices on name-brand sporting goods, including golf

items, won't put a hole in your pocket. For instance, Titleis
woods were $142 and a Ben Hogan Tour Wood Vector Shaft
Foot Joy Super Softies cost $53. They also sell tennis stuff along with
squash and racquetball gear. We hear every racquet is stocked. How
about a Wilson T-2000 for $38.95? Or a Head Competition 3 for
$62.95? The accessory line is complete from nets to bags to ball
machines. Gut and nylon string prices are the best we've seen so far:
gut was $16.25 and nylon went from $2 to $8.75. Don't drive, just
putt your order in at Lombard's for savings of 30% to 60%. **Free C, B
$1** (mailings of periodic fliers)

MOUNTAIN CAMPER
P.O. Box 291
Seymour, TN 37865
(800) 251-1021
(800) 332-6006: TN residents
(615) 573-3028

"We're great outdoors," says President John Hall of his successful
company, which now has 23 outlets around the country. Fine quality
camping goods like tents, sleeping bags, and outer wear are shipped
factory direct by a leading manufacturer from the hills of Tennessee.
We found a 10-by-16-foot two-room deluxe canvas tent (sleeps nine)
for $229; $300 elsewhere. Goose-down jackets in sizes XS to XXL
started at $49.50. The fine quality sleeping bags tucked in the back of
their *Preview Catalog* were an exceptional value from $22 to $90.
Everything shipped is first-quality. In their outlets around the country, you can pick up closeouts, such as a pair of Montblanc hiking
boots for $25, floor models and samples at further reductions. Full-
color catalogs twice a year and special promotional mailers to those
who have bought. Full refunds if not satisfied. **C**

NEW ENGLAND DIVERS INC.
131 Rantoul St.
Beverly, MA 01915
(800) 343-8122
(617) 922-6951: MA residents

When in a sink-or-swim situation, give special tanks to New England
Divers. They advertise as the world's largest distributor of diving
equipment. Dive in for famous brands like U.S. Diver's, Dacor,
Swimaster, Farallon, Poseidon, and Mako and bubble over their 10%

to 20% discounts. If you don't see it in their catalog, call them and they can probably fish it out of stock for you. **C**

PRO SHOP WORLD OF GOLF
8130 N. Lincoln Ave.
Skokie, IL 60077
(800) 323-4047
(312) 675-5286: IL residents

High prices are enough to knock the dimples off any Titleist, so why fall into the (sand) trap of paying retail? Stay away from the rough— you can stop driving and start to putter around at home if you trust a Pro. Hazards are few with such names as Wilson, Lynx, MacGregor, Ben Hogan, Ping, Ram, Spalding, and other brands in clubs, golf carts, golf balls, drivers, wedges, utility irons, shoes, and gloves. We saw MacGregor M.T. Copper Face clubs (eight irons, three woods) listed in their catalog for $619.99 ($750 manufacturer's list). They do not give refunds, but will make exchanges. We noted Hogan and Powerbilt Golf Bags were $49.99, and since all merchandise is first-quality, you won't find a hole-in-one. **B**

RAYCO TENNIS PRODUCTS
1436 University Ave.
San Diego, CA 92103
(800) 854-6692
(714) 295-4777: CA residents

Zing went the strings of our tennis rackets so we called Rayco and they didn't rake us over the coals. Now you can tighten up your purse strings, too, and save up to 50% on all sorts of racket stringing machines, tennis balls, and other equipment needed on the court. **C,** **B, PQ**

REED TACKLE
P.O. Box 1348
Fairfield, NJ 07006
(201) 227-0409

The ultimate in dyed-fly buys, Reed Tackle gives you reel-life excitement offering a product list as fascinating as it is useful. Materials for flies include imitation polar bear hair, moose mane, peacock tail, and pheasant feathers. Among more mundane but equally practical items are rod and reel accessories, floaters, hooks, lines, and sinkers. We wormed it all out of them. **C**

REI CO-OP
P.O. Box C-88125
Seattle, WA 98188
(800) 426-4840
(800) 562-4894: WA residents

REI has one of the best outdoor sporting goods catalogs covering high-technology hiking, climbing, and camping gear, cross-country skiing, bicycling items, and fashion sportswear. Many famous products: Jansport, Sierra Designs, Kelty, Chounard, and Mountain House and with the mounting cost of pursuing outdoor recreation, you can save quite a bit on their own brand "Peak Value," which offers the same quality but at reduced prices. Also, for a $5 membership fee, you will be mailed a 10% refund on your total year's purchases at year's end. **C**

SANDAN ASSOCIATES
P.O. Box 986
Delray Beach, FL 33444

Starry, starry nights in the Chevy or on the levee will be more enjoyable with the right stuff. Astronomy and binocular buffs will clearly see the savings on spotting scopes, monoculars, binoculars, and telescopes discounted up to 50%. Brands we spotted: Swift, Bushnell, and Bausch & Lomb. Write for their price quote. **PQ**

THE SHOTGUN NEWS
P.O. Box 669
Hastings, NB 68901
(402) 463-4589

We got a kick out of the reaction they triggered. This high-caliber publication aims to offer "the finest gun buys and trades in the U.S." Shoot, for only $15, you'll be hit with 36 issues; that's one issue three times per month (or 72 issues for $29.50). You can really get loaded on 108 issues for $44. If you want a sample copy to rifle through before you subscribe lock, stock, and barrel, send $3.

STUYVESANT BICYCLE
349 W. 14th St.
New York, NY 10014
(212) 254-5200: sales
(212) 675-2160: parts

Don't let your exercise program be gone with the Schwinn. Get into gear with quality bikes, exercisers, rowers, treadmills, mopeds, scooters, wagons, and tricycles wheeling such names as Atalia, Raleigh, Bianchi, Ross, Tunturi, Carnelli, and Puch. Accessories, too, at a 10% to 30% discount. A spokes-man said, "We want all our customers to be satisfied. If an item is defective, we will replace it. Common sense and reason must prevail." Stuyvesant has been in business for over a 40-year cycle. **C $2.50** (refundable)

TAYLOR CUTLERY MANUFACTURING CO.
P.O. Box 1638
806 E. Center St.
Kingsport, TN 37662
(800) 251-0254: orders
(615) 247-2406: TN residents

Whittlers, outdoorsmen, and knife fanciers will appreciate Taylor's sharp selection of their own cutlery and Elk Horn knives at whole-sale prices (50% lower). Using only top-grade surgical steel blades, slashing prices in half is not uncommon. The Elkhorn Falcon with a smooth bone handle, lock back, brass liners, and nickel silver bolster sold for $7.50 (retail $15). The minimum order is $25.00 and must be submitted with a certified check or money order for prompt delivery. Ask for the dealer wholesale catalog for a deal that's a cut above the rest. Money-back guarantee. **C $1**

TBC
Box 13
1514 E. Chocolate Ave.
Hershey, PA 17033
(800) 233-2175
(717) 533-8339: PA residents

At first we thought "TBC" meant "The Best Chocolate," but they say it's "The Best Choice." Their free catalog won't melt in your hand but you will find mouth-watering savings on running, tennis, and hiking shoes as well as clothing for men and women. Choices include Nike, Adidas, New Balance, and Bill Rodgers, among others. Bite off a 15% to 20% discount on clothing, a 20% discount on shoes. Restocking charge, $5. **C**

THOS. D. ROBINSON & SON, LTD.
321 Central Ave.
White Plains, NY 10606
(914) 948-8488

Hooked on fishing, but high prices leave you green around the gills? Cast your eyes on these guys. With prices averaging 30% to 40% less than at retail stores, we found the best prices we've seen on all types of fishing gear, from rods and reels, tackle and tackle boxes to camping equipment and shooter's supplies. We found big names like Diawa, Penn, Fenwick, Orvis, Zebco, Garcia, and Eureka to hook onto. So stop floundering around and drop them a line. **C**

TIMBERWOLF
P.O. Box 757, Dept. 20
Clanton, AL 35045
(800) 633-4266: orders only
(205) 755-6533: AL residents call collect
(205) 755-7758

Tim-ber! Watch out for Macho Meany, a 1½-inch stainless steel knife, $12.99 (retail $22.50). Spend Saturday night as the Samurai Tailor with a $39 sword, listing at $79.95. A Ka-Bar fighting knife was $24 (retail $39.95). Uncle Henry Bear Paw, a popular hunting knife, was $18.99 (retail $37.95). Not only are these knives a "cut above" in quality, they are discounted up to 50%. Brands included Buck, Ranger, Schrade, Camillus, Connecticut Valley Arms, Case, Browning, Carvel Hall, and many others. Boots, jeans, tents, backpacks, and other hunting accessories are also shown. The toll-free number has a $25 minimum. **C**

TROPHYLAND USA, INC.
7001 W. 20th Ave.
P.O. Box 4606
Hialeah, FL 33014
(800) 327-5820
(800) 432-3528: FL residents

By now you must be accomplished in reading catalogs. Give yourself a medal or trophy from Trophyland—you earned it. They carry a complete line of trophies, medals, plaques, desk sets, charms, and show ribbons at factory-direct savings. All wood is walnut, with the marble imported from Italy. Free engraving. **C**

8.

HOME LIVING

Bed and Bath

Bed and bath bargains abound between the sheets in this section. Take comfort in outfitting your bed and bathrooms at half the price. Salute the four-star savings at the 50%-off outlet for Dresher brass beds or march up to the decorated deals on Martex towels, Nettlecreek bedspreads, or Springmaid sheets. At these prices, you can change with the weather.

ACME QUILTING CO.
240 E. Chestnut St.
Hanover, PA 17331
(717) 632-8691

Since July of '63, the Acme Quilting Co. has been turning out the textiles. Over 5,000 bedspreads alone are available for the great American coverup. Inventory also includes bedspreads, towels, drapes, pillows, sheets, comforters, quilts, and blankets from Nettlecreek, Beau Ideal, Bloomcraft, Bates, Acme, and others. Save 30% to 50% on first-quality merchandise and 50% to 70% on irregulars. (Who cares if your bottom sheet has faded at the corner!) Liberal exchanges and refund policy with shipment by UPS (tack on an additional 50 cents for carton and handling). Sleep tighter if you're a tightwad. **B**

CAMEO, INC.
503 Grandville S.W.
Grand Rapids, MI 49503
(616) 451-2759

When we gazed at this Cameo, our faces were etched with relief. This well-established company pillow-ried high retail prices with 25% to 30% savings on piles of bed pillows, decorative pillows, down comforters, and rocker and chair pads, while names like DuPont, Sontique, Adoration, and Cameo gave us quality we could re-lie on. There's a $15 minimum on custom orders, no restocking charge, and a guarantee against defective workmanship. For a decision you can sleep on, try the mail—if you don't, you may have fluffed it. **PQ**

CANNONDALE'S
Route 3, Box 448C, Suite UG
Selbyville, DE 19975
(302) 539-0105

Sleep perchance to dream of 25% to 40% savings on complete brass beds (from $275 up) in 21 very attractive pure brass (70% copper, 30% zinc) styles. These beds have a baked enamel, "diamond lite" finish for easy maintenance (just wipe with cloth). At any given time, they are likely to be holding a sale, which saves you even more. Whether it is nobler in the mind to pay cash or use your charge card is up to you. These are faithful reproductions of turn-of-the-century classics. "One hundred percent safe delivery and satisfaction guaranteed" is their policy. Thirty-day money-back guarantee. They also have an installment plan. Visit the Senwick Island, Delaware, showroom just north of Ocean City, Maryland. **B**

CLASSIC QUILT CO.
P.O. Box 82
Spencertown, NY 12165
(518) 392-2749

When you're feeling down, snuggle in a 100% down quilt and let the world goose someone else. Discounts were 20% to 25% on quilts, pillows, and quilt slipcovers. An all-down quilt selling for $250 retail was tucked away in Classic Quilt's brochure for $190. Refunds within 10 days if not completely satisfied. No minimum order; no restocking charge on returns. All products are guaranteed for 10 years providing there is no abuse. **B**

COLUMBIA FACTORY OUTLET
Route 462 and Oswego Drive
Columbia, PA 17512
(717) 684-6341

Hail, Columbia! These folks change inventory at their outlet barn faster than most people change their sheets. That's why they can't catalog their large selection of bedspreads, sheets, mattress pads, comforters, blankets, curtains, drapes, towels, and throw rugs since many of them are discontinued patterns and styles. They do have a brochure or you can write or call for specific styles. They carry the Bates bedspread line at 20% to 50% below retail, as well as J.P. Stevens and Cannon labels in towels and linens. **B**

ELDRIDGE TEXTILE CO.
277 Grand St.
New York, NY 10002
(212) 925-1523

For a Bloomie, big selection for the boutique bed, bath, or boudoir, this is a really big show! Four floors and over 10,000 square feet full of first-quality merchandise to floor you. But the buck doesn't stop here. Shop the ground-floor opportunities for name-brand and designer towels, sheets, area rugs, blankets, pillows, and closet accessories. Move on to the main attraction for kitchen curtains, tablecloths, bed and bath boutique items, and placemats (lots of imports and even linen from China). Climb the ladder of success to the second floor laden with bedspreads, drapes, verticals, and wallpaper. Names read like a "Who's Who" in home decorating. Shipped UPS by weight; returns accepted if not used and still saleable. **PQ**

ELECTROPEDIC ADJUSTABLE BEDS
907 Hollywood Way
Burbank, CA 91505
(800) 423-2725
(213) 845-7488: CA residents

Open your own chiropractice by ordering direct from this manufacturer who sells "America's best-built electric adjustable bed." There is a five-year guarantee on lift motors (which can be replaced easily by an all thumbs teen-ager) and a one-year guarantee on heat pads according to their literature. A 39-by-70 twin regular bed was $899 (priced retail at $1,498). A special offer to *Underground* sleepers, a twin long for $800 (regularly sold for $949). Add approximately $75 for shipping for rest-assured delivery. Ask about their other products, one of which was described briefly as an at-home massage unit that kneads out the competition. We don't want to rub it in but we have a hands-off policy here. **C**

FRANCO TEXTILE
294 Grand St.
New York, NY 10002
(212) 226-3370 or 226-9413

Uh-oh! You'll think about Franco all the way to the bank-o. Deposit the savings up to 40% after you purchase some of the name-brand sheets, towels, pillowcases, blankets (including electric) by Fieldcrest, Martex, Springmaid, and Croscill. You're only a phone call away from decorating tips and custom-made items from their sheets or your own fabric. **PQ**

HARRIS LEVY, INC.
278 Grand St.
New York, NY 10002
(212) 226-3102

With only two complaints (both resolved) in 89 years, we'll Levy this granddaddy on Grand Street our finest honor. Harris Levy throws in the towel, as well as the sheets, comforters, and other B&B items in between at 25% to 50% off. They carry every major brand in the business but you must be specific when ordering by mail or by phone. Their custom order department can fill special requests for table linens, draperies, shower curtains including monogramming. Returns are handled on an individual basis within 30 days as long as the item is returned in its original condition. **PQ**

J. SCHACHTER CORP.
115 Allen St.
New York, NY 10002
(212) 533-1150

Is there a Schachter in the house? You bet. Since 1919, you can find them in the bedroom buried under the largest fabric selection for comforters in the country. Over 200 to choose from as well as the other accessories to complete the ensemble: shams, ruffles, table covers, drapes, and a decorator if you're color blind. Also carries both custom and stock comforters, pillows, and linens by Wamsutta, Martex, Cannon, and Dan River without Schachter-ing your budget. Save 25% to 40% with no returns accepted on custom or special orders but credits issued on out-of-stock unopened merchandise. Take two bedspreads and call them in the morning. **PQ**

PENNY WISE WAREHOUSE
2819 Blystone
Dallas, TX 75220
(214) 352-4515

Brass will last where money is concerned; a penny saved is indeed a penny earned. Penny Wise carries brass beds, mattress sets, and upholstered furniture at surp-Wise-ingly low prices. Give a hoot and save 40% to 50% on Dresher, Swan, Sunshine, Spring Air, Serta, Carlton, Bassett, Norwalk, and others. They also are owlish on their enormous selection of trundle, iron, and brass beds by Hallmark and Corsican. They'll send a bed anywhere in the continental U.S. and Canada and tuck in a one-year full replacement guarantee or a two-year guarantee on Dresher products for defective materials or workmanship. Delivery price $40 within Texas; other delivery charges quoted upon order. Customer satisfaction guaranteed. **B, PQ**

RAFAEL
291 Grand St.
New York, NY 10002
(212) 966-1928

Put your money worries to bed and dream of Rafael who offers seductive savings of 25% to 40% off the nightmarish cost of bed and bath creations. Take comfort-er, as well as sheets, pillowcases, towels, table linens, and more from the houses of Bill Blass, Dan River, Vera, Burlington, Martex, and Springmaid. Write or call for your particular passion. **PQ**

RUBIN & GREEN, INC.
290 Grand St.
New York, NY 10002
(212) 226-0313

Rubin & Green has a complete decorating service and carries an extensive line of draperies, carpeting, towels, and sheets plus other home furnishings at 20% to 40% off. They sell only first-quality items bought directly from the manufacturers. A catalog is not available but they have a pamphlet for custom-designed comforters made from goose down, lamb's wool, or dacron. Friendly personnel take your MasterCard, Visa, or C.O.D. phone orders and will ship same day if order is in stock. If you spot a European bedspread or other special items in a magazine or department store, call for availability and prices. They state: "We stand behind our manufacturers' guarantees and warranties." (Since the manufacturers are presumably also standing behind their products, when's the parade?) **PQ**

SHORE LINENS TEXTILES
274 Grand St.
New York, NY 10002
(212) 226-0228

Don't sink into retail. Swim to Shore and get your linen closet in ship-shape. Shore Linens waves 25% to 35% off the price on home furnishings, sheets, towels, and blankets from Fieldcrest, Martex, Springmaid, and others. Yes, they even accept special orders with a liberal 60-day return policy. **PQ**

THE WHOLESALE HOUSE
1319 Broadway
Hewlett, NY 11557
(800) 645-3372
(516) 569-2688: NY residents

Gimme shelter! The Wholesale House is a welcome refuge from reigning retail prices. Their beautifully photographed, 56-page, full-color catalog features the latest designs in bedroom linens, pillows, comforters, blankets, towels, table linens, etc., from such leading designers as Laura Ashley, Bassetti, Porthault, Rosie, Tricia Guild, Collier-Campbell, Mary McFadden, Jay Yang, and Bill Blass. Famous mills represented included Martex, Burlington, Wamsutta, and Springmaid. Savings were substantial, ranging from 20% to 40%. Wamsutta's Protocol line in twin flat or fitted sheets was $14.95 (retail $22) and the Prairie Land line by Springmaid in twin flat or fitted sheets was $10.95 (retail $20). Bathroom accessories were available and their custom shop creates custom-made headboards, pillows, draperies, and comforters, too. **C 75 cents**

China and Silver

If your cupboards are down to the bare essentials, it's time to bone up with china. From antique English to patterns that have gone by the wayside, there are folks who find your long-lost place-settings. Others offer super deals on current patterns. Most carry name-brand silver, china, and stemware. If you're looking for something special, be very specific in your correspondence. Replies from Europe can take a while, so be patient. It is always a good idea to enclose an SASE for expediency.

A.B. SCHOU
4 NY Ostergade
1101 Copenhagen
Denmark

Big savings of 30% off U.S. retail on crystal by Royal Copenhagen, Lladro, Herend, Waterford, Lalique, and Orrefors. This company sells more than a dozen Waterford stemware patterns and miscellaneous serving pieces. "Seconds" figurines with minimal flaws by such makers as Royal Copenhagen are reduced an additional 20%. Full satisfaction or money back; no restocking charge; no minimum order. The catalog price is refundable with your order. All prices include surface postage and insurance costs. **PQ, B, C $4** (refundable)

ALBERT S. SMYTH CO.
29 Greenmeadow Drive
Timonium, MD 21093
(800) 638-3333
(301) 252-6666: MD residents

These folks can dish it out, but they can't take it. Your money, that is. (At least not much of it.) We dug through a world of catalogs and came up in china. Albert S. Smyth carries china, crystal, and gifts in such well-known names as Lenox, Minton, Royal Doulton, Wedgwood, and others at 20% to 25% off retail. Their 24-page black-and-white catalog displayed some beautiful items at good savings off the suggested list price. Thirty-day full-refund written policy. Member, National Bridal Service. Feel free to write for a-dish-ional information. **C**

AMERICAN ARCHIVES
5535 N. Long Ave.
Chicago, IL 60630
(800) 621-5809: credit card orders
(800) 972-5858: IL residents

When you polish up on silver, you soon tarnish the myth that all that glitters is gold. Sterling silver tabletop and giftware items at 15% to 75% lower than suggested retail from this 79-year-old company definitely are a cloud with a silver lining. We dug deep into their catalog and dreamed of getting mother loded with a punch bowl at $299.95 ($350 retail). A stunning silver candelabrum was a miner miracle at $39.95 ($55 retail). As Underground Shoppers, we're paid to be pick-y, but our Hunt was not in vein with this catalog. **C**

BEN MORRIS JEWELRY CO.
P.O. Box 7305
4417 Lovers Lane
Dallas, TX 75209
(214) 526-7565

Morris isn't the Cat-alog man but he will put more money in your purrs. He carries fine lines of sterling silver, stainless flatware, silverplate holloware, china, crystal, diamonds, and watches. We saw brands like Gorham, Reed & Barton, Wallace, Towle, Kirk-Stieff, International, Lenox, Royal Doulton, Aynsley, Minton, and Oxford. China and crystal is about 20% off, Seikos and jewelry were about 30% off, and prices on sterling silver, flatware, holloware, and stainless were discounted about 31%. There's no minimum order and no restocking charge (they only make exchanges with the sales slip). Owners welcome all inquiries on specific brands, lines, or models, and although they don't have a catalog, they'll share information on current sales. **PQ**

CARL'S HOUSE OF SILVER
86 W. Palisade Ave., Dept. C
Englewood, NJ 07631
(201) 568-5990

Are you panning for gold to afford silver these days? You'll find the silver lining at Carl's House. Polished folks know about his lower prices of 20% to 50% off retail on silver, gold, flatware, jewelry, and other fine giftware. Notable names carried are Armatel, Wallace, Towle, Gorham, International, and Lenox. A Gorham silverplated Paul Revere 6½-inch bowl for $21.60 ($36 list), sterling silver barbell cufflinks for $27.50 ($40 list), and a 5½mm pearl choker with 14K gold clasp for $169 ($265 retail) were some of the goods that outshined them all. There's no minimum order and no restocking charge, but they don't give refunds—only credit. You won't find any goldbricks in this House of Silver. **C 50 cents**

CHINACRAFT OF LONDON
Parke House
130 Barlby Road
London W10 6BW, England
Phone: 960-2121 (dial "01" for operator assistance in making this call)

We thought a China craft was a junk. Oh, no way! They Yangzte prices way down and they don't paddle the prices to begin with. If you are yin-terested, they yen-k the prices down at least 50%. We're willing Tibet you will find a lot to yak about in this catalog. Ask for price quotes on gorgeous china and hand-cut crystal from Wedgwood, Spode, Royal Worcester, Royal Doulton, Baccarat, Waterford, and Stuart. A guide price list is enclosed to give an indication of the approximate cost. **C, PQ**

EMERALD MAIL ORDER
Ballingeary
County Cork
Ireland

No sham, rock-bottom prices in the Emerald Isle. Drink in full line of Waterford crystal and Belleek china as well as Aynsley, Coalport, and Limoges featured at 40% discounts. You won't get leprechauned by these fine folks. Now you can thank your lucky stars and eat 'em too (from a Belleek bowl). Minimum order for charges, $20. **C** (free by surface mail, $2 refundable by airmail)

FORTUNOFF
681 Fifth Ave.
New York, NY 10022
(800) 223-2326
(212) 758-6660 ext. 242: NY residents

Patterns from Gorham, Towle, International, Reed & Barton, Kirk-Stieff, Lunt, and Oneida are put out to pasture at passionate prices. Other goodies go for full fare. Twice-a-year (spring and Christmas) catalogs fortunately arrive on time to herald in each major shopping season. Choose from their over 500 patterns of flatware in sterling, silverplate, or stainless steel, or choose a gem from their beautiful collection of fine jewelry priced at less than you'd imagine. Others will make a Fortunoff you, but this company specializes in contemporary and antique silver and boldly exclaims, "No one sells sterling flatware for less." **C**

GOOD SHEPHERD'S STORE
P.O. Box 96
Manger Street
Bethlehem, Israel

While Good Shepherd's Store watches their stock by night, wise men won't have to travel far for their mother-of-pearl. But, we would have walked a mile for one of their camels, starting at $6, or a Holy Bible, $14 ($21 at U.S. flea markets) both in olive wood. Chess sets, candlesticks, religious figures, jewelry boxes. An inlaid mother-of-pearl cross was $4. Minimum order is $30. **C $2**

GREATER NEW YORK TRADING CO.
81 Canal St.
New York, NY 10002
(212) 226-2808

What's greater than the Big Apple? The Empapaya State Building? Orange, New Jersey? Grape Neck, Long Island? What could be greater than tableware by: Gorham, International, Lenox, Lunt, Mikasa, Minton, Noritake, Oneida, Orrefors, Reed & Barton, Rosenthal, Royal Worcester, Kirk-Stieff, Towle, and Wedgwood to name a few fruits looming around at 50% off. Top-banana small and large appliances, too. **PQ**

JEAN'S SILVERSMITHS
16 W. 45th St.
New York, NY 10036
(212) 575-0723

Jean blows the others to smith-ereens with over 100 current and discontinued patterns in sterling silver flatware, new and used silver, and antique jewelry. We inquired about International's discontinued Silver Rhythm pattern; were quoted $38 each for place spoons (quoted $52 elsewhere) and salad forks ($48 elsewhere). You can send an outline of items you want to match, noting knife blade types, bright or dull finish, stainless or sliver plated. **PQ**

MICHAEL C. FINA
580 Fifth Ave.
New York, NY 10036
(800) 223-6589
(212) 869-5050: NY residents

Fina-lize your wedding plans here. All that glitters can be found in this distributor's catalog: sterling silver tea services, crystal stemware, bone china, even a set of pewter goblets. Low prices, a large selection, and the special Personal Gift Catalog Service solves the gift-giving dilemma, Fina-lly. It's a super idea for those hard-to-buy-for, picky types. Catalogs are available in the states of Maryland, Virginia, Texas, Illinois, New York, and the District of Columbia. All manufacturers' price fluctuations are beyond their control and may change without notice. Sterling silver flatware fluctuates with the silver market. C $2 (refundable)

PATTERNS UNLIMITED
P.O. Box 15238
Seattle, WA 98115
(206) 523-9710

Now you don't have to take a slow boat to China to match discontinued patterns of china, crystal, silver, and earthenware from all makes and manufacturers. Just send a long, self-addressed stamped envelope to Patterns Unlimited. Tell them what you want. They might keep you from being at odds finding a place to replace odd china patterns. You'll pay a 20% restocking charge for your mistakes. Add 20% ($15 minimum) for finder's fee, packing, shipping, and insurance. PQ

REJECT CHINA SHOP
33-34-35 Beauchamp Place
London SW3 INU
England
Phone: 581-0733 (dial "01" for operator assistance in making this call)

In this Reject China Shop, you will not find a chink out of sync, only some of the best imports in town. Get on their mailing list and become pen pals with Spode, Aynsley, Coalport, Royal Worcester, Limoges, Wedgwood, and Denby discounted 15% to 50%. Prices vary with shipping but are very worthwhile according to our British correspondent. China settings and porcelain are their specialty. Chipped goods get full refund. **C $3**

RICHARD YERXA JEWELRY AND SILVER
5100 Belt Line Road, Suite 840
Dallas, TX 75240
(800) 527-5913
(800) 442-5799: TX residents
(214) 386-6995

In spite of its close proximity to Texas' own Sakowitz Village, have no "fear of buying." They wrote the book on name-brand silver like Reed & Barton and Gorham with chapter headings, "Save 30%." Sterling silver and silver plate, Seiko and Bulova watches from 20% off and holloware at 30%. **PQ**

ROBIN IMPORTERS
510 Madison Ave.
New York, NY 10022
(212) 753-6475
(212) 752-5605

Robin Importers Sher-wood save the rich and the poor from poverty, not by robbin' but by offering 20% to 60% discounts on a large selection of stainless steel, china, cutlery, crystal, giftware, and bakeware, and even tablecloths. Hard-to-find discounted Sabatier and Swiss army knives, Val St. Lambert stemware and giftware were a sight for sore pocketbooks. Some of the brands in this forest of imports include Wallace, Gorham, Mikasa, Wedgwood (Midwinter and Stonehenge), and Arabia, in patterns that have made marryin' so wonderful. Write (SASE) or call Robin with a description of what you want and his merry men will help you. **PQ**

ROGERS & ROSENTHAL
105 Canal St.
New York, NY 10002
(212) 925-7557

We took a slow boat down the Canal to find china and silver discounted up to 40%. Set an exquisite table even when there's so many hungry Maos to feed. The shop features every major advertised brand for 25% off retail. Send for price list but you must be specific

about what you want. Allow from one to eight weeks delivery while
they're Peking your order. **PQ, SASE**

ROGERS STERLING MATCHING SERVICE
P.O. Box 1665
Mansfield, OH 44901
(800) 537-5783
(800) 472-5667: OH residents

If your name isn't Hunt, the next best way to buy silver is to go the
refinished route. Silver from the old days, the estate sale, or the
wedding that wasn't can be restored or replated. This company had
the best prices and most efficient service we found. Refinished
versions are from ⅓ to ¼ the price of new silver, which they also carry.
Brands carried: Oneida, Reed & Barton, Gorham, Towle, Wallace,
and others 25% to 50% off. We ordered a teaspoon, $20, from our
discontinued pattern (current pattern price was $120) which was
located minutes after we called and put on reserve. It arrived
promptly and in perfect condition. You'll pay postage, handling, and
insurance. Restocking charge after 15-day return period ends. Also,
new silver plate and stainless flatware as well as new sterling flatware at discount prices. **PQ**

ROSS-SIMONS OF WARWICK
136 Route 5
Warwick, RI 02886
(800) 556-7376
(401) 738-6700: RI residents

At Ross-Simons "the money-back policy is guaranteed even if the
wedding isn't." We got a factory sealed teaspoon by Oneida, Damask
Rose pattern, for $35 (retail $120) plus $2.50 for postage and han-
dling. Discounts on fine china such as Aynsley, Lenox, and Royal
Doulton and crystal by Atlantis, Stuart, Waterford, and others about
25% below retail. A friendly clerk told us about upcoming promotions and the 90-day layaway. **PQ**

THE ROYAL TABLE
26 Kennedy Blvd.
East Brunswick, NJ 08816
(201) 846-5886

Royal Table's private club enables members to save 30% to 70% on fine china and crystal from England's most prestigious manufacturers, including Royal Worcester, Spode, and others. For a $5 fee, you'll receive "for members only" mailings four times a year. Members also receive 35% off on any item in stock during the year. **C**

SAXKJAERS
53 Kobmagergade
1150 Copenhagen K
Denmark

Have a Danish. Trying to cut down? Try Saxkjaers for Royal Copenhagen (RC) and Bing & Grondahl (BG) porcelain collector's plates at 40% below the U.S. retail price. RC Christmas plate 1981, $32.50 (retail $52.50), BG Mother's Day plate, $22 (retail $35). New designs every year and destroying the mold after each issue makes these plates very valuable. Original hand-crafted Swedish lead crystal and Lladro porcelain figurines were also described and pictured in the brochures we received. Prices include shipping, insurance, and door-to-door delivery. **C**

SHANNON MAIL ORDER
Shannon Free Airport
Ireland
Phone: 011-35361-61444 (dial direct)

The luck o' the Irish will have you Dublin your pleasure and saving nearly 50% on handmade Irish lace, Waterford crystal, French perfumes, pure Irish linen, Irish and Norwegian pewter, mohair-wool blankets, Goebel and Hummel figurines, and German music boxes. One place setting of Wedgwood bone china, Wild Strawberry pattern, was $50 for five pieces. Adding duty tax made it $69. At Neiman-Marcus, Dallas, it was priced at $105. Order your catalog and look it cl-over. Follow your nose to Opium 1/4-ounce perfume, $46.50; Orrefors perfume bottles, $39.95; Bal a Versailles 1 ounce, $97. **C**

STECHER'S
62 Independence Square
Port of Spain
Trinidad, West Indies

Some of the best buys in the world can be found at the many duty-free shops located in the West Indies, and Stecher's is no exception. They carry china by Wedgwood, Belleek, and others, silver by Georg Jensen, watches by Seiko, Piaget, and more. Their cargo usually goes for 30% to 50% off. Write to them with specific information about what you want for a price quote. **PQ**

STEPHEN FALLER (EXPORTS) LTD.
Mervue
Galway, Ireland
Phone: 091-61226 (dial "01" for operator assistance in making this call)

Stylish Irish! We fell for this Faller and his beautiful, full-color mail-order book packed with fine collectibles: Waterford crystal, Belleek china, Lladro figurines, tableware from Minton, Wedgwood, Spode, and Worcester, Beatrix Potter collectibles. Traditional Irish linens, tweeds, Aran knits, and more at 30% to 40% off. Glory be, they've been in business for 100 years. **C $1** (surface), **$2** (airmail)

TREASURE TRADERS LTD.
P.O. Box N-635
Nassau, Bahamas
(809) 322-8521 (dial direct)

Treasure you'll hold to your chest at 25% to 40% off: china, crystal, and silver by Georg Jensen, Gorham, Towle, Tuttle (silver), Wedgwood, Coalport, and Royal Worcester, crystal by Baccarat and Boda. You must request specific manufacturers' brochures to get their free price list. **B**

UNIVERSAL SUPPLIERS
P.O. Box 4803
GPO
Hong Kong
Phone: 001-852-5-224-768 (dial direct)

Susie can't go Wong with this Hong Kong supplier of ivory carvings, photographic and stereo equipment, Seiko and Rolex watches, eyeglasses, and contact lenses, with a one-year guarantee on everything. Rolex stainless steel case with steel oyster bracelet, $589 ($800 locally); French eyeglasses 14K gold-plated frame by Morel,

$32.70; replacement contact lenses (by American Optical), $20 per lens, $32.50 per pair. Save 50% on eyeglassware. Hand-carved ivory ball earrings, $7.50 ($33.95 in U.S.). Note the intricately carved ivory chess pieces, dragons, fans, figurines, vases. "Sori for printing errors" or so their story goes. **C $1.50**

WALTER DRAKE SILVER EXCHANGE
Drake Building
Colorado Springs, CO 80940
(800) 525-9291
(800) 332-3661: CO residents

Maybe you weren't born with a silver spoon in your mouth, but over the years, you've acquired a set and need to replace one now. Specializing in pattern matching, Walter Drake will help you identify, locate, and purchase the pattern at substantial savings. The Exchange also will buy sterling and silver plate flatware and holloware if you want to trade your set in for a new one. When you contact them with the pieces, pattern, and manufacturer you're interested in, they will feed the information to their computers and give you a complete itemized price list reflecting the outstanding savings. We priced six Damask Rose teaspoons by Oneida/Heirloom at $39.15 (retail $120). No C.O.D.s; add $1.50 for postage and handling with all orders. **C, PQ**

Furniture and Accessories

From high-tech to traditional, you can decorate your home with fine furniture by mail from manufacturers like Broyhill, Heritage, Henredon, Thomasville, Stanley, Thayer Coggin, and others. Send for catalogs or go shopping locally. When you find the perfect sofa and chair, get the manufacturer's name, description, model numbers, and fabric swatches and see if you can't find it by mail. Your house can be beautiful at half the price if you're willing to wait—often as long as 4 to 5 months.

ALEXANDER'S
701 Greensboro Road
High Point, NC 27260
(919) 882-0915
(919) 882-2313

Alexander's has no rag-time brands—they carry mid-to-upper-eche-
lon lines in accessories, bedroom furniture, chairs, dining-room furniture, floor rugs, lamps and lighting, mattresses and sleep
products, office furniture, patio and outdoor furniture, rattan and
wicker, sleepers and sofas, tables, upholstered furniture, and wall
systems. There are about 200 brands carried, including such names
as Chapman, Hayim, Henry Link, and Thomasville. Alexander's is
great . . . with "35% to 45% discounts, plus freight." Restocking
charge of 25% for stock items and 50% on special orders. **B, PQ**

ARISE FUTON MATTRESS CO.
37 Wooster St.
New York, NY 10013
(212) 925-0310

When you're too tired to stand up and be counted, you can always lie
down and be discounted. Arise sells its own make of contemporary
mattresses that fold up into couches: Five different styles of futons
(Japanese bed rolls) in sizes ranging from crib- to king-size and
occupying different price categories—twin-size futons ranged in
price from $89 to $225 at approximately $30 intervals. Arise also
carries sofa and bed frames, futon covers, down and cotton quilts and
quilt covers, as well as bolster pillows, throw pillows, and a variety of
cushions. Perusing their brochure triggered a host of possibilities to
unfold. Our favorite sofa and bed frame bore the name of king-sized
Kinko and was $625. By federal law, mattresses are not returnable;
other products acceptable for store credit. **B $2**

BLACKWELDER'S
U.S. Highway 21 North
Statesville, NC 28661
(800) 438-0201
(704) 872-8921: NC residents

This is the shiny black book for all you wood-be weekend decorators.
Features walnut, mahogany, cherrywood, rosewood, ash, maple,
wicker, and rattan furniture at prices that are knot bad. They even

branch into brass beds, Persian rugs, Kimball pianos, mirrors, and lamps—all from the family tree of famous names at 30% to 45% off retail. They're known by the companies they keep: American of Martinsville, Barcalounger, Chromcraft, Frederick Cooper, Fitz & Floyd, Henredon, Hickory, Pulaski, Selig, and more. Open six days a week and with customers calling from every nook and cranny in the country, this family-owned and operated business begs for your patience if their four in-bound WATS lines are busy. Shipping handled by their own truck line or by special contract rate (can even be lower than a common-carrier rate) with North American Van Lines. You may even see a driver unload wearing white gloves. "The customer is our highest priority," says John Blackwelder. **C $4 (refundable)**

BOYLES FURNITURE SALES
727 N. Main St.
P.O. Box 2084
High Point, NC 27261
(800) 334-3185
(800) 334-5135: DC, DE, SC, TN, VA, WV, MD, GA residents
(919) 889-4147: NC residents

Another North Carolina company carrying over 150 lines including Henredon, Heritage, Drexel, Century, Henkel, and 18th-century reproductions at 40% off (if you live in North Carolina or surrounding states); 30% off list if you live elsewhere. Shipping charges averaged $110 for 200 pounds including set-up or $80 by common carrier. Expect anywhere from an eight- to 12-week wait at the earliest and as long as five to six months at the outside. An interesting quirk: we found higher (35%) discounts during February. Will the South rise again in March? **B**

COLONY HOUSE FURNITURE
322 North Center St.
Statesville, NC 28677
(800) 438-5352
(704) 873-1863: NC residents

Here's a house that's worth looking into. They are a major discounter of fine home and office furnishings. Well over 300 of the top names in town at prices 25% to 40% off retail. Expect to pay a 50% deposit and the balance due upon delivery. Over a quarter of a century of savings with decorators on hand by phone or in their showroom to assist you. Delivery most anywhere—by company truck in local areas and to select geographical centers at no additional charge. Outside their regular trade area, delivery by common carrier. Deposit refunded if order canceled within 15 days. **B, PQ**

CONRAN'S
145 Huguenot St.
New Rochelle, NY 10801
(800) 431-2718
(914) 632-0515: NY residents call collect

Why wait for your knight in shining armoire to arrive at your door. Shop at home from this purveyor of things high and tech-ish. Technically, you might even be buying some original fabrications by Sir Terrance Conran himself. From mundane settees to the most contemporary upwardly mobile pit groups, you'll find both quality and value are their buy-words. From the modular groupings to heavy upholstered looks plus the helpful money-saving decorating tips and bend-over-backward service, Conran's your man. **C** January **$2,** others **$1** (quarterly issues)

THE EDGAR B. PLANTATION
Highway 158
P.O. Box 849
Clemmons, NC 27012
(800) 334-2010
(919) 766-0513: NC residents

Edgar B. Plantation features some of the finest reproductions of 18th-century furnishings available in America today. Befitting Scarlett O'Hara's Tara, they carry fine pieces (at 40% off) from over 100 mid-to-upper-end manufacturers like Henredon, Thomasville, Century, Davis, and Hickory at affordable prices. Eight-piece Thomasville bedroom suite retailing for $3,250 was $1,950 plus a $200 to $300 freight cost giving the buyer a $1,000 savings. Also, a large selection of classic, ornate wall units at an average of 40% off was available. Frankly, my chair, I don't give a dime. But at these prices, your decorating dollars won't be gone with the wind. **C $3**

ELKES CARPET OUTLET
2910 Archdale Road
High Point, NC 27263
(919) 434-4104

You've heard of having an uncle in the business, now you have an ant-

Furniture and Accessories 285

ler in the business. The Elkes have really racked up 50% savings and more on top-choice irregulars, closeouts, discontinued colors, and promotional styles of name-brand contract carpet. They've got a selection that is coming out of their ears (or should we say antlers). If you don't see what you want, call or write for a price quote since they have access to most major lines. If you caribou-t saving on most major brands, (commercial, industrial, and institutional lines) with names like Galaxy, Alexander Smith, Columbus, Wunda Weave, Philadelphia, send for their brochures. A catalog is planned. **B**

FRAN'S BASKET HOUSE
295 Route 10
Succasunna, NJ 07876
(201) 584-2230

Rattan is dandy and wicker is quicker to rearrange from parlor to patio. Find all your lightweight furniture here including dressers, headboards, chaise longues, porch furniture, even unusual baskets imported direct from Hong Kong, Poland, Spain, and the Philippines. Fran's considerable savings and selection does her Pier, one up. **C 50 cents**

FURNITURELAND SOUTH, INC.
2200 S. Main St.
P.O. Box 790
High Point, NC 27261
(800) 334-7393
(919) 885-0116: NC residents

When furniture comes from Furnitureland, does it follow that it's "soiled" and dirt cheap? We hope not, because we liked what we saw here. Aside from furniture, they carry lamps, accessories, and room-size rugs at savings averaging 35% to 50% off retail. They have a showroom with special prices on already discounted samples and closeouts. Orders require a 25% deposit (lower than many other firms), with the balance due upon delivery. There's a 20% restocking charge (plus freight). If they don't travel to your area with their trucks and crews, they'll connect with truck lines who do in-home set-ups. **B**

HENDRICKS FURNITURE, INC.
Route 6, Box 11
1500 N. Main St.
Mocksville, NC 27028
(704) 634-5978

This may sound Sealy but we found bargains on the Barcaloungers and Brown Jordans to be at least 40% below retail. That same chairful bit of news goes for over 200 lines including Drexel, Burlington, American of Martinsville, Simmons, Century, Pennsylvania House, Thomasville, Heritage, and more represented in their 18,000-square foot showroom. Brochures available from all the major manufacturers they represent. Freight charged by weight and distance: $25 to $45 per 100 pounds is the average. Remember, you will be saving sales tax if you are not a resident of NC. If the dining room suite is $5,000 retail plus sales tax of 5% ($250) and Hendricks' price is $3,000 and the weight is 800 pounds, you will only be paying $315 for freight. The proof of the savings is in you pocketbook. **PQ**

INTERNATIONAL VENTURES OF CALIFORNIA, INC.
P.O. Box 426
14240 Shakeridge Road
Jackson, CA 95642
(209) 267-0720

Rejoice, the price of those lovely handmade silk pillows seen only in decorator's showrooms before is now on the recline. From the laid-back land of California come elegant silk-covered pillows to enhance your rooms. There's a whole lot of pillow talk going on with 20% discounts to readers of this book. Each pillow is 16-by-16 and comes in a variety of print patterns ($20), 45 plain colors ($18), and a contemporary abstract design ($28). Minimum order is two pillows. Shipping by UPS. **C $1**

JAMES ROY INC.
15 E. 32nd St.
New York, NY 10016
(212) 679-2565

James has no Version of a catalog to serve as your Bible on prices, but he will send you (SASE) a free list of over 60 name-brand furniture and carpet lines discounted 33% to 40% off (⅓ off is guaranteed). Members of King James' Roy-al entourage include Broyhill, Heritage, Henredon, Thomasville, Stanley, and Pennsylvania House. He requires model, style, and color codes before he'll issue a proclamation on prices. Shipping time varies with the manufacturer. **B, PQ SASE**

KING'S CHANDELIER CO.
Highway 14, P.O. Box 667
Eden (Leaksville), NC 27288
(919) 623-6188

Let's shed some light on the subject of chandeliers. King's no jester— every crystal piece in the place is their own design. Lighting fixtures are crystal, brass, and pewter combinations. Chandeliers and sconces hold court in either brass or silver finish. Their catalog is filled with every style chandelier you can swing from as well as royal testimonials from customers such as Beverly Sills. Their prices are good when compared to similar quality merchandise in a retail show-room and their designs are often better. They pay shipping charges east of the Mississippi River. Chandeliers may be returned within five working days after receipt for a full refund (customer pays shipping). Debby Boone lights up your life—King's lights up your k-night. **C $2**

LAMP WAREHOUSE
1073 39th St.
Brooklyn, NY 11219
(212) 436-2207

Watt's a nice girl like you doing in a place like Brooklyn? Saving 25% off Stiffel lamps and every other major name-brand lighting fixture and shade available. Lamps are no light load, so figure on spending about $9 for shipping. There's a $10 restocking charge on returns and although they don't give refunds, they do give credit. **PQ**

LOFTIN-BLACK FURNITURE CO.
941 Randolph St.
Thomasville, NC 27360
(800) 334-7398
(919) 476-3117: NC residents

Loftin space? Less-than-lofty prices is one reason for lofting a letter to Loftin-Black. This 35-year-old firm can furnish you with furniture, lamps, and Oriental rugs from over 300 major manufacturers. Prices generally run about 35% below retail. Their price quotes include freight charges and they require a 50% deposit before they'll ship. They have their own trucks and will set up your purchase in your home in 26 states (they use common carriers or van lines in the remaining states). **B**

MALLORY'S
P.O. Box 1150
Jacksonville, NC 28540
(800) 334-2340
(919) 447-2136: NC residents

Mallory's should watch their calories: Some of their furniture looks positively stuffed. This firm carries Baker, Drexel, Heritage, Henredon, and over 35 other lines of high-end merchandise. Prices are discounted to 40%. They have 30,000 square feet of showrooms in Jacksonville and Havelock, North Carolina. Their slick 24-page catalog is beautifully photographed; get one, plop down at the kitchen table, and sample their furniture buffet. There's a 40% restocking charge if custom ordered. If an item is returned, customer is responsible for freight and safe return. **C, PQ**

MURROW FURNITURE GALLERIES
3514 S. College Road
P.O. Box 4337
Wilmington, NC 28406
(800) 334-1614
(919) 799-4010: NC residents

To Murrow, to Murrow, I'll be there, to Murrow, it's only a stamp away. Murrow represents over 500 reputable manufacturers in the heart of this country's home furnishing industry. Resident decorators available to assist you on choices of furniture, carpeting, and accessories at an average of 40% savings. Deposit with order required, balance due upon delivery. Custom-made upholstery requires eight to 12 weeks for production and delivery. Brochure gives a partial list of brands and company policies. Write Annie time. **B**

NITE FURNITURE CO.
P.O. Box 249
611 S. Green St.
Morganton, NC 28655
(704) 437-1491

Good Nite, ladies. Merrily these folks have rolled along for over 35 years giving discounts on first-quality furniture. For a refundable $25, they will ship 10 pounds of catalogs, although they have brochures from each manufacturer that are free. Over 200 manufacturers represented with brands such as Drexel, Heritage, Henredon, and Frederick-Edward. They also carry bedspreads, fabric, carpets, lamps, and wall coverings. "It's smart to shop at Nite." **C, B**

NORTH CAROLINA FURNITURE SHOWROOMS
1805 N.W. 38th Ave.
Ft. Lauderdale, FL 33311
(305) 739-6945

These tarheels are well-heeled in furniture with 409 leading furniture manufacturers represented. Discounts range from 20% to 40%, so when you order from their wealth of inventory you won't land in the poorhouse. They require a 25% deposit to place an order: all sales are final. Call for a price quote and be sure to ask about sale prices on samples and closeouts for further discounts. Manufacturers' brochures are provided. **PQ**

PLEXI-CRAFT QUALITY PRODUCTS
514 W. 24th St.
New York, NY 10011
(212) 924-3244

Plexi-Craft sells a variety of lucite and plexiglass acrylic products including furniture, cubes, tables, kitchen and bathroom accessories, and more at prices below what you would pay in department and hardware stores. They also do custom orders; send a sketch of what you want molded into plastic and they'll send you a price quote. Average 50% discount, all house brands. **C $2**

PRIBA FURNITURE
5 Wendy Court
P.O. Box 13295
Greensboro, NC 27405
(800) 334-2498
(919) 855-9034: NC residents

Don't be a La-Z-Boy and pay retail for your home furnishings. Priba offers discounts up to 40% across the table—that sounds good sofa-r. They carry major brands of furniture, lamps and accessories, carpets, fabrics and leather, shades and blinds, wall coverings, and bedding. A 30% deposit is due when placing an order, balance is due prior to shipping. Write or call for the price list or price quote. Brochures on request but you must specify the manufacturer. **B, PQ**

QUALITY FURNITURE MARKET OF LENOIR, INC.
2034 Hickory Blvd., S.W.
Lenoir, NC 28645
(704) 728-2946

Just because you're Quality doesn't mean you can't have Quantity and this army of four-legged (predominantly wooden) soldiers definitely got our attention. We were furnished with a list of about 130 notable names in furniture, porch and patio lines, and area rugs fit to outfit the home fort. As a general overview, we saw such major brands as Barcalounger, Chromcraft, Broyhill, Drexel, Henredon, Heritage, La-Z-Boy, Levolor blinds, Sealy, Serta, and Huntley/Thomasville, to trumpet but a few. Prices on these decorated heroes are approximately 40% off retail. All orders must be paid in full before shipment. They operate on a "cost plus" basis, which means prices are subject to change by the manufacturer. **PQ**

RICHARD B. ZARBIN & ASSOC.
225 West Hubbard St., 5th Floor
Chicago, IL 60610
(312) 527-1570

"Crate day in the morning! It's here, Maude, it's finally here! Our furniture's come to live with us and we won't have to sleep in the bathtub anymore!" This company can save you 40% on furniture or almost as much on a number of other items. Over 100 brands are available including Thomasville, Baker, Heritage, Drexel, Henredon, Stiffel, Sealy, Flexsteel, and Lane. Lees & Masland carpet is offered at 75 cents per yard over cost. Write them with manufacturer and model number and they'll quote a price. Crated shipments from the factory cannot be made to private homes (other than in the Chicago area) where someone is not always available to assist in unloading. The average delivery time is 10 to 16 weeks. **PQ**

ROSE FURNITURE CO.
P.O. Box 1829
214 S. Elm St.
High Point, NC 27261
(800) 334-1045
(919) 882-6871: NC residents

You can Bette your fiddler it ain't owned by Midler. Owner Bill Kester is the grandson of the founder and he's discounting 300 manufacturers' lines to the tune of 40%. If you're on a Rose bud-get, spend $800 to $1,000 on purchases and save $200 to $300 after freight charges. They require a 20% to 30% deposit for orders to be placed. Rose has eight trucks and two-man teams to set up furniture in your home. With an average of 1,000 pieces to deliver per week, it's no wonder their sales Rose last year. **B, PQ**

SHAW FURNITURE
131 W. Academy St.
Randleman, NC 27317
(800) 334-6799
(919) 498-2628: NC residents

By George, Bernard! I think Shaw's got it! Not only does "the largest furniture discount house in the Carolinas" sell up to a 45% discount (not including sales tax, not required outside North Carolina), they'll even make motel reservations for me and My Fair Lady if we plan to visit their galleries. Shaw represents over 300 major-brand furniture companies (except Thomasville) and they also carry brass beds, clocks, lamps, mirrors, bedding, lighting—even grand pianos. They set the stage for savings with the prop-er discounts. They require a check for half of the purchase when ordering, then the balance before shipment. **B, PQ**

SOBOL HOUSE
140 Richardson Blvd.
Black Mountain, NC 28711
(704) 669-8031

Sobol sells furniture from over 150 companies at 40% to 45% off
retail (you pay shipping) or 30% and Sobol picks up the tab, So-
bolster your savings. Select from Century, Thomasville, Pennsylvania House, Broyhill, Sealy, Clayton Marcus, American Drew, and
others. They'll also furnish you with carpeting, wallpaper, drapes,
blinds, and bedspreads. There is a 20% restocking charge for
returns. A helpful "request for quote" form is sent by the company
along with instructions on how to go about shopping by mail from
them. **C** ($$ varies depending on manufacturer)

TODAY'S FURNITURE GALLERY
208 E. Green
High Point, NC 27260
(919) 885-8711: readers call collect

If your furniture has that frazzled look from yesteryear, update your
upholstered furniture to today. Today's Furniture Gallery specializes
in medium- to high-end contemporary lines of furniture. Notable
names include Finesse (upholstery is in natural fibers only), Ello (for
mirrors), and Carson. Prices are 35% to 45% off retail and selection
is tremendous: They have a 24,000-square foot showroom and a new
warehouse of 40,000 square feet of discontinued, overinventoried,
and special sale items. A 50% deposit is required to order, balance on
delivery. Their trucks regularly travel to Maryland, Washington, DC,
and Florida—they'll set up in your home. Common carriers are also
used. The restocking charge is 20%, plus the freight back. **B**

UTILITY CRAFT, INC.
Route 1
Willard Road
High Point, NC 27260
(800) 334-3897
(919) 454-2390: NC residents

Hounded by high prices? Buy Bassett. Reverent of time? Try Colonial
clocks. Walking the streets for bargains? Have a Hooker. A-Nile-ated
by expenses? Riverside's on your side. Exercising restraint in buying
new bedding? Simmons says, "We bend over to please." Up in arms

over costly carpets? Get in step with West Point Pepperell. If you think buying furniture and accessories involves an endless stream of questions, call the Utility company. They can turn on the bright lights and offer discounts on most major manufacturers. They specialize in solid wood, 18th-century, and colonial reproduction pieces. **B**

VARNER WAREHOUSE SALES INC.
2605 Uwharrie Road
High Point, NC 27263
(800) 334-3894
(919) 431-8113: NC residents

If you want to garner the wealth of Silas Marner, then you're gonna wanna' pay a visit to this Varner. When furniture prices drove miserly Silas buggy, he steered his way to VW. (He had a rabbit interest in saving money.) Discounts were 30% to 40% on first-quality furniture and accessories such as upholstery, carpets, lamps, etc. An extra 20% discount was offered on selected floor samples, usually the cream of the crop, used to impress buyers at trade shows. Varner snares some particularly good buys (50% to 60% off) on showroom samples. **B, PQ**

WAYSIDE INTERIORS
P.O. Box 207
High Point, NC 27261-0207
(919) 882-8823
(919) 885-6716

It's not hard to imagine that George Washington slept in one of the rooms pictured in the "Drexel 18th-Century Classics" brochure we received promptly from this company. By the Wayside policy, almost any line on the market can be obtained and is discounted 30% to 40%. "Martha! Bring my slippers while I prop up on this Boling chair. Items from that Forge Company are revolutionary. See, they have Liberty furniture and the brochure is free. By George, there's the Royal line (usually costs a king's ransom)." **B**

YOUNG'S FURNITURE AND RUG CO.
P.O. Box 5005
High Point, NC 27262
(919) 883-4111

If you're Young at the heart of the furniture industry, the future belongs to you. This is an ageless source for indoor, outdoor, rattan, and office furniture, as well as bedding, lamps, clocks, and carpet at discounts up to 40% off (special orders receive similar discounts). In the heart of furnitureland, though not as Young as they look, these folks have been in business 37 years and carry over 150 better-quality lines, among them such old-time favorites as Baker, Henredon, Kittinger, Heritage, Drexel, Henkel-Harris, Century, Councill, and Hickory. They require a ⅓-down payment on all orders and have an excellent delivery system with shipping time generally varying from two to five weeks. If you're vacationing in the area, a look at their 25,000-square foot furniture showroom could be the High Point of your trip. **C**

Hardware and Tools

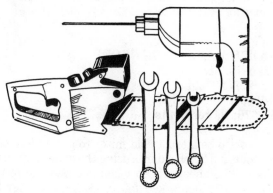

If you're considering renovating your home or just building a classy sandbox, tools and hardware can be expensive and often hard to find discounted locally. Hook up with these listings for brass and porcelain faucets, chain saw winches, hydraulic presses, underwater sweepers, or a pair of woodchopper's chaps.

ASSOCIATED DISTRIBUTORS
401 Augusta St.
Cincinnati, OH 45202
(513) 621-0677

Discounts are the tools of their trade. We don't want to drill it in but why tool around paying retail when you can get a $44.50 air hammer from Associated for $25.50? Air ratchets at $47.85 (retail $79.95). Sanders, grinders, wrenches, jacks—everything for the mechanically inclined at least 20% less. **C $2** (refundable)

ASSOCIATED MARKETING GROUP
100 W. Franklin St.
Hackensack, NJ 07601
(800) 331-1000: orders only
(201) 488-0626: NJ residents

You don't have to be a crusty old miser to get a piece of the pie. If you've got four and 20 blackbirds using the shower, or just one, your water bills will be cheep, cheep when you use one of these water misers. Order a trademarked faucet ($12.95), shower ($14.95), or toilet ($10.95) miser and save up to thousands of gallons of water per year, reduce your fuel costs up to $125 per home and cut water usage in half per flush. Send $29.95 plus shipping for all three. Help conserve our water supply and your money supply at the same time. **B**

B

BAILEY'S, INC.
P.O. Box 550
Highway 101
Laytonville, CA 95454
(800) 358-1661
(707) 984-6133: CA residents

Paul could have saved himself some Bunyans by using this cata-log for supplies. We saw items ranging from extra large dogs (claws) preferred by experienced timberfallers on down to a toy chain saw for the little cut-up. Woodsmen can lumber along in Chippewa-brand boots at savings approaching 25% off list price. Significant discounts on chain saws didn't go against our grain, either. McCulloch, Pioneer, Homelite, in fact, all brands (except Stihl), were carried and were waiting for the right jerk to make them roar to life. A chain saw winch was a cinch at $349 and a pair of protective forester chaps was

$33 to $46, depending on size. Be the first chip off your block to axe for a catalog. **C**

CONTINENTAL LAWN MOWER MANUFACTURING CO.
3205 E. Abrams
Arlington, TX 76010
(817) 640-1198

Great grass-cutting prices on riding lawn mowers are not a continent away; they are but a phone call away. This is the manufacturer cutting corners by offering their mowers by mail as well as to customers who save freight by driving to their 43,000-plus square foot factory. Construction on the eight horsepower basic is all steel, parts are under warranty for one year from the factory. The engine is a four-cycle Briggs & Stratton with authorized dealer warranty. It has a three-position with reverse transmission, chain drive, safety clutch, adjustable cutting height, can carry 500 pounds, and comes assembled. Basic price was $420 in September 1982. From here, it's like buying a car. You add to the options and price. Pneumatic wheel, four-wheel rear drive, padded and/or spring seat, grass catcher, and high-speed sprocket are some choices. **B, PQ**

GILLIOM MANUFACTURING INC.
1700 Scherer Parkway
St. Charles, MO 63301
(314) 724-1814

Keep this number handy, man. If you're into power tools, Gilliom has the plans and tools for build-it-yourself band saws, lathe drill presses, wood shapers, circular saw tables—all designed to save you $50 to $250. Aside from power tools themselves, there were kits of metal parts for construction of home workshop power tools. We saw plenty of parts and accessories, such as V-pulleys, line shafts, work lights, motors, sanding drums. All parts are guaranteed for five years against mechanical failure due to defect. There's no minimum order and a 10% restocking charge on returns. This is definitely a place for things that go bump and grind in the night. **C $1, PQ**

MASTER MECHANIC MANUFACTURING CO.
P.O. Box A
280 S. Pine St.
Burlington, WI 53105
(800) 558-9444
(414) 763-2428: WI residents

Mastermind a plot to save about 20% on a wide range of mechanical items and tools. We saw hydraulic presses, winches, drill presses, air compressors, electric motors, pumps, electric tools, etc. The Master Mechanic alternators can guard against disaster in case of power outages. The 1,500-watt direct drive generators (four horsepower with two-year warranty) were $391 and we spied a 14-inch Remington gas chain saw for $69.50. A $2.50 invoice service charge is added to all orders under $20. Their 72-page catalog is electrifying. C

RENOVATOR'S SUPPLY
Millers Falls, MA 01349
(413) 659-3961

They've got the handle on everything: brass door knobs, drawer pulls, brass and porcelain faucets, chandelier prisms, door hinges, fancy letter boxes, weathervanes, brass bolts and hooks, copper lanterns, and the "world's largest selection of brass switch plates." Everything a renovated home needs to feel pretty, at savings up to 70% (knock on wood). Most of the unique items are specially produced for owners Claude and Donna Jeanloz: the others are imported from around the world. They'll exchange items, give credit, or refund the purchase price if not satisfied. Their new magazine, "Victorian Homes," is for young couples renovating old homes. C $2 (refundable)

SAFE EQUIPMENT CO., INC.
Route 1, P.O. Box 61
Wallace, NC 28466
(800) 682-5001: NC residents
(919) 285-5679

Better Safe than sorry. Don't go down the tubes financially paying full price for pumps, suctions, and Briggs & Stratton engines when you can save 35%. An old wives' tale says there's safety in numbers so you must order a minimum of 10 items to receive the discount. Happy motoring, folks. B

U.S. GENERAL TOOL AND HARDWARE
100 Commercial St.
Plainview, NY 11803
(516) 349-7282: orders
(516) 349-7275: inquiries

After 25 years, this General has a plan of attack to battle high prices. The lieutenant who answered our phone request could hardly be awarded a medal of honor. His rudeness smacked of the enemy. Nevertheless, we found an army of name-brand hand and power tools and hardware marching to the tune of 40% off in the 195-page coded catalog, which lists late-model items from Black & Decker, Rockwell, and others. Those items coded with a "D" are shipped directly from the manufacturer to avoid double shipping costs. Also check into additional discounts with the Volume Discount Plan for orders exceeding $300, you'll receive an additional 2% discount; 3% off for $500 or more, and 4% for $1,000 or more orders. Yes sir, that's American. C $1 (refundable)

WORLD ABRASIVE CO.
1866 "U" Eastern Parkway
Brooklyn, NY 11233
(212) 495-4301

Thankfully, the people here aren't noted for their abrasive personalities, even when they're worn out. (They certainly didn't rub us the wrong way.) They've got sanding belts, discs, sheets, rolls, and other sanding accessories at nitty-gritty savings. True grit prices on sanding discs: $3.46 for 25 fine 6-inch discs ($6.75 elsewhere). Of course, their world also includes wire wheels, goggles, oil stones, and grinding wheels for those who like the grind of everyday life. Prices were about 30% to 50% off retail; there's no restocking charge or minimum order and they'll refund or exchange on returns. C

ZIP-PENN INC.
P.O. Box 15129
Sacramento, CA 95851
(800) 824-8521
(800) 952-5535: CA residents

When Charlene the Chain Saw needs a new wardrobe, Zip-Penn zips in with accessories to outfit her in style. We saw discounts up to 50% on accessories, protective clothing, and parts that made our chain saw break into a snaggle-toothed smile. Write for their famous "Zip-o-Gram" listing many bargains. Other locations at 1372 Blounstown Highway, P.O. Box 4248, Tallahassee, FL 32303 or 2008 E. 33rd. St., P.O. Box 10308, Erie, PA 16515. **PQ**

Housewares

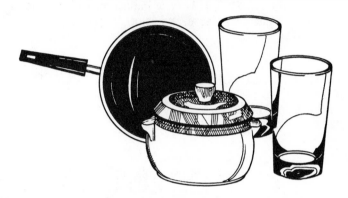

Why go to Belgium for waffles when you can iron them out on your own. Or how about Sabatier knives for slicing that elegant pâte en croute? Celebrate St. Patrick's Day with a set of Irish ale tankards. Raise your cooking to haute cuisine with Calphalon cookware. Americans are entertaining in-house more and more and singing, "Someone's in the kitchen with china." Here's your chance to add to your collection of housewares and be the envy of the next progressive dinner party.

A. BENJAMIN & CO.
80-82 Bowery
New York, NY 10013
(212) 226-6013

Don't throw in the Towle. Get 25% to 50% off name-brand silver-ware, china, and crystal. We went on a buying "Benj" with Gorham, International, Reed & Barton, Wallace, Heirloom, Lunt, with a minimum order of $100. It is very important to have the model or style number, pattern, pieces, and colors. **PQ** (with SASE)

ALEXANDER BUTCHER BLOCK AND SUPPLY CO.
176 Bowery
New York, NY 10012
(212) 226-4021

This family-owned store is a chop off the old retail block. They fashion their own first-quality furniture, tools, and kitchenware using 100% maple, oak, and some Formica. Find 100 different styles of chairs alone. Alexander says they can custom-make a piece of furniture to your exact specifications in a day's time and will "beat anyone's price" claiming 50% off department store tickets. Write or call them with your wood-be specifications. There's a 20% charge for returned tables. **PQ**

BACHMAIER & KLEMMER
Postfach 220
D-8240 Berchestesgaden-2
West Germany
Phone: 8652-5079 (dial "01" for operator assistance in making this call)

Birds of a feather clock together at this German clock factory, which sells a variety of plain or painted cuckoo clocks. Prices are 45% to 50% lower than comparable American clocks. There's a guarantee on material and workmanship for one year and they'll exchange during this period. If the clock has been damaged in transport, they'll replace (but official transport claim by a local post office must be made). There's no minimum order and no restocking charge. So speak now or forever hold your timepiece. **C $1**

BOARDMAN, LTD.
833 Broadway
Albany, NY 12201
(518) 462-6771

The Albany store offers discounts by mail across the board, man, on everything from adult games to yogurt makers, with clocks, jewelry, pasta machines, stereos, typewriters, and whirlpool baths in between. Ladies' Seiko watches won't get you ticked off at $186 (retail $225). A Rival crockpot was cooking at $21.50, bentwood rocker was rockin' at $67.60 (retail $140), Panasonic mini tape recorder plugged in at $36.66 (retail $52.95). **C $2**

THE CHEF'S CATALOG
3915 Commercial Ave.
Northbrook, IL 60015
(800) 331-1750: credit card orders
(312) 480-9400: IL residents

Cuisine is an art and the Chef's Catalog has restaurant cookware supplies from around the world to aid you in your next gourmet masterpiece. Sometimes it's better to give and to receive: Give them your name and address and receive a retail catalog and a series of special sale catalogs, too. From chafing dishes to choppers to Victorian food molds, all the wonderful brands like Cuisinart and Calphalon are served up with tempting reductions. A Belgium waffle iron by Nordic Ware was $31.50, plus $4.50 postage (regularly $37 plus tax in the retail stores). An introductory special featured the Cuisinart DLC7 Pro Food Processor for $225.95 plus $9.50 shipping for a savings of $50. Recipes for everything from peas and rice to Peking Duck appear periodically. **C $1**

CHINA CLOSET
6807 Wisconsin Ave.
Bethesda, MD 20815
(800) 368-2722
(301) 656-5400: MD residents

Why have a China Closet when you could have a great wall of china? Discounts of 20% to 40% might be one reason. Although we had a yen for china, we found their newspaper brochure more heavily populated with pictures of kitchenware products such as woks (Ah so! A wok-in closet!), knives, pots and pans, spatulas, and other assorted accessories. China Closet has an open door policy on returns: If you don't like your purchase for any reason, you have 30 days to return it for a refund or replacement. Now that's a guarantee that won't Confucius. **B**

CLOTHCRAFTERS
Elkhart Lake, WI 53020
(414) 876-2112

Smile and say "cheesecloth" for only $2 for two yards. This cloth can be used for straining, keeping salad and parsley fresh for weeks, plus a variety of other purposes. For pots that are too hot to handle, order denim potholders, $2, or casserole cushions, $2.50. Excellent buys on 100% seamed cotton flannel sheets compared to expensive imports. Twin (70-by-108) was $11 in white; in blue or yellow, $13. Full or queen (90-by-108) in white was $13 and $15 in blue or yellow. Pillowcases were $6 a pair in white, $7 in blue or yellow. A white cotton shower curtain needing no liner was $20. There's no minimum order, no restocking charge, and refunds are issued on request. **B**

COLLINSWORTH
109 N. Broad St.
Lancaster, OH 43130
(800) 228-5444: orders only
(614) 687-2032: OH residents

Buying glassware at retail prices can be a real pain in the pocketbook. Collinsworth (a division of Anchor-Hocking) for 18 years has helped shatter the high cost with classic hand-cut glassware at see-through savings of up to 50%, plus special discounts for those buying in quantity. Ashtrays, ale tankards, drinking glasses, decanters, candleholders, and bud vases. A few crystal-clear bargains: a half-litre wine carafe with four wine glasses at $14.50 ($29 value), monogrammed sangria pitcher with six glasses at $28.50 ($57 value), a 10-inch monogrammed oil lamp for $9.25 ($18.50 value). Each set comes with a card signed by the artisan who cut the glass. What class! Minimum order, $15. **C**

GRAND FINALE
P.O. Box 34257
Farmers Branch, TX 75234
(214) 934-9777

Designer clothing, fine furnishings, and elegant accessories bow out in the pages of Grand Finale, the first catalog company formed exclusively to offer luxury merchandise at significant savings. Designers' names are not always given, but imagine ordering a blouse and finding out it's an Albert Nipon! A recent catalog featured curtain calls by Anne Klein fashions at 40% off, a 20-piece set of ironstone by Wedgwood for $49.90 (retail $146), and a designed and stamped Baccarat crystal perfume bottle for $39.90 (originally $50). Write for their smashing catalog. You'll ask for an encore. **C $2**

HANDART EMBROIDERIES
Hing Wai Building, Room 106
36 Queen's Road Central
Hong Kong
Phone: 011-852-5-235744 (dial direct)

We're not above taking a Handart with items like these. This company stocks embroidered table cloths, kimonos, shirts, blouses, and other Oriental items at about 20% below retail. We saw in their Xeroxed catalog of price sheets a 72-inch round hand-crocheted lace table cover available for only $25. Children's Kung Fu style pajamas were $8 (sizes 2 to 14). We also saw hand-crocheted doilies and placemats as well as ladies' pure silk printed flower scarves for $12. Satin sheets for a queen-size bed were $36. Jade ornaments and ivory hand-carved ornaments were priced reasonably, too. They go out on a limb to offer a full money refund if the customer is not satisfied for any reason. **C**

IMOCO INC.
2201 Parkside St.
P.O. Box 2052
Irving, TX 75061
(214) 254-0151

Imoco, you're ok. Imoco sells housewares primarily, carrying Corning Corelle Livingware 35-piece sets of Wildflower and Spice-O-Life designs at $89.95 and $79.95 (retail price of $178). A 20-piece set of New French White Corning Ware is also offered at $69.95 ($156 retail), as is Corning's Special Occasion set, which includes a giant turkey roaster, that can be gobbled up for $69.95 ($105.96 retail). Corning Rangetoppers are carried in Wildflower and Cornflower patterns. Pots, pans (waterless cookware), and handmade porcelain china are also available, along with Oneida silver, Montrose stoneware, Cannon towels, and Samsonite luggage at discounts of approximately 50%. Thirty-day full-refund/replacement if defective. **C $2, B**

KITCHEN BAZAAR
4455 Connecticut Ave., N.W.
Washington, DC 20008
(800) 424-3777: orders only
(202) 363-4625: inquiries

Mark it on your colander to write for this catalog of kitchenware including gourmet cook and serve ware. Sift through the retail to find the reductions and get on their mailing list for periodic sales simmering up to 70% off. January is traditionally their clearance month where they've gathered all the losers and slashed prices to the bone. Sabatier knives were cut from $15.98 to $7.99, a French Madeleine pan from $6.99 to $5.99, a Romertopf clay cooker from $49.68 to $34.99, a copper paella pan from $50 to $39.99, and stock pots and crockpots, stack pans and rack pans. Last call on Le Creuset/Cousances at 50% off was really cookin'. Shipping charges from $3 to $7 should not grate on you. **C**

KUSTOM KRAFT CO.
P.O. Box Y
Edgemont, SD 57735
(800) 843-8312
(605) 662-7235: SD residents

Kustom offers black walnut serving ware at prices you wood not believe. These are factory-seconds on sale at 30% to 50% below retail, and often having small, insignificant blemishes you might not even notice. Lettuce look at salad bowls: An 11-by-5 bowl will serve you at $23.50 and 11-inch salad tongs were $7.50. Taking a slice at cheese board prices, an 8-by-16 cheeser with dome and knife, accented with inlaid maple strips was $28.75. Plenty of pepper mill sets, wine racks, candleholders, cutting boards, and other decorative accessories. **C**

LINEN AND FABRIC OUTLET
100 E. Louisiana
McKinney, TX 75069
(214) 542-4516

Remember the hit song by John Linen, "I Want To Hold Your Pan?"

Now there are potholders for every color scheme along with placemats, aprons, tablecloths, napkins, card table covers, and other coordinated accessories discounted 40% to 60%. What did John Linen say when his wife spilled something on the tablecloth? Yoko, oh no! If you live in a yellow submarine, you're bound to find something to match in their color catalog. **C $1**

MONSANTO PLASTICS AND RESINS CO.
800 N. Lindbergh Blvd.
St. Louis, MO 63166
(314) 694-1000

OK, maybe you never made it as a football hero. Just because you didn't bask in glory in the past doesn't mean you can't bask on the grass in the present. For $1.50 per square foot, you can put stadium Astroturf remnants around your pool area, in the kitchen, or on the patio. Rolls are 10 feet to 350 feet long and in 15-foot widths. These folks prefer not to cut existing pieces to exact dimensions, but to select the piece(s) that best meet your requirements. It's not returnable, so if you don't like your rug—turf luck! (Still . . . while you may never be able to cut like O.J. Simpson, you won't have to cut like your Lawn Boy, either.) "So let's go, men, and remember: When the going gets turf, the turf gets going. Get out there and kick As-troturf!" **PQ**

PARIS BREAD PANS
500 Independence Ave., S.E.
Washington, DC 20003
(202) 544-6858

Founder Clyde Brooks writes that having lived in Paris many years, he grew fond of French cuisine—especially the light, crusty bread that the French are noted for. He devised his own formula and, unable to find pans comparable to those used in France, he designed his own. A set of two pans costs $11.20, including postage and a four-pan set was $16.20, much lower than in retail gourmet shops. New items offered include a San Francisco sourdough pan and recipe, $9.25; oversize cookie sheets to utilize the whole oven, $7.50 to $8.50; and the slice-a-slice machine for cutting store-bought bread slices in half, $9.50 to $12.50. Our Mr. Brooks says you can save plenty of dough by baking your own. **B**

PFALTZGRAFF PFACTORY STORE
3325 W. Market St.
York, PA 17404
(717) 792-1440

They say it's "pfabulous, pforever, pfantastic!" It's Pfaltzgraff stoneware, glassware, and copperware. Every piece is made from natural materials, hand-finished and hand-decorated. They offer a world of ware for your kitchen counter or dinner table—platters, soup tureens, casserole dishes, wine goblets, gravy boats, mugs, copper candlesticks, and cookie cutters. Stoneware is safe in microwave ovens, freezers, and dishwashers and is chip resistant. **C**

THE UNDERGROUND
311½ S. 11th St.
Tacoma, WA 98402
(206) 383-2041

Hey, wait a minute. With a name like that, Jon and Karen Fayth must be doing something right. Keep the Fayth because some juicy bargains are in store for health nuts who want to prepare nutritious foods at home. Champion juicers, for example, were priced 20% lower to put the squeeze on the competition. Flour children who want to make the daily grind a little finer will barley be able to contain themselves after seeing the Mil-Rite food grinders also discounted. **C $1**

WESTON BOWL MILL
Weston, VT 05161
(802) 824-6219

Super Bowl any day! You wooden strike out at Weston Bowl because their housewares aren't your everyday run of the Mill. Maple, birch, elm, and beech sacrifice their roots to become salad bowls, cheese boards, knife holders, pine sugar buckets, stools, coffee tables, shelves and racks, canisters, and jewelry boxes. Beautiful quality in your choice of natural or dark lacquer finish or no finish. Prices are a chip off the old buck, too. There's a $5 service charge on all orders under $50, with a minimum order of $3. **C 50 cents**

Windows and Walls

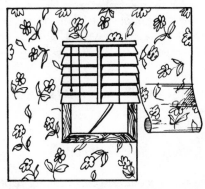

Here's a tip on how to measure your windows when buying blinds. To avoid any possible confusion when stating the sizes for your blinds inside a window, remember the *width* is the measurement taken from left to right, the *length* is taken from top to bottom, the *sill height* is the measurement taken from the floor (or counter top) to the window sill. Ask for free installation instructions when ordering your blinds. It's not difficult and will save you labor charges.

ALEXANDERS WALLPAPER
2964 Gallows Road
Falls Church, VA 22042
(703) 560-5524

This may sound a little spacey, but if you get high, you can unroll your own grasscloth. This company carries Arirang, their own design of grasscloth handmade in Korea, as well as another type of grasscloth, plus cork, two lines of silk string, and hand-sliced woods. Prices are 50% to 70% lower than retail stores. The minimum order is a unit package, which is one double roll. Their refund policy is 30 days from invoice shipment if unopened, with a 20% restocking charge. Come on along. **C $2.25**

AMERICAN DISCOUNT WALLCOVERINGS
1411 5th Ave.
Pittsburgh, PA 15219
(800) 245-1768
(412) 471-6941: PA residents call collect

We didn't give this discounter their walking papers with brands like Schumacher, Walltex, Katzenbach, and Warren with woven woods and mini-blinds from Kirsch, Graber, Bali, and Flexalum at 20% or more off. All goods are first-quality. Give them the length and width of the window, pattern name, color, and trim specs and you'll get a price quote quicker than you can say Levolor, Levolor, Levolor. There's no minimum order. There's a 20-day exchange or refund period on full bolts of wall covering (less 20% restocking charge), with no returns on custom window treatments. **PQ**

BEST BROS. PAINTS
312 E. Walnut St.
Lancaster, PA 17602
(717) 393-2792

What the Best Bros. lack in modesty they more than make up for in savings. Specializing in paint, wall coverings, and miscellaneous supplies in names like Best Bros., Walltex, Wallmate, and Eisenhart. These folks sell at 40% to 75% lower than full-price retail stores (and if there's one thing we hate, it's wall-owing in high prices). There's a full refund on in-stock items and a 20% handling (restocking) charge on specially ordered merchandise. Paint the town red with the money you save on paints, or walls across the country with the bargains on discontinued wallpapers. **PQ**

THE BLIND SPOT
2067 N. Central Expressway
Suite 102
Richardson, TX 75080
(214) 669-1383

If you want elegant window treatments at affordable prices, you've got it made in the shade with The Blind Spot. Among the brands we spotted: Levolor and Bali mini-blinds, Louverdrape, Graber, and Flexalum, vertical blinds, woven woods and window shades at up to 60% off of suggested list. Everything's first-quality, custom made. Supply style, color, size, and model number and the store will send you an informative product brochure that also tells you how to measure your windows for blinds and shades. They'll also send you a price list to determine the cost. Great selection of fabrics, bedspreads, baskets, feather dusters at discounted prices. Send style, color, size, and model number. **B, PQ**

HARMONY SUPPLY INC.
18 High St.
Medford, MA 02155
(617) 395-2600

She'd rather use Harmony than his money when 60% to 80% savings are in store. When the wallpaper hangs limp like a wilted wallflower and hides in the corner in shame, write this company and give your roomful of blues something to sing about. Harmony carries over 2,500 patterns in wall coverings (plus grasscloth), as well as Flexalum and Levolor blinds. Discounts on special orders run 30% to 50% off, while in stock merchandise is an even bigger bargain. In-stock merchandise can be returned for a full refund; however, there's a 20% restocking charge on special orders. No brochures or price lists; send them a pattern number and Harmony will send you the pitch. **PQ**

INTERIORS BY SANZ
P.O. Box 1794
701 Greensboro Road
High Point, NC 27261
(919) 883-4622

From inside out, Interiors by Sanz turns all others into inferiors.

Prices were an incredible 30% to 90% below manufacturers' suggested list prices on wallpapers, fabrics, and grasscloths. Hang out with such famous names as Brunschwig & Fils, Scalamandré Silks, Louis Bowen, Schumacher, Waverley, Eisenhart, York Wallcoverings and Imperial Papers, as well as almost 60 others (with more added monthly). Over 150,000 rolls in stock so they're worth calling if you know the pattern number. No minimum order. Complete refund on in-stock orders within 30 days; 20% restocking charge on special orders. It makes Sanz to shop at Sanz. **B, PQ**

MUTUAL WALLPAPER AND PAINT CO.
812 W. Main St.
Louisville, KY 40202
(502) 583-0523

Ninety-eight models of veneer on the wall, 98 models of veneer. That's how many different patterns this company offers in their catalog and we'll drink to that! No sheepish followers allowed at this well-flocked catalog store. Do a whole room (12-by-14-by-8) for as little as $35. Both regular and prepasted varieties, strippable vinyls and flock, fabric-backed vinyls, and all the tools of the trade. Savings up to 50% is Mutual-ly agreeable. **C $1** (actual vinyl and flock samples); **C 35 cents** (for pictures of vinyl and flock)

PAINT & PATTERN
2901 Avenue K
Plano, TX 75074
(214) 423-2684

Step right up, friends! You say you want fabric and upholstery? Carpets and floor coverings? Wallpaper and wall coverings? Drapes and blinds? Well, folks, they've got all that and more! Waverly, Delmar, Levolor, Armstrong, Congoleum—you name it, they've got it. Designer Solarium floor covering was just $9.95, that's $16.50 in many other shops. And carpet was only 10% over their cost! Yessir—builders' prices to everyone! And if we didn't paint a good picture with our patter, why, write with the item, model, and pattern description and see for yourself! **PQ**

ROBINSON'S WALLCOVERINGS
225 W. Spring St.
Titusville, PA 16354
(814) 827-1893

Tired of being just another brick in the wall? Break out of the mold and let the real you shine through with Robinson's vinyls, flocks, and fabric patterns at discounts up to 50%. All papers come in pre-trimmed and prepasted rolls and some styles come with matching fabrics (special order). Unpasted rolls were $2.35 to $2.85. They also have coordinated cabinets, mirrors, sconces, curtains, mini-blinds, and other accessories to perk up your surroundings. **C $1**

RONNIE DRAPERIES
145 Broad Ave.
Fairview, NJ 07022
(201) 945-1900
(212) 964-1480: NY residents

Ronnie sells its own original designs in draperies, bedspreads, and curtains at 20% to 50% savings. Wide selection, many styles comparable to goods offered in the best retail stores. Bedspreads and draperies come lined or unlined and they also offer thermal insulated draperies. Check the section in their 64-page, full-color catalog on how to measure for draperies before ordering. **C $1**

SHIBUI WALLCOVERINGS
P.O. Box 1638
Rohnert Park, CA 94928
(707) 526-6170: call collect

Shibui knows the paper chase can leave you climbing the walls. Shibui carries hand-crafted textiles, grasscloths, and string wall coverings (all imported from the Orient) at approximately 50% of the normal retail price. Wall coverings are natural in texture, color, and material. Their kit of 80 samples of wall coverings costs $1, which is deductible from your first order. Do-it-yourself instructions and tools are available, along with a special program for licensed decorators. No minimum order though a 10% surcharge on returns is generally assessed. **C $1** (refundable)

WALLPAPER NOW
3507 S. Main St.
Archdale, NC 27263
(919) 431-6341

Also known as Hang-It-Now Wallpaper stores, this 2-year-old company is no baby to discounts. A whopping 30% to 80% discount is lopped off the top of each roll. Don't put off until tomorrow what you can Wallpaper Now. This company offers a huge selection of 25,000 different papers and coverings at a discount. Brands like Sunworthy are worth looking into and Schumacher will sure make you order. Wallpaper Now will match the cuttings you send and will also mail out samples. Prices from 96 cents to $8.95 for a single roll, with quality ranging from "paint store" inventory and up. **PQ**

WELLS INTERIORS, INC.
1983 N. Main St.
Walnut Creek, CA 94596
(800) 547-8982

This company is a leading supplier of window, wall, and floor covering products at blinding discounts of 40% to 60%. And that includes free UPS shipping—unless items are too large for UPS specifications. Orders accepted by phone, but use of the order blank ensures no possibility of error. Brands carried include Levolor, Louverdrape, Kirsch, and Del Mar woven woods, Joanna custom shutters are in stock, and exquisite machine-made Oriental rugs (100% wool) are pending. Remember, measure windows correctly as there are no returns on custom-cut orders. All's well that ends at Wells. **C, B, PQ** $2 (refundable)

WINDOW WORKS
210 Fifth Ave.
New York, NY 10010
(212) 258-5679

We shutter at the thought of paying blindingly high retail prices on window treatments. Window Works can beat the daylights out of the others and save you 45% to 50% on mini-blinds (including Levolor), woven woods, Louverdrapes, and the new "softlight" by Del Mar. They even offer five-year written product guarantees on Levolor Riviera 1-inch blinds. Write or call for their "Magic with Windows" kit for complete measuring instructions and product lines. Your $1 will be credited toward your purchase. We can't draw the drapes on that sunny deal. **PQ, B $1**

9.

DO-IT-YOURSELF

Kits and Kaboodle

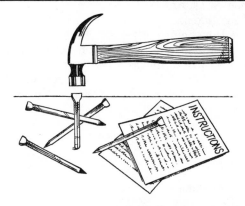

Remember that first do-it-yourself project? You were 5 and you used half a paper plate and some crayons on a gift for your mother and she thought that it was the most beautiful paper plate-half in the world. You're probably more skilled at paper and paint—and wood and cloth and cooking and brewing—by now. (And maybe it's time for another gift for Mom.) Do-it-yourself has come a long way from paper plates and crayons. You can, for example, build a grandfather clock or a baby's cradle, assemble an arbor, ferment some wine, repair an antique trunk, construct a computer, wire a stereo, even build a houseboat or an A-frame mountain home. Though not purporting to be discounted, kits can save you money.

THE BARTLEY COLLECTION
121 Schelter Road
Prairie View, IL 60069
(800) 228-2606: MC and Visa orders only
(800) 642-8777: NB residents
(312) 634-9510

You take the lowboy and I'll take the highboy from this elegantly photographed catalog of 18th-century antique furniture reproduction kits. These gleaming wood pieces will hold your candles, brandy, and the White House china (in reproduction of course), while the tray table shelves your murder mystery collection. All kits are complete—order them finished or unfinished. The hardware's included as well as masterful instructions for the assembling servants. There's even a form for the possibility of missing pieces. Thirty-day return for refunds. **C $1**

BETTER HOMES & GARDENS
Craft Kits Department
P.O. Box 374
Des Moines, IA 50336
(800) 247-5099
(800) 532-1526: IA residents

Enough animals for a wave of arks, enough flowers to cover several estates, and enough sunsets to close down many a planet's days fill this queen of crafts catalogs. Ride a white horse—a unicorn of course—on backgammon boards, Cluny tapestries, needlepoint pillows, cross-stitched eyeglass cases, and long-stitched doorstops. A wide and colorful array of kits enables you to hook a rug, deliver a doll, and even mix a batch of magical potpourri. **C**

BREWMASTER
162 Steam Mill Road
Odessa, NY 14869
(607) 594-3743

Ale, ale, the gang's all here. Is this for you? Of Coors it is! Nip those beer prices in the Bud. Many men become Hamm's after just one try. You won't be a Lone Star when those other guys find out either. You'll want to invite your best St. Pauli Girl to the party. A Rolling Rock gathers no moss, but a brewmaster beer-making kit is great fun, Gus. And we heard through the grapevine, they carry wine-making supplies, too. A random sampling of items for s-ale: Chablis kit, $28.95; lite-beer kit (20 gallons), $14.95; Old English Stout kit (6.5 gallons), $10.25. The year-end sale offered 10% discounts on all merchandise. Nuts to you, too. **B**

BURRO
14143 21st Ave., N.
North Plymouth, MN 55441
(800) 328-3592
(612) 559-0026: MN and Canada residents call collect

If you load up a Burro with all your vacation supplies, you won't have to make a jackass out of yourself. This lightweight trailer costs less to tow than its heavier relative and it can be led by hand. A day or two of assembling will put this beast of burden in working order and if you're not in the mood to burro-w through the parts yourself, company people will offer a bray of hope by assembling it for you. The basic kit starts at $2,596. **B**

CANE AND BASKET SUPPLY CO.
1283 S. Cochran Ave.
Los Angeles, CA 90019
(213) 939-9644

In a Testament to the Genesis of evil, Cane was Able to weave himself a tale of woe. Fortunately, you won't become a basket case if you make the right sacrifices and stay out of trouble. Boasting "the largest selection of caning and basket supplies in the world," these folks offer guidance in hand-weaving chair seats, choosing the appropriate tools and materials, and suggesting oils and varnishes for finishing touches. (And that's the unvarnished truth!) Prices are 20% to 40% lower than in craft stores carrying similar products. They also sell complete kits of woods and weavings for footstools and chairs, for those who want to keep their idle hands busy in their own and not the Devil's workshop. Returns, no questions asked. Customer pays postage. **C $1** (refundable)

CHARING CROSS KITS
Main Street
Box 798
Meredith, NH 03253
(603) 279-8449

Clothkits, as the English parent store is known, was started at home by a young woman and now has a small but devoted clientele world-wide. Clothing kits for men, women, children, and even dolls at 30% to 50% savings. In their winter catalog, there was a machine-washable corduroy skirt kit for women for $29.50 (we've seen similar skirts on sale in stores for $40 or more). All kits are silk screened on the fabric—no layouts to bother with. The Charing Cross shop was opened by a Clothkits fan and both shops sell the same styles and send out color leaflets in September and March. **C $2**

COLONIAL WOODCRAFT
11229 Reading Road
Cincinnati, OH 45241
(513) 563-6666

We cannot tell a lie. Colonial took a tip from good old George Washington and has cut down a forest of black, wild cherry trees for you to assemble and polish into rockers, tilt-top tables, washstands, desks, quilt rods, cheval mirrors, a butler tea cart, and a beautifully detailed crib. A Shenandoah rocker was $169.95 ($7.75 shipping) for the kit, $500 retail value. **C**

COLORADO SUNKITS
Box 3288
Boulder, CO 80307
(303) 494-5476

Singing—and running—in the rain (and all other weathers) will be comfortable, cheerful, and definitely cheaper with Sunkits sew-it-yourself sportswear. Parkas, running suits, and tennis togs with all the trimmings are featured and when you sew your wild oats, you save at least 50% off ready-to-wear. They sell synthetic fabric by the yard as well. **C**

CONSTANTINE'S
2050 Eastchester Road
Bronx, NY 10461
(800) 223-8087
(212) 792-1600: NY residents

Constantine's claim is "everything for better woodworking" and who would disagree? This 170-year-old company offers kits and materials and tools and books on everything from backgammon table tops to dollhouse miniatures. Build a model ship or a guitar, create a cabinet or a clock. Inlays, overlays, cane and rush supplies. Their library is as extensive as their selection of specialty tools. There's a $15 minimum order with charge card; a $10 minimum with cash. Full refund or replacement if not satisfied. **C $1**

COUNTRY WAYS, INC.
15235 Minnetonka Blvd.
Minnetonka, MN 55343
(612) 935-0022

The president of this company would like to remind you to "Get out and boat today." Create with your hands and you "create an adventure," says this nicely photographed catalog. They offer easy-to-make kits for canoes, kayaks, sailboats, skis, and bamboo ski poles, sleeping bags and fanny packs, backpacks, wooden ducks, banjos, dulcimers, maple-sugaring equipment—even snowshoes and snowshoe furniture. **C**

DECOYS UNLIMITED
P.O. Box 69
Clinton, IA 52732
(319) 243-3948: inquiries only

No, this is not an organization parodying Ducks Unlimited. This company supplies cast aluminum molds and materials to make your own durable waterfowl decoys (goose, mallard, and bluebill). These decoys have won blue ribbons for their realistic appearance and there's no minimum order on decoy kits. The brochure is loaded with information and the price is refundable with the first order. **B $1** (refundable)

E.C. KRAUS
Home Winemaking Equipment
9001 E. 24 Highway
P.O. Box 7850
Independence, MO 64053
(816) 254-7448

Distill, my art! A loaf of bread, a jug of watermelon wine, and thou art on the way to enjoying the fermented fruits, flowers, and vegetables of thy labors. Kraus features a library of information plus a large supply of yeasts, extracts, equipment, and accessories for personal beer and wine production. You supply the women (or men) and song. **C**

EMPEROR CLOCK CO.
Emperor Industrial Park
Fairhope, AL 36532
(205) 928-2316

Look at the Emperor's new clocks from the world's largest manufacturer of grandfather clocks. Kits at this 12-year-old factory start at prices from $264 to $589 (retail $800 to $1,500) with movement included as well as wall clocks in cherry, walnut, and other fine woods. Or buy the clocks assembled and still save a great deal, from 30% to 50%. Also carries butler tables, chests, gun cabinet kits. Complete instructions, screws, and hardware included. **B**

FOUR SEASONS GREENHOUSES
910 Route 110
Farmingdale, NY 11735
(516) 694-4400

Their greenhouses or sunspaces aren't just for flowers anymore. They can be free-standing rooms or lean-to designs. They incorporate maintenance-free features and accessories for collecting solar energy, leisure living activities as well as growing plants. Tempered safety glass is 10 times stronger than ordinary glass, totally weatherproof, and almost unbreakable. Easy-to-erect pre-fab kits vary in price according to size and model. Custom orders accepted. Five-year limited warranty and small discount offered for full payment. **C**

FROSTLINE KITS
Frostline Circle
Denver, CO 80241
(303) 451-5600: orders only

Baby bunting and clothes for hunting, saddlebags for mopeds, backpacks for dogs, robes and booties for humans, comforters and tents and even a do-it-yourself (imitation) bear rug are among a wide variety of outdoor clothing and equipment ready-to-sew to take the chill off. **C**

GERRY SHARP, TRUNK DOCTOR
8489-95 Culebra Road
San Antonio, TX 78251
(512) 684-1470
(512) 681-5770

Do you suppose Gerry became unhinged when Houdini told her he had an engagement and he couldn't get out of it? The trunk doctor has never lost a patient after 15 years. If your Pandora's box is getting a little creaky in the joints, Gerry Sharp, T.D. (Trunk Doctor) has leather dyes, straps and hinges, brass nails, slotted handles, drawbolts, corners, and ball-bearing casters, plus various closures for antique trunk restorers. "Trunk Trix," a truncated manual, was packed with Sharp tips for $5. **B**

GO CART
9140 W. Dodge Road
Omaha, NB 68124
(402) 397-3911

Wheels of fortune we doubt, but you can save a few turns on a go-cart kit complete with three-horsepower engine, clutch, and chain. Or order a la cart without the engine, $179.95 (retail $239.95). Direct from the factory and ready to be bolted. **C $3** (refundable)

GOLF DAY PRODUCTS, INC.
3015 Commercial Ave.
Northbrook, IL 60062
(312) 498-1400

Join the club of savvy swingers who do their own golf club repairs. Save up to $40 per set of 14 new golf grips, according to the company's 48-page repair manual/catalog of over 1,000 golf items. Save up to $36 on refinishing three woods. Golf Day tells how to do tricky repairs and offers the supplies by mail. Credit cards are accepted. **C 50 cents**

THE GREEN PEPPER
941 Olive St.
Eugene, OR 97401
(503) 345-6665

I'm a pepper, you're a pepper, but these folks are Green Peppers (and when you're hot, you're hot!). Buy the patterns alone or the complete kits to make colorful, fashionable clothes for camping, galloping, pedaling, crossing the country, or skiing the slopes. This company specializes in active sportswear patterns, fabrics, and notions in brands like Green Pepper, Gore-Tex, Klimate, Thinsulate, and Dacron II Holofill. Prices reflect 50% or more savings over comparable ready-mades. We saw sewing kits for vests, jackets, parkas, ski suits, running suits, as well as book bags, saddle bags, and cargo bags all designated by asterisks to denote degree of difficulty. Beginning to experienced sewers can find something in this 20-page slick, black-and-white photographed catalog. The Green Pepper has no minimum order, no restocking charge, and refunds or exchanges are made on merchandise returned in its original condition (shipping charges are not included in the refund). Wouldn't you like to be a Pepper, too? **C $1**

GREEN RIVER TRADING CO.
Boston Corners Road
Millerton, NY 12546
(518) 789-3311

Have a barn-building party (or put up a garage for a noble steel steed) with kits from Green River. They specialize in rustic-looking log cabin kits and will sell you blueprints or help you design your own. Prices range 20% to 40% under conventional prices. There's no minimum order; no restocking charge on returns, and exchanges or refunds are honored up to 60 days after delivery. All materials are warrantied for one year. For those who wish to avoid slivers from timbers, Green River sells novelty log siding—for the log look without the log. **C $5** (refundable)

HARDWOOD CRAFTSMAN LTD.
121 Schelter Road
Prairie View, IL 60069
(800) 228-2606
(800) 642-8777: NB residents
(312) 634-3050: inquiries

Hardwood Craftsman sells colonial-style furniture kits of solid cherry, oak, and birch that come ready to be assembled. Their brochure says this can be done in one evening. You can save even more money by taking advantage of the frequent sales. Prices generally run 30% to 50% off the cost of finished furniture. There's a 30-day period for full refunds. **B**

H. DECOVNICK & SON
225 B Alamo Plaza
P.O. Box 68
Alamo, CA 94507
(415) 837-1244

DeCovnick & Son doesn't stop time in its flight with only grandfather clocks but also includes a whole family of models from grandmas to grandchildren. They sell components for all the major brands like Seth Thomas and others as well as oils, wood fillers, and polish. Numerals and pendulums swing out the savings when you mark your own time. No pits here—even their black-and-white illustrations were minutely exciting. **C $1**

HEATHKIT ELECTRONIC CENTER
6825A Green Oaks Road
Fort Worth, TX 76116
(817) 737-8822

There's not a room in your castle, inside or out, that wouldn't welcome a project from this grand old name in home kit electronics. Solar water heaters, weather indicators, desk computers, metal locators, doorbells, air cleaners, chess challengers, clocks, cradles, radios, and television sets are just a few of the possibilities. Easy-to-build equipment kits also are available for computers, televisions (Zenith System III), automotive items, marine test instruments, furniture, stereo, ham radio, and weather equipment. They even offer home study courses. Prices generally range from 30% to 40% lower than retail and they have a complete inventory of replacement parts and repair facilities. There is a liberal return policy with a restocking charge only when a kit has been opened and extensive repacking is required. Parts are guaranteed for 90 days. **C, PQ**

HERITAGE CLOCK CO.
Heritage Industrial Park
Drawer 1577
Lexington, NC 27293-1577
(704) 956-2113

Time flies when you're having fun building your own timepiece from Heritage's oak, cherry, and walnut grandfather clock kits. Do-it-yourself kits (those without movements) sell from $339.50 to $699.50. Solid brass West German movements sell from $234.50 to $1,474.50. Wall and mantel kits with movements sell from $49.50 to $329.50. If you don't have the time to assemble and finish the clock, you may purchase completely assembled finished clocks to grace your home. They also have a large selection of carriage clocks, cuckoo clocks, ship's clocks, anniversary clocks, barometer clocks, and tambour clocks. Major credit cards accepted. Their 40-page full-color catalog is a klock-out. **C $1**

HOLLYWOOD FANCY FEATHER CO.
512 S. Broadway
Los Angeles, CA 90013
(213) 625-8453 or 625-2883

This is no fly-by-night operation. Birds of a feather and maybe even Elton John flock here for their wardrobes. They sell fancy feathers: pheasant, ostrich, guinea hen, turkey, and others. Get your head out of the sand and take flight with ostrich feathers at $6 to $20 per dozen; over one dozen colors to choose from including turquoise, gold, and burgundy. Sounds plum-e fit for a peacock! You won't feel fowl parading in your plumage along with their exotic pheasant skins ($12 to $25 per skin) and marabou boas. **PQ**

JIM WALTER CORP.
P.O. Box 22601
1500 N. Dale Mabry Highway
Tampa, FL 33622
(800) 237-2771
(813) 871-4612: FL residents call collect

Jim Walter homes and cottages are built to almost any stage of completion from the shell home to one that is 90% complete. They construct the outside from foundation to roof including outside doors, windows, roofing, siding, and outside paint. From this point on, you tell them where to stop and you take over to finish. The more you do, the more you save. You can take over painting the interiors, wallpapering, installing wallboard, hooking up the plumbing, purchasing and installing doors, or have them do it. They build on customer-owned property only and qualified property owners can have instant mortgage financing. **C**

KUEMPEL CHIME CLOCK WORKS
21195 Minnetonka Blvd.
Excelsior, MN 55331
(612) 474-6177

These grandfather clock kits are fabricated by real grandfathers! The catalog welcomes you into the company of these little old clock makers, tells you how the business began, and offers happy tributes from customers. You can buy just the clock plans, or just the moulding packages, or an entire kit of all case pieces. A selection of melodic clock works is sold separately. The beauty of the photographed clocks in this slick, full-color catalog is almost beyond words. Get to work; your talent and time will tell. **C**

LEE WARDS
Needlework and Crafts Catalog
840 N. State St.
Elgin, IL 60120
(800) 621-5146: orders only
(800) 972-5855: IL residents
(312) 888-5858

Don't be crewel to these colorful kits and we won't have to embroider tales about them. You'll need no needling to work up a smashing sampler, an elegant ornament, or an affable afghan among many others. Full kits, accessories, and equipment will keep you in stitches. **C**

LUGER BOATS
3800 W. Highway 13
Burnsville, MN 55337
(612) 890-3000

The decks and hulls are done; you install the interiors in these molded fiberglass getaways. Luger features live-aboard boats, seaworthy surfriders, sailboats, and sport fishing models. **C $1**

MILAN LABORATORY
57 Spring St.
New York, NY 10012
(212) 226-4780

Discover the secrets of Forbidden Fruit, Roman Punch, and other magical nectars of gods and concoct them in the confines of your own kitchen. Milan is a complete headquarters for little ol' wine makers. They have chemicals, extracts, preservatives, barrels, corks, and a host of other supplies to make your alcoholic elixir-making easier. Their $2.50 catalog devotes a whole page to extracts you mix with alcohol, sugar, and water to make instant (and discounted) liqueurs and cordials. Discounts fermented at 50%. Brands are Milan's own. Their wine doctor can diagnose and remedy ale-ments if you suffer from sick spirits. **C $2.50** (if mailed), **$1** (at store), **B**

MILES HOMES
P.O. Box 9495
4700 Nathan Lane
Minneapolis, MN 55440
(612) 553-8300

Miles to go before you sleep in one of these ranch, split-level, one and one-half, and two-story houses, available with decks, vaulted ceilings, and even separate dining rooms in some cases. The Miles people specialize in making your impossible dream of home ownership a four-walled reality. Mostly modern and simple designs but solid and homey-looking. **C $3, B**

NEW SHELTER MAGAZINE
33 E. Minor St.
Emmaus, PA 18049
(215) 967-5171

Want to put a gym where the living room once was? Or move the bedroom outdoors for the summer? Maybe you just want to go passive on your energy bills. Here's a comprehensive publication for the do-it-yourself-better-for-less lifestyle. Topics such as, "What Makes Wood Rot," "Bug-Proofing a House," and "Outdoor Lighting" in a pleasant format supplemented by advertising. Published by Rodale Press. One year for $10.

PYRAMID PRODUCTS
3736 S. Seventh Ave.
Phoenix, AZ 85041
(602) 276-5365

With a Pyramid foundry set, mechanics, hobbyists, artists,

inventors, jewelers, and sculptors can make metal molds of models or model parts, figurines, plaques, etc. Their furnaces allow casting in iron, bronze, aluminum, copper, gold, white metal, and silver. Books and tools also available. **C**

ROLLERWALL, INC.
P.O. Box 757
Silver Springs, MD 20901
(301) 649-4422

What do you get when you cross a wallpaper pattern with a paint roller? Rollerwall, of course! It's the perfect craft: the company claims you don't need any talent and they guarantee "delightful results." A wide variety of designs and two choices of applicators enable the user to apply paint on plain walls in intricate designs. Satisfied customer letters include some from set designers and hotel owners. There is a full refund for goods returned within 30 days. **B**

SPEAKERLAB
P.O. Box C-30325
Wallingford Station
735 N. Northlake Way
Seattle, WA 98103
(800) 426-7736
(206) 633-5020: WA, HI, AK residents

You and Speakerlab can make beautiful music together. Often resembling clones (or at least cousins) of that mysterious monolith from *2001,* these elegant-looking you-build-'em speakers are projects to please both audio and visual buffs. Their catalog manages to look extremely professional and sound down-home friendly at the same time and is filled with "sound" information as well as convincing sales copy. **C**

STAVROS KOUYOUMOUTZAKIS
Iraklion, Crete
Greece
Phone: 011-30-81-284-466 (dial direct)

You'll ab-Zorba the Greek bargains here. You won't have to go up and down the Isles, just flip through the Greek pages. We'll be dis-Crete in describing their beautiful and unusual weaving and knitting yarns from Crete and Australia that would cost twice as much in the States. **C**

TEXAS GREENHOUSE CO.
2731 St. Louis Ave.
Fort Worth, TX 76110
(817) 926-5447

Red-faced over greenhouse prices? There is no reason to be hot-headed over hot houses with Texas Greenhouse kits. (When you build your own greenhouse, only your plants will get steamed.) Since 1948, this company has manufactured their own greenhouses and accessories so all prices are factory direct (plus *Underground Shopper* readers get a 5% discount on greenhouses on request). There's a 15% restocking charge on returns and a 50% deposit with order, balance due upon delivery. **C**

TURN-O-CARVE TOOL CO.
P.O. Box 8315
Tampa, FL 33674-8315
(813) 933-2730

The turn of a few screws here will get you beautiful furniture legs, candlesticks, etc. Enough ingenuous language and some innocently misspelled words in their material give the impression of a few craftspeople really devoted to giving personal service. Their major product is wood turning duplicators; they also sell brackets, tracer tools, and chisels. **C**

VERITECHNOLOGY ELECTRONICS CORP.
P.O. Box 167
St. Joseph, MI 49085
(616) 982-3740

Those wonderful folks who bring you Heathkits now bring you projects that need no batteries and have no plugs. Star of the show in the catalog was an Early American platform cradle; other kits included a banker's rolltop desk with an extraordinary rolltop desk chair, a Victorian octagonal oak dining room set, and a horizontal hall mirror with hooks for your top hat and white gloves. Brass and glass items, as well as clock kits. **C**

VIKING CLOCK DIVISION
Acromag Viking Inc.
The Viking Building, Box 490
Foley, AL 36536
(205) 943-5081

It's easy to tell what makes Viking tick—a collection of clock kits from grandfather-size to wall-mounted to mantelpiece models. They offer top-quality Queen Anne furniture in Pennsylvania cherry and a Tennessee oak chair kit with a cane seat. They'll chip off the new blocks and send them your way. There is a 30-day refund for items that are returned postage paid and in their original condition. **C**

WESTERN CLASSIC HOMES
6000 Western Place
Fort Worth, TX 76101
(817) 737-2668 or 467-4400

These folks sell these shells by the seashore (or even inland). Victorian-styled shells are unfinished wooden homes that you complete yourself. Allow four to six weeks from the time you place your order. The shells range in price from $16,700 to $44,000 and there are 12 different floor plans in sizes ranging from 968 square feet on up to 2,880 square feet. The company builds it on your lot, which amounts to a 40% to 50% savings off the cost of conventional housing. A 2,049-square foot house shell costs $29,500 with estimated finishing costs of $16,500 to $24,750. Since a conventional house would probably cost at least twice as much, you can lay a pretty firm foundation for savings. **B**

WILDERNESS LOG HOMES
Rural Route 2
Plymouth, WI 53073
(800) 558-5881
(800) 852-5828: WI residents

Here is the stuff in which presidents are born—or in which mere taxpayers are made into satisfied dwellers. However, these are not the rough-hewn, thatch-as-thatch-can variety, but with hand-crafted logs and custom design. Conservation-aware, they're available with up to five bedrooms, cathedral ceiling, study, dining room, and great room. **C $5**

10.

THE BIG BUYS

Surplus and Volume

If you've ever wondered where to find uniforms for medical technicians, seafood restaurant waiters, or French maids, Portuguese camouflage berets, utility paint tanks, deluxe naked leather and down vests, Korean War vintage genuine U.S. Army issue hand-powered generators, and grenade belts from World War I, you've come to the right places. Buying overstocks or buying in multiples usually means financial benefits, as you will see from the following dealers.

AIRBORNE SALES CO.
P.O. Box 2727
Culver City, CA 90230
(213) 870-4687

You'll take off for Cloud Nine when you see the prices on Airborne's aircraft tachometers, pressure gauges, and flight jackets. They also offer new and used surplus automotive hardware, manufacturing and industrial items, as well as all sorts of marine goodies. Need a nuclear radiation survey meter? Only $54.50 ($119 U.S. government cost). Their customers include large corporations, foreign and the U.S. government. There's a $10 minimum order and a 15% restocking charge on returns. Visit their Surplus Store in L.A. at 10341 Venice Blvd. **C** $1 (refundable)

ANKA CO.
90 Greenwich Ave.
P.O. Box 89
West Warwick, RI 02886
(800) 556-7768: orders only
(401) 737-8107: RI residents

Pull up the Anka and sell away. Anka sells a wide variety of inexpensive sterling silver or 10K gold-filled and goldplate rings geared toward the person who wants to resell at a profit. Pearl, opal, star sapphire, and jade jewelry sets were discounted up to 80%. Plus "kiddie rings" and a line of jewelry for men. From engagement/ wedding sets to professional truck driver rings ($72), this company also provides literature on how to become an Anka dealer. Their claim to fame is "200% below retail" discounts. The minimum order is $20 ($40 for credit card orders). **C** $1 (refundable)

BLAIR
1000 Robins Road
Lynchburg, VA 24506
(804) 845-7073

Mary, this is o-Kay. Without being caddy, we were in the pink with all these beauty products at wholesale prices. This plan operates as a dealership but you determine your own quota. You can buy for yourself or for gifts at their wholesale prices. They offer cosmetics, fragrances, health aids, food products such as spices, costume jewelry, home products, and small gifts. Blair guarantees products to both dealers and customers and has been in business since 1920. **B**

BRIGADE QUARTERMASTERS
266 Roswell St.
Marietta, GA 30060
(404) 428-1234

Masters at shaving almost a quarter off the retail price, Brigade buys from U.S. military suppliers and sells American surplus, imports, and goods made exclusively for them. Usual array of army surplus clothing, noted for being cheap, durable, functional and, as of late, very fashionable (top designer Perry Ellis uses genuine army khaki in his clothing). They also have survival equipment and camping gear. Satisfaction guaranteed 100%; no restocking charge. **C $2**

BUDGET UNIFORM
941 Mill Road
Bensalem, PA 19020
(800) 523-5750
(215) 245-0300: PA residents

This catalog salutes men and women in uniform. Not the military kind, but for those employees in the restaurant, hotel, and medical business. And the respectably low prices and volume discounts of 5% offered will make you salute, too. They've got the look: be it nautical, calico folksy, western, classic tuxedo, colonial tavern, saloon scene, upstairs maid, sleek cocktail waitress, or south-of-the-border gringo. All styles of aprons, vests, tunics, blazers, chef's hats, lab coats, and Florence Nightingale whites. No discounts before 12 uniforms. May they take your order? **C**

CAMEO
381 Park Ave. S.
New York, NY 10016
(212) 889-9280

Diamond deals, sapphire sales, opal offers—Cameo will make a gold-filled jeweler out of you. They guarantee that you'll earn over $600 in your spare time in the first month selling their rings and other pretty things. You buy at 10% of their suggested retail price, then set your own price for resale. Claims of 900% profit are inspiring. **C**

JERRYCO, INC.
5700 Northwest Highway
Chicago, IL 60646
(312) 763-0313

Gosh, we didn't fight a battle at Jerryco and our wall-ets came a tumblin' down on the counter to buy army and industrial surplus goods at up to 95% off (in the case of some exotic and military surplus items). Their half-a-buck pun-filled catalog, *Superfluity,* was a bewildering collection of curious goods that may or may not be useful to someone—perhaps those on scavenger hunts. Anyone for a 1979 calendar, some nichrome wire, or gumwall cleaner? A later catalog, *Sir Plus,* included such beauties as Do-It-Yourself Clone Kits, pickled frogs, and antique railroad relays. They're open to suggestions for future offerings. Since many of their products are limited stock items made by manufacturers out of business or out of production, there are no guarantees; but if you return a purchase within 30 days in the same condition, you can get your money back. Their 48-page catalog is a delight. **C 50 cents** (free at American Science Center stores)

POOLEY GLASS ENGRAVERS
Glassware Factory Outlet
122 Greenwood Ave.
Bethel, CT 06801
(203) 794-1391

Raise a toast to discounted glassware, the perfect gift for weddings, anniversaries, or any special occasion. You won't be ashamed to show your mug around town or gulp from an engraved goblet from PGE. Engraved 12-ounce goblets were $3.75 each including three initials. The discount schedule: 50 to 100 pieces, 10%; 100 to 200, 15%; over 200, 20% off their price or about 40% below retail. There is no minimum order, no restocking charge, and returned items are exchangeable. No need to Pooley your resources, the catalog is free. **C**

PURE PLANET PRODUCTS
1025 N. 48th St.
Phoenix, AZ 85008
(602) 267-1000

If you want your diet to be Pure, Planet! This company offers such items as edible starch papers ("for vegetarians who do not wish to use animal gelatin capsules"), a porcupine pneumatic oval hair brush (I bristle at the thought of not having one), and that ambrosial tongue-tickler, bee secretion (containing Chinese ginseng extract, royal jelly, and such scrumptious herbs as Astragalus, Cordyceps, Dong Quai, Fo Ti, and honey). They had a good selection of herbs, soaps, and other natural products, too. Prices are up to 30% off retail although discounts depend upon order size. There is a $2 handling charge on orders under $10. **C 25 cents**

THE SURPLUS CENTER
1000-15 W. "O" St.
P.O. Box 82209
Lincoln, NB 68501
(402) 474-4366

Surplus plus—not quite from A to Z but from air-operated tools to wire. In between, you'll find paint spray guns and pulleys, batteries and blowers, tanks and telephones, hacksaws and horns at up to 85% off retail prices. Overall, their slant is more toward electrical and mechanical items for business, industry, farm, and home as opposed to military gear like clothing and weaponry. Their 100-page catalog is both attractive and straightforward. **C**

UNCLE DAN'S LTD.
2440 N. Lincoln Ave.
Chicago, IL 60614
(312) 477-1918

Uncle Sam's not the only uncle in the army surplus business. "We can get you anything you desire," they say, in army-navy surplus, camping goods, and recycled clothing. Generally speaking, some of their prices reflect the status quo but we salute Uncle Dan on some relative-ly good buys: 100% wool "like new" army pants, $15.98, other new army pants were $16, brand new government-issue camouflage army pants and jackets were $28.95 each, and Coleman lanterns were $33.75 ($45 retail). You'll OD on the olive drab. **C**

WEISS AND MAHONEY
142 Fifth Ave.
New York, NY 10011
(212) 675-1915

Weiss and Mahoney, "the peaceful little army and navy store," sells the usual items of war sold by army surplus stores including clothing, camping equipment, and much more. They have regulation uniforms for all the armed forces and flags from over 50 countries. In their free catalog, we found uncamouflaged brand names such as Schott (outer wear) and Kirkham (tents and camping equipment) but the big discounts went undetected. **C**

11.

CHAPTER ELEVEN

Hard-to-Find

While the following companies do not sell discounted merchandise, we felt the goods they carried were unusual enough to merit a listing in this book. We've been telling you all along that variety is the name of this game and if you absolutely can't get it wholesale, well, at least you *can* get it. There are times when you can't find a suitable ladies' size 4 business suit in the local department store. Have you ever gone out to buy a ventriloquist's outfit and wound up feeling like the dummy? Before you throw your voice, time, and money away, check here first. Shop by mail and you'll have more luck finding that four-leaf clover, however small (a club for thimble collectors) or large (a truckload of hamburgers) it may be.

BEITMAN CO., INC.
840 Main St.
P.O. Box 1541
Bridgeport, CT 06601
(203) 333-7738

Tired of button your head against the wall? Let Beitman and the Boy Wonder blast out of the Beit-cave in their Beit-mobile and race to your aid. This company custom-covers belts and buttons from fabric, leather, suede, or even plastic you supply. Everything is made-to-order, except leather tabs and some buckles. Prices are often lower than those found in custom sewing shops. There's a $5 minimum order and all merchandise is guaranteed machine washable. Pick up the Beit-phone or write to put these not-so-comic superheroes in stitches. **C**

THE COLLECTOR'S CHOICE
1313 S. Killian Dr.
P.O. Box 12600
Lake Park, FL 33403-9986
(305) 845-6075

Jack be thimble, Jack be quick . . . This firm specializes in collector's bells, spoons, thimbles, plates, showcases, scrapbooks, figurines, and other collectibles. Manufacturers include Hummel, Belmar Editions Ltd., Schmid, Gorham, and Simons to name a few. Norman Rockwell spoons were $14.99 each or $89.99 for a set of six, while Prince Charles and Lady Diana Royal Nuptial Commemorative Thimbles, Ronald and Nancy Reagan silver-plated spoons, and Elvis Presley and John Wayne thimbles, spoons, and bells were also available. Sculptured ram, elk, and unicorn pewter bells looked interesting. Prices on par with retail; less with a Collector's Circle membership. A $20 minimum order with credit cards; no minimum when payment's enclosed. The catalog's free to readers of *The Underground Shopper.* **C $1**

IMPORTED BOOKS
P.O. Box 4414
2025 W. Clarendon
Dallas, TX 75208
(214) 941-6497

A great source for foreign-language books, mostly in Spanish, such as the Porrua series of Spanish classics and Sopena dictionaries plus some difficult-to-find modern Mexican fiction. Shelves are always krauted with other language books including German, French (including the Larousse dictionaries), Portuguese, Italian, and other smaller volumes in Japanese, Russian, even Vietnamese. This 48-page catalog offers same-day shipping though does not guarantee against damages or accept credit cards. Special orders, if coming from abroad, take longer. C'est romantique, n'est-ce-pas? **C**

JOHNSON SMITH CO.
35075 Automation Drive
Mt. Clemens, MI 48043
(313) 791-2800

Here I thought my hometown had nothing funny but the smell. After getting a whiff of their catalog, I was ready to place my order for a Herculean wrist band, rotating spaghetti forks, a leather bullwhip, a ventriloquist's dummy, live "sea monkeys," character masks (for those with minor personality disorders, I presume), phony blood, alien ears, monster teeth, motorized shark fins, an electric talking toilet, liquor lollipops, and The Last Supper purse wallets. Over 1,600 unusual offerings from around the world. This 69-year-old company has two catalogs: their *World of Fun Catalog* and *The Lighter Side*. No minimum order with satisfaction guaranteed. Give my regards to the Colonial Hotel and the Clinton River. And does anybody remember the Emcee Theater? **C**

THE JUGGLING ARTS
612 Calpella Drive
San Jose, CA 95136
(408) 267-8237

This company really goes for the juggler vein with their range of juggling equipment like spinning plates, clubs, fire torches, balls, and such. Their merchandise is slightly less expensive than other mail-order firms, with their claim that "there are no props of equal quality in retail stores." A set of three cloth balls filled with rice was $10.95, while a set of three rings 11 inches in diameter was $14.95. Fire torches (designated not for the beginner) were $10.50 each. A 100% refund if requested. **C $1**

THE NON-ELECTRIC HERITAGE CATALOG
Lehman Hardware and Appliances
Box 41
Kidron, OH 44636
(216) 857-5441

If your electricity has just been turned off or if you've been turned off to modern times, get back to basics and reacquaint yourself with some quaint and useful appliances. Among the many offerings we found: dough mixers, noodle makers, corn dryers, lard presses, hand-operated clothes washers, hog scrapers, apple parers, and cream separators. A six-quart ice cream freezer was a bargain at $80. Wood stoves were also a good buy, to electric bills that is. The Lehman family operates two stores in Holmes and Wayne counties right in the heart of Ohio's Amish country. Wire you waiting? Send for their unique catalog today. **C $2**

PAPRIKAS WEISS IMPORTER
1546 Second Ave.
New York, NY 10028
(212) 288-6117

From the wooden shelves of this renowned gourmet food shop come some of the world's finest delectables. Owner Ed Weiss "has to be the greatest and fastest and most complete and thorough source of food information in the world," wrote Maida Heatter, the famous creator of the *New York Times* recipe series. The imported foods and cookware (hard to find on many local fronts) included many Hungarian specialites like double-smoked Hungarian bacon, paprika paste, fresh-baked Dobosh torte (seven-layer cake), even a dumpling machine. Plus cheeses, pâtés, coffees, teas, and candies. Corporate gifts available. Not discounted fare. **C $1**

RED FLANNEL FACTORY
73 S. Main St.
Cedar Springs, MI 49319
(616) 696-9240

In response to a futile attempt by a New York writer to find red flannels to cope with the blizzard of 1936, the town of Cedar Springs piped up and became a specialist for the bright undergarments. In 1949, a shop opened and later became the Red Flannel Factory, which now manufactures pajamas, undergarments, robes, and shirts in white and red flannel for the entire family—even the dog. Fabric can be either the 100% Sanforized cotton flannel, a knit with 50% polyester/50% cotton, or muslin. Three-button shirt with long sleeves and knit bottoms, $13.75; long johns, $29.25; long flannel gown, $18.25; nightcaps, $5 to $7.25. **C**

RUVEL
3037 N. Clark St.
Chicago, IL 60657
(312) 248-1922

Boy, did the military serve us when we enlisted the help of their catalog. Clothing (flier's jackets, pith helmets), camping goods (sleeping bags, snowshoes), dummy grenades, gas masks, knives, poison-resistant full-body aprons, and blood-pressure kits are just a few of the items from their wide selection. A 100% down-filled vest (80% Northern goose, 20% other down) was $29.50 and electric socks were $14.95. No license or permit necessary for any of their items. Thirty-day return policy on items in same condition as when shipped; items ordered in error or returned for a refund are subject to a 20% restocking charge. **C $2**

UNIQUE PETITES
Plaza Petites Mail Order Co.
5625 N. 19th Ave.
Phoenix, AZ 85015
(602) 745-4500

When someone said good things come in small packages, he must have been talking about this company. This is the missing link for junior sizes 0 to 14 or 5 feet 4 inches and under. A little fashion goes a long way . . . and their catalog features a great big selection of the newest petite styles in coordinates, sportswear, lingerie, coats, and dresses all wee-sonably priced. **C $1**

WHITE CASTLE HAMBURGERS
915 W. Fifth Ave.
Columbus, OH 43212
(614) 294-3753

Sammy Davis loves them. Frank Sinatra feels the same. The late Hubert Humphrey used to "buy 'em by the sack." These delectable burgers have a cult of devotees who will actually travel miles out of their way for the 28-cent sandwich. In an effort to capitalize on this demand, the company has started a mail-order service. Fully-cooked hamburgers in their little white boxes are frozen (just zap 'em in the microwave) and shipped in an attractive container, which can be used as a cooler afterwards. Although the hamburgers are still just 28 cents each, you pay $61 to ship up to 100. Recently a convoy of three 18-wheelers trucked 99,999 hamburgers and 1 cheeseburger to Fountain Hills, Arizona, for a local fundraiser. Next time someone offers you his castle for a hamburger, take him up on it. **PQ**

12.

SAYING OUR GOOD-BUYS

National Chains:
Your Hometown Link
to Savings

Now that you know how to shop the underground by mail, how about turning up some new turf in your own town or when you're on the road again. There are "off-price retailers" located in most major cities and you can save anywhere from 20% to 90% if you know where to look.

Just what is sold at an "off-price outlet"? Is it always a dumping ground for seconds, irregulars, or out-of-date merchandise? That assumption couldn't be further from the truth. Most outlets carry current, first-quality goods (just like those shipped to retail stores) and are generally staffed by friendly, knowledgeable salespeople. Occasionally, you might find an outlet selling damaged goods, but look for rock-bottom reductions tagging along.

Almost anything can be found at the stores we've included in this section. You'll find sources for suits, shoes, shirts, pants, underwear, bathing suits, china, crystal, pottery, gifts, linens, fabrics, wallpaper, hardware, appliances, sporting goods, toys, and much more located a few miles from where you live. Just check the telephone directory or write to the company (where addresses are given) for a complete list of store locations. When planning your next trip consult this section and don't leave home without it.

—B—

Banker's Note: Bank on Banker's Note (regionally in Texas, Georgia, and Florida) for discounts around 25% on first-quality women's fashions in such brands as Ralph Lauren, Calvin Klein, Ellen Tracy, Chaus, Liz Claiborne, J.G. Hook, Evan Picone, and more in sizes from 6 to 16.

Barry Manufacturing Co.: You can pick berries, but we pick Barry's for their private label men's clothes starting at $65 for your basic corduroy suit. Shirts starting at $7.95; slacks starting at $12.95. For a list of their stores write: Barry Manufacturing, 5700 Airport Freeway, Fort Worth, TX 76117.

Bass Shoe Factory: Women's career and casual-style shoes in sizes 5 to 9½ and men's corporate to casual sizes 9 to 13 narrow and 7 to 13 medium. For a list of their 28 stores write to: Bass Factory Outlet, Box 678, Wilton, ME 04294.

B & F Shoes: First-quality shoes for men and women like Topsiders, Garolini, Corelli, Beene Bag, Bass, and Florsheim sell for 20% to 50% less than retail here. Handbags are also a good buy. Sixty-four stores around the country.

Blue Bell Factory Outlet: Not an ice cream store, but thousands of pairs of Wrangler jeans can be found for 20% to 40% off here lickety-split. Sizes 1 to 50 for the entire family. Irregulars from their own manufacturing and closeouts of other brands. Fourteen stores. For a list write to: Blue Bell, Box 21488, Greensboro, NC 27420.

Brenda Allen: It's Allen a day's work, discounting first-quality misses, ladies', and junior fashions, that is. Large-volume purchases and low overhead translate to 40% to 60% off lines such as Villager, Sasson, Chic, Lee, and Liz Claiborne. Nineteen stores. For addresses write: Benny Barton, Sam's Style Shop, 1625 Atwood, Pensacola, FL 32504.

—C—

Calico Corners: Fabrics purchased from famous designer labels are 30% to 60% off. In this Corner, there were crewels from India, Belgium linens, and prints from England. Fifty-four stores. For listings of their stores write: Calico Corners, Bancroft Mills, Drawer 670, Wilmington, DE 19897 or call (800) 821-7700, ext. 810.

Carter's Factory Outlet: The Carter's (not Jimmy and Roz, the other ones) sell their own branded sleep wear, underwear, outer wear, swim wear, and sportswear in sizes infants to 14 (girls) and infants to 16 (boys) at 30% off retail. Other brands are discounted 10% to 20%. Write for store locations (55 in existence and 12 more planned): William Carter Company, 963 Highland Ave., Needham Heights, MA 02194.

Chocolate Soup: Factory-direct prices from this popular manufacturer of children's fashions amounts to 50% or more off. Besides carrying the Chocolate Soup label, they have out-of-house brands like Izod and Calabash. Ten stores across the country. Write for your list to: Chocolate Soup, 5960 Royal Lane, Dallas, TX 75230.

Con-Co Shoes: Quality, nationally advertised footwear for the family (and no Con job, either). Bass, Dexter, Nike, Nunn Bush, Child Life, Buster Brown, and others discounted 20% to 50%. They also carry casual sportswear for men and women. Eleven stores in the Minneapolis-St. Paul area; three around the country.

Cosco Outlet Store: A recent addition to this nationally recognized leader in men's, women's, and children's apparel opened at the Duofold Distribution Center in Utica, New York (which is fast becoming a center for factory outlets). There are 33 stores located primarily in the Southeast, Northeast, and upstate New York. Notable brands include: Arrow, Lady Arrow, Gold Toe, Donmoor, and Dobie—"everything from outer wear to underwear" discounted up to 50%. Cosco also distributes the Duofold line of ski underwear in their outlets. For a complete list of stores, write to: Cosco Outlet Store, 1122 Route 22, Mountainside, NJ 07092.

Crackers: All the major children's lines can be found at one time or another here: Billy the Kid, Luv It, Rob Roy, Calabash, Tulip Top, Jordache, Buster Brown, Calvin Klein . . . sizes 4 to teen (girls) and 8 to 20 (boys). Discounts of 30% to 50%. One location near Albany, New York, and others planned for Texas, Washington, D.C., and upstate New York.

Cutting Corners: Fine fabrics of all designs and makes including Wamsutta, Burlington, La France, and Cohama discounted 50% to 75%. Six stores around the country. For a list of stores write: Cutting Corners, 13720 Midway Road, Dallas, TX 75234.

—D—
Daffy Dan's: Only two in New Jersey but what they lack in numbers they make up for in labels. Ralph Lauren, Dior, Perry Ellis, Liz

Claiborne, Halston, Kasper, Calvin Klein, and others similarly in-Kleined all at savings of 20% to 80%.

Dansk Factory Outlet: Dance to any of Dansk's 17 stores around the country to find housewares, gifts, china, plastics, linens, cookware, candles, glassware, lamps, and kitchen utensils at considerable discounts.

Doe Spun Outlet Store: Better children's sportswear under the Doe Spun label at factory-direct prices, about 40% to 70% off. They also carry other famous brands. Twenty-three stores, some under the name of The Kid's Stop.

Donasan Fashion Outlet: Junior and missy fashions discounted 30% to 70% with an emphasis on Calvin Klein, Gloria Vanderbilt, Liz Claiborne, Stewart Lang, and hundreds of other active sportswear lines. Regionally in Texas.

Drug Emporium: Not an emp-ty shelf in sight at this 24,000-square foot emporium of over 28,000 items sure to be dubbed hypochon-driac's heaven. Savings measured about 35% on health and beauty aids, stationery, sunglasses, greeting cards, sundries, over-the-counter drugs, and yes, Rx. National chain based in Columbus, Ohio.

—F—

Factory Outlet Shop: Better sportswear and dresses for juniors and misses discounted 30% to 50%. Sizes 4 to 20, juniors 3 to 15. Nine stores in Texas, Oklahoma, Illinois, and Missouri. For addresses write: Factory Outlet Shop, 4949 Beeman Ave., Dallas, TX 75223.

Fayva Shoes: Do yourself a Fayva and set foot inside one of their many stores across the country for Converse, Nike, Ponies, Kan-garoos, and their house brand of sport shoes. Lots of imports but you'll save 10% to 50% on shoes for the entire family.

Finale Shop: This is the Finale of finales with discounts of 25% to 50% on gourmet foods, kitchenwares, linens, toys, decorative accessories, jewelry, lounge wear, and executive desk items. Check the three stores around the Dallas-Fort Worth area and the mail-order division (214) 385-2700 (see the Grand Finale listing under Housewares). A division of the Horchow Collection.

5 & 10 Shoe Store: They don't nickel and dime it here. Famous ladies' shoes by Nina, Candies, Marquis, Corelli, and more priced from $5 to $20. They accept returns and give refunds. Fifteen stores around the country.

For Peanuts: Buy greeting cards (Hallmark, Drawing Board, Current), party ware, gift wrap and gift ware, accessories, and brass ware for peanuts at For Peanuts. Candles priced at four for $1 to $5. With discounts of 50%, check their 15 stores in Texas and two in Oklahoma.

—H—

Hit or Miss: Mrs. and misses sizes 3 to 16 in first-quality labels like Reed Hunter, Margaret Chadwick, Reference Point, Bill Blass, Gloria Vanderbilt, Burlington, Electric Sok, Utex, Cyclone, and Sasson at 20% to 50% off. A Zayre Corporation specialty chain. Over 240 stores from New England to the Midwest, for the location nearest you, write: Marketing Department, Commonwealth Trading Co., 100 Campanella Parkway, Stoughton, MA 02072.

—I—

Inlook Outlet: Look for ladies' clothing and sportswear from the Jerell Company in brands such as Levi, Chic, and Jordache as well as their own lines: IBJ, Melissa Lane, and Straight Lane. Look for their 13 stores around the Texas, Oklahoma, and Tennessee areas.

—J—

J. Brannam: Look here for big savings on Just Brand Names in menswear like Arrow, Calvin Klein, and Levi as well as discounts on women's labels such as Gloria Vanderbilt, Evan Picone, Liz Claiborne, and many more. Domestically speaking, they have Martex and Fieldcrest labels, too. You'll find 20% to 60% off department store prices. Thirty stores. For listings write to: J. Brannam, 12750 Merit Drive, Suite 222 LB 20, Dallas, TX 75251.

—K—

Kuppenheimer: Their Kuppen runneth over with men's suits, slacks, shirts, and accessories from designers and famous makers. Large inventories in their pipe-rack operation with names like Pierre Cardin, Sussex, Yves St. Laurent, Stanley Blacker, John Henry, and others. Fabrics from polyester to cashmere. Discounts to 40% nationwide.

—L—

Linens 'N Things: Outstanding variety of linens, kitchen, bed, and bathroom accessories from some of America's leading manufacturers. Floor-to-ceiling shelves, tiered baskets of napkin rings, attractive floor displays in canisters and baskets. Prices averaged 25% off on first-quality; more on select irregulars.

Loehmann's: Nationwide ladies' discount apparel chain featuring top designers such as Perry Ellis, Calvin Klein, Yves St. Laurent, Ralph Lauren, and Christian Dior priced one-third less than retail. Sizes 4 to 16 in misses and juniors. Community dressing rooms and Back Room for "haute-y couture." For list of 59 stores write to: Loehmann's, 2500 Harsey St., Bronx, NY 10461.

—M—

Marshall's: One of the fastest growing discount operations in the United States, this off-price department store stocks a wide variety of famous-name apparel, lingerie, jewelry, shoes, handbags, housewares, linens, and gifts discounted up to 60%. In addition to fashions for the entire family, they're one of the few national sources we recommend to females with fuller figures. They call that department Woman's World. For a list of their stores contact: Marshall's, 83 Commerce Way, Woburn, MA 01888.

Maternity Discount Center: The Dan Howard line of maternity fashions includes dresses, lingerie, pants, tops, and swimsuits priced from $10 to $45. Discounts average about 30% on sizes 4 to 24. Over 50 stores across the country. For store listings write: Dan Howard Industries, 710 W. Jackson, Chicago, IL 60606.

Maxine's Shoes: Max-imum savings were afoot in this Dallas area shoe store chain (operates under the Lottie's, Dottie's, or Steinhart name in Tennessee and the Chip's name in Boca Raton, Florida). Names like Ferragamo, Andrew Geller, Naturalizer, Selby, Vanelli in a wide variety of styles should keep your feet footloose and fancy-free. Savings from 30% to 60%.

Michael's: March to Michael's to find 50% discounts on macrame jute, crewel kits, silk flowers, baskets, frames, artist's materials, and candy molds. Check any of their eight stores around the country.

Microwave Cooking & The Kitchen Korner: The micro-wave of the future. Little Jack Horner could sit in this corner eating his microwave-zapped curds and whey. Savings of 20% to 50% on major manufacturers of microwave ovens and accessories like Litton, Amana, Toshiba, and Quasar. Other gourmet products by Revereware, Calphalon, Robot Coupe, Henckel, and others also available. Locations in Dallas and Washington, D.C. For listings of stores write to: Microwave Cooking & The Kitchen Korner, 3100 Independence Parkway, Plano, TX 75075.

Mountain Camper: Take a hike to Mountain Camper for 50% discounts on down outer wear, backpacking and camping equipment, and tents. They specialize in gear for family campers and offer an additional 10% discount to Boy Scouts. Twenty-six stores around the country.

Munsingwear Factory Outlet: Send an undercover wire by Vassarette or Hollywood to ladies, or the famous Munsingwear underwear and accessories to men. Quiche lovers will love to bare their souls with savings of 50%. Corporate offices will direct you to the outlet nearest you. Call (612) 340-4700.

—P—

Pfaltzgraff Pfactory Store: Pfamous hand-crafted stoneware at pfabulous savings. Locations in New Jersey, Pennsylvania, Maryland, Virginia.

Pic-A-Dilly: Pic from famous brands like Dawn Joy, Enchante, JD Too, and Rehearsals at up to 60% discounts. You can find designer dresses, suits, separates, and sportswear at any of their 200 stores nationwide. Some bargains of e-pic proportions.

Pix: Pix-ie and Dixie didn't bristle over the selection here. Florsheim, Bandolino, Bernardo sandals, Nunn Bush, and Naturalizer in mostly first-quality men's and women's shoes in both current sizzlers and last year's fizzlers. Savings from 10% to 40%; more during sales. Nike, Adidas, and Pumas, sport, too.

Plus Sizes: A good source for large-size ladies' sportswear, PS carries Lady Devon, Gloria Vanderbilt, Sasson, Jordache, Joyce, Coronet, and other lines in sizes 16½ to 32½ and 38 to 52. Discounts from 20% to 50%. Also carries a full line of lingerie with labels from Glamorize and Playtex, dresses and coats. For store locations contact: PS Plus Sizes, Plus Savings, 85 Union Ave., Memphis, TN 38103.

Polly Flinders Factory Outlet: Girl's hand-smocked dresses at manufacturer's factory-outlet prices, usually 40% to 60% less than retail. Also carries slips, tights, and sleepwear bearing the Polly Flinders label. One outlet in Cincinnati, Ohio, and 16 in Florida.

Pottery Plus Bargain Bazaar: With only one discount store in Texas and two in Oklahoma, the excellent bargains are limited to a few lucky recipients. Mikasa and Franciscan china (some seconds) are discounted 33% to 70% along with canister sets, pottery, and copper. For listings of their 13 retail stores write: Pottery Plus, 13235

Montfort Drive, Dallas, TX 75240.

Prince Fashion Outlet: Single-mindedness pays off. The Prince brand ruffled shirts, silk trousers, jackets, blazers, and even jogging suits are marked down 50% when bought direct from the manufacturer in one of nine outlets around the country. Write for store listings to: Prince Fashion Outlet, 1201 N. Interstate 35, Carrollton, TX 75006.

—R—

Red River Pottery: You won't find gold in Red River but you will find priceless savings on pie pans, pottery, pots and dishes, silk flowers, brass pieces, and framing services. Prints, frames, and glass are all red-uced. Check their three Dallas area stores or 10 others around the country.

—S—

Sassafras: Smart and sassy sportswear for both juniors and misses with such mint names as Bar Harbor, D'Shwa, Modern Junior, Villager, and Sir for Her. Prices tipped the scales at a reduced rate of 40% to 60%.

SportPages Final Edition Shop: Don't check this sports page unless you are looking for discounts of 20% to 80% (from their SportPages catalog left-overs) on tennis shoes, jogging wear, gift ware, and lots of accessories. Sportswear by Bill Blass and Christian Dior wind down finally at 180 Spring Creek Village, Dallas, Texas 75240.

Suzanne's: Working girls have been marching to the tune of this Suza's phone for years. Famous brands like Sasson, Brittania, Chic, Lee, Chaus, Jones New York, Evan Picone, and JH Collectibles are 30% off retail. See their 37 stores around Texas.

Sym's: Hymns to Sym's good selection of European and American designer fashions such as Cardin, Cerruti, Giorgio St. Angelo, YSL, Gant, Ralph Lauren, and Ted Lapidus for men, women, and children. Suits, overcoats, slacks, shirts, sweaters, shoes, hats, gloves, pajamas, and underwear discounted 30% to 70%. Eleven stores in New York and New Jersey.

—T—

Tennis and Ski Warehouse: You'll love to net the 15% to 30% savings on court rackets, balls, and supplies, ski accessories, too, and apparel for both sports. In Texas and Oklahoma.

T.J. Maxx: The second of the giant Zayre corporation's discount stores (Hit or Miss is the other) or maybe it's the first, it nevertheless has made a hit across the country. Offering family apparel through their 30 outlets in 11 states: Massachusetts, Connecticut, Rhode Island, New Hampshire, North Carolina, South Carolina, Maine, Georgia, Illinois, Ohio, and Michigan. Addresses are available from their Advertising Department, Box 878 Framingham, MA 01701.

Toys 'R' Us: This national chain can be your undoing if you need to tinker with toys. Everything but the missing link for little ones at a savings of 20% to 30%. If it's toys u want, they r r choice 4 u.

Tuesday Morning: Check your local newspapers for the gift ware show of shows. Forty-one stores across the country offering quality linens, ceramics, crystal, glassware, skiwear, brass ware, kitchenware, toys, baskets, china, and pottery. Periodic sales during peak shopping seasons where savings soar to 90%. Everything in the store is 50% and more off the retail price.

—V—

Van Heusen Outlet Store: Men's and women's sportswear including shirts, sweaters, ties, and belts in sizes S to XL. Twenty-six locations. Write to Van Heusen, Box 2201, New Brunswick, NJ 08903.

Virginia Alan: Excellent buys on quality women's apparel by Gentry, Emotions, Evan Picone, Elle's Belles, and Sports Galore in sizes 4 to 16. Savings averaged 40% to 60%. A wool gabardine suit was $129 (retail $250). Stores throughout the country. For listings of stores write: Virginia Alan Ltd., 40 Mead St., Stratford, CT 06497.

—W—

Wallpapers to Go: Wall-to-wall wallpaper can be found at Wallpapers to Go. Discounts of 10% to 40% on grass cloth, vinyls, flocks, and more. With 1,200 patterns, check their other 100 locations.

Webster Warehouse Outlet: Check to see if your mall has a Warehouse location. That's where the bargains are! Volume deals in men's clothing from sportswear to suits at 35% to 75% off make the pages in our book. No irregulars. Quality designer and brand names like Brittany, Oleg Casini, Members Only, and Coverage to name a few.

SALES-BY-MAIL

It's as easy as one-two-three to get the special catalogs from the "Big Four" major catalog/retail stores (JC Penney, Sears, Montgomery Ward, and Spiegel). In addition to their regular books, they all put out sale and special-edition catalogs that are smaller, but you have to know how to get them. Each company has different rules on who receives these catalogs and you have to remember there are always expiration dates on the items offered. Here are the rules:

J.C. PENNEY: You must place at least a $30 order from any regular catalog every six months from the same address.

SEARS: You must place a catalog order of $25 or more every three months. Extra copies of sale catalogs are available at their retail stores in the catalog department.

MONTGOMERY WARD: You must place three catalog orders every six months to receive the Christmas book, two Big Books, and all the sale catalogs.

SPIEGEL, Box 6340, Chicago, IL 60680: You must place two orders of $25 each within six months to receive their Christmas and summer sale catalogs.

"TOIL FREE"
800 NUMBERS

A surprising number of major manufacturers have toll-free lines for consumers. If you call 800 information, 1-800-555-1212, you will need the corporate name exactly as it is listed. For your copy of *The Toll-Free Digest*, which lists over 25,000 toll-free numbers, send $6.50 plus 40 cents postage to: Toll-Free Digest Co., Inc., Box 800, Claverack, NY 12513. Another suggestion is to look on a side panel of a product to see if an 800 number is there. These lines are to deal with questions about their product(s), but sometimes you can get an answer to a general question, request a refund, or register a complaint. Some useful numbers we found:

• Procter & Gamble lists this number for bar soap and household cleaners: 1-800-543-1745 (Ohio 1-800-582-0345). Another number, 1-800-543-7270 (Ohio 1-800-582-1891), is for beauty and health care products.

• General Electric has an Answer Center, 1-800-626-2000, which cleared up instructions we received with a GE battery recharger and control settings on a GE refrigerator. This is a 24-hour line and we didn't get the cold shoulder, either. In the Whirlpool Cool Line, a telephone troubleshooter listened patiently to an ailing Whirlpool dryer. Calling him on 1-800-253-1301 (Monday through Friday, 8 a.m. to 9:30 p.m.; Saturday, 9 a.m. to 4:30 p.m. EST) saved calling a serviceman and that, in turn, saved a lot of static.

• A bad case of the frizzies was helped by calling 1-800-243-5320 and asking Cheeseborough Ponds' advice. This is a hair and cosmetic question line operating Monday through Friday, 8:30 a.m. to 4:30 p.m. EST. Clairol does this, too, with its 1-800-223-5800 number specializing in rescuing do-it-yourself color jobs and permanents.

• Prescriptions for ailing lawns, gardens, trees, and shrubs are given by phone with the Scott Lawn Care attendant at 1-800-543-8873 (TURF).

• Polaroid's 1-800-225-1384 hot line will clear up cloudy pictures you might have with their cameras.

• And if you get bleary after answering baby's room service cries at 3 a.m., maybe you'll get relief by listening to one of Beech Nut Baby Food's most popular recordings: "Sleeping through the Night." Another on their most requested list is "Solid Foods." These and others can be requested 9 a.m. to 4 p.m. EST at 1-800-523-6633. Questions are centered around newborns to 2-year-olds.

READER'S RESPONSE

1. Overall, I thought the book was _____ excellent _____ good _____ fair _____ poor.

2. I would like to see more listings in the following categories:

   a. _____ d. _____

   b. _____ e. _____

   c. _____ f. _____

   I would also like to see discount mail-order sources for the following

   lines or labels _____

3. I (did/did not) _____ like the way the book was organized.

4. I have bought merchandise from the following stores in your book and would rate them as (excellent, good, fair, poor):

   a. _____ rating _____

   b. _____ rating _____

   c. _____ rating _____

5. I have had a problem with _____.

   (Please describe) _____

6. I have had an interesting, funny, unusual experience dealing with one of

   the listings. (Describe): _____

   _____.

7. Some good overseas bargain stores are _____

   _____.

8. I consider the most important categories to be: _____

   _____.

9. Your book saved me $_____ on a purchase of

   $_____ bought from _____.

10. I will recommend *The Underground Shopper* to my friends.

    Yes _____ No _____

11. Would you like to have Sue Goldstein speak to your organization or company's national meeting or convention? A well-known consumer advocate, Sue Goldstein speaks regularly on shopping and saving money to groups across the country as well as appearing on major radio and television talk shows.

    I would like to know more about engaging Sue Goldstein as a speaker for

    _____.

IT'S CHIC TO BE CHEAP (and fun to be an Underground Shopper)! Help spread the word about discount mail-order shopping. Share your finds with our staff so we can include them in the next edition.

WE NEED YOUR LEADS _____

_____

_____

Your name _____

Address _____

City, State _____ Zip _____

Phone ( ) _____

Mail your responses to: SusAnn Publications, Inc.
                         3110 N. Fitzhugh
                         Dallas, TX 75204

INDEX